The Harrowsmith Northern Gardener

By Jennifer Bennett

Camden House

Second printing 1988
Third printing 1989
Fourth printing 1993 (updated)

Canadian Cataloguing in Publication Data

Bennett, Jennifer
The Harrowsmith northern gardener

Includes index.
ISBN 0-920656-22-6

1. Vegetable gardening–Canada. 2. Organic gardening–Canada. 3. Vegetable gardening–Northeastern States. 4. Organic gardening–Northeastern States. 5. Vegetable gardening–Northwestern States. 6. Organic gardening–Northwestern States. I. Title.

SB321.B47   635.0971   C82-090119-9

Printed and bound in Canada by
D.W. Friesen & Sons Ltd.
Altona, Manitoba

Printed on acid-free paper

Published by Camden House Publishing
(a division of Telemedia Communications Inc.)

Camden House Publishing
7 Queen Victoria Road
Camden East, Ontario K0K 1J0

Camden House Publishing
Box 766
Buffalo, New York 14240-0766

Trade distribution by
Firefly Books
250 Sparks Avenue
Willowdale, Ontario M2H 2S4

P.O. Box 1325
Ellicott Station
Buffalo, New York 14205

Design by Michael G. Bowness

Cover art by Heather Cooper

Colour Separations and Complete Film
by Herzig Somerville Limited

To R.T.

Acknowledgements

In a small publishing enterprise such as Camden House, the efforts of each person involved in producing a book like this are essential and very much appreciated by the author. First, I would like to thank our outfielders: *Harrowsmith* magazine's contributors from across the country; Douglas Green and Hubert Earl of Kemptville College of Agricultural Technology, who kindly read the manuscript; freelance food consultant Anne Borella, who checked the home preserving information; Ruth Geddes, who helped with typesetting; Sharon McFadzean, who proofread the copy; and Inez Platenius, who prepared the index.

Closer to home, I want to thank all the employees of *Harrowsmith* magazine who helped with the book, either directly or indirectly.

Contents

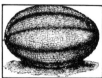

Introduction

The intention to produce a vegetable gardening book has been a part of the plans of *Harrowsmith* magazine for quite some time. We knew that the need existed for a comprehensive guide just for Northerners; readers had made that quite plain and our own scanning of library shelves had confirmed it. There was nothing on the market that really filled the bill, especially for those gardeners who prefer to work without synthetic pesticides. After four years as *Harrowsmith's* gardening editor, I have finally gathered enough material to present you with the essence of what I have learned from my own garden and from readers and scientists working all across the North.

The word "north" is relative, of course, as the magazine's readers living "north of 60" have taken pains to point out. What exactly is a Northerner? The most specific we can be is to state that for our purposes the northern gardener lives anywhere in Canada or the upper third of the United States. More generally, a northern gardener has a twilight sufficiently long for him to thin all his carrots after the sun sets but before dark, has at least one trick up his sleeve for protecting his tomatoes from fall frosts, and has lost most of his garden topsoil to Pleistocene glaciers that deposited it somewhere around the corn belt. He may find his gardening endeavours squeezed into a growing season some would consider little more than wishful thinking, but it is certainly sufficient to thaw his spirits and produce an abundance of fresh, home-grown food.

Written for seasoned gardeners and beginners alike, the book makes no presumption that a "green thumb" is a prerequisite for successful backyard food production. It is not. A green thumb is little more than digital reference to the sum of experience, confidence and intuitive understanding of weather and plants that finally comes to everyone after a few gardening seasons.

The aim of this book is to inspire the reader to grow a garden that is as economical as it is enjoyable; that is free of gimmicks and fads; that is a very personal expression of the reader's own likes and dislikes, climate and environment. The garden should be able to supply its caretaker with wholesome food without its surroundings being harmed in any way, biologically or aesthetically. A lovingly tended garden is a living work of art that repays the gardener in manifold ways.

— *Jennifer Bennett*

Strategies & Speculations

> "We shall have about three acres ready for spring-crops. . . . This will be sown with oats, pumpkins, Indian corn and potatoes"
>
> – Catharine Parr Traill,
> The Backwoods of Canada, 1832

Having written *The Backwoods of Canada* and *The Canadian Settler's Guide* well over a century ago, Catharine Parr Traill might seem to have little in common with today's gardener blessed with how-to manuals, nursery-grown transplants, quality-controlled seeds and engine-driven cultivators. Traill's declaration that her new country was capable of "producing almost everything which can minister to the comforts and luxuries of life. . . ," seems remarkable when one considers the difficulties that faced any pioneer of her time: no electricity, no rotary tillers and never a frosty lager at the end of a hot day of digging.

Today, when the "comforts and luxuries of life" come more frequently from the store than from one's own labour, the gardener still has a great deal in common with Traill. He or she is a pioneer who harvests a little more knowledge with every crop. As in Catharine's day, each garden is a singular, distinct bit of land that must be understood gradually. Still, there are skills to be learned, hardships and disappointments to be endured, harvests to be celebrated. Land must be brought into condition and some hard, manual work must be done.

If you are fortunate enough to have fallen heir to an existing plot, you already have a head start. But more likely the beginning gardener will agree with Traill's words soon after she arrived in Upper Canada: "This spring, there is so much pressing work to be done on the land in clearing for crops that I do not like to urge my claim on a pretty garden." The modern gardener may have a suburban plot whose topsoil was removed by developers, a wind-swept apartment balcony, a city back yard, a piece of impenetrable bush or a country field choked with weeds and old tractor tires. Take heart. If Catharine, fresh from England, managed to produce a lush garden from the tangled Ontario forest, there is hope for you as well. But you, too, must limit your priorities at the outset.

Start Small

Great expectations may be inspiring, but they can also be intimidating. To expect that your first garden will look just like the one Aunt Minnie has been tending since you were knee-high to a Colorado potato beetle is an invitation to discouragement. A horticulturist at the University of Michigan puts it this way: "First-time gardeners, particularly, tend to take on larger gardens than they can handle. A workable rule of thumb is to decide how large a garden you think you can manage and then cut that roughly by half."

During your first year, then, limit your endeavour so that you can keep it manageable and enjoyable. Rather than attempting to produce your own first crop of tomato and onion transplants, buy them from a nursery or have an experienced neighbour grow a few extra for you. Every year, grow a plant just for fun, a leafy "pet" whose survival will not be critical to the home food supply, but whose progress will be a matter of interest: perhaps sunflowers, bottle gourds or husk tomatoes. And always plant a flower or two in odd garden corners — marigolds, nasturtiums, or gladiolas will cheer the gardener and may also act as pest deterrents.

This is going to be your garden, a very personal, living extension of your property, your soil, your tastes, experiences and way of life. It won't be quite like anybody else's garden and, like any living thing, will not be truly mature for some time. Have patience. Many organic farmers estimate that it takes at least four years to make a real impression on the soil and crops. Remember, too, that gardening gets easier as it goes along. Not only will your garden progress as you acquire skills and knowledge, but also, well-tended soil becomes progressively more free of weeds, easier to work and more fertile. One of the greatest ironies of gardening is that it is the beginner, with the fewest gardening skills, who also must cope with the worst gardening conditions. The gardener and the garden grow together.

The Best Site
Whether establishing a new garden or enlarging the old, the gardener must begin the process by taking stock of his particular situation — its possibilities and shortcomings — and then making the best of it. In almost every instance, some compromises will be made, but the closer the garden comes to meeting the ideal the better its potential will be for producing healthy crops that mature quickly.

Light The garden's most pressing necessity is light. Unlike houseplants, most vegetables need at least six potential hours of sunshine during the hottest part of the day, and will do better with more. In the North, where the growing season is short, vegetable plants simply cannot receive too much light. In-

deed, it is because of the longer days of the northern summer that gardens in these latitudes survive as well as they do. Plants that are allowed too little light become spindly and weak, are slow to mature, are susceptible to garden pests and diseases, and often end up producing no fruit at all.

Because shade can retard vegetable growth appreciably, garden plans must take solar exposure into consideration

The best orientation for the garden, then, is south or, almost as good, southeast or southwest. A garden that slopes slightly toward one of these directions is ideal. If you are able to remove or avoid overshadowing objects you should do so, although many gardeners simply have to make the best of a plot surrounded by buildings and trees. Unfortunately, nearby trees not only shade the garden but also tap soil nutrients at the expense of vegetables. If possible, situate the garden beyond the tree's drip line. If shade is unavoidable, plan to use that area for shade-tolerant plants such as bunching onions or the leafy vegetables: lettuce, spinach and Chinese cabbage. These crops actually do better in shade during hot weather. Foil reflectors and mulches have been shown to be some help in increasing light in shady areas.

Garden rows are usually planted in a north-south orientation for equalization of light, but even if the rows are oriented differently, it is important that tall plants are situated toward the north side of the garden where their shade will not inhibit shorter-growing plants. Corn, asparagus, sunflowers, Jerusalem artichokes and staked plants such as tomatoes, cucumbers, peas and pole beans are all tall items that should go at the north end of the garden. Leafy crops, root crops and onions are among the shortest vegetables, while bushy plants – beans, potatoes, broccoli and such – fill in the mid-range.

Wind In exposed gardens, especially on the Prai-

peratures slightly above freezing. For instance, in an experiment at the University of California, five-day-old tomato plants were killed by seven days' exposure to 34 degrees F (1 degree C).

The average base temperature (the point below which plants cease growing) is 41 degrees F (5 de-

As long as they do not prevent the vegetables from obtaining their required sunlight, small trees or berry bushes can provide an attractive windbreak for exposed gardens

Although they are frost tender, cherry tomatoes are quick to mature

ries and in the far North, harsh winds can damage garden plants. A row of trees or bushes, called a shelterbelt, should be planted on the windward side of the garden and could even extend around the north, east and west sides of the garden, at a sufficient distance to prevent shading but close enough to be effective; it has been demonstrated that for every foot of tree height, a distance of 50 feet on the leeward side of the shelterbelt is protected to some extent from wind damage. Berries such as currants, serviceberries, cranberries or Saskatoons can be both protective and productive. Where trees or bushes are impractical, Agriculture Canada suggests the substitution of a 4- to 6-foot-high fence. At the lowest topographical point in the shelterbelt, leave a space between the trees or in the fence to allow the passage of cold air out of the garden.

Warmth Keeping the plants warm is the gardener's next priority. Not only will seeds germinate slowly (if at all) in very cool soil, but growing plants also are extremely dependent upon temperature for health and growth. Some, those termed "tender" vegetables because they can be killed very quickly by a frosty night, may die a slow death even at tem-

grees C) for all plants, but actually varies with different species. The base temperature of spinach is 36 degrees F (2.2 degrees C); of peas 42 degrees F (5.5 degrees C); of corn and beans 50 degrees F (10 degrees C) and of tomatoes and pumpkins 55.4 degrees F (13 degrees C). What this means is that if the average temperature does not rise above 50 degrees F (10 degrees C) during July, the corn, beans, tomatoes and pumpkins will either deteriorate or simply rest in suspended animation until August – providing the weather improves then. Pests and diseases, however, will not be so dormant and may finish off the stunted plants before they can progress.

If little can be done about the weather in such situations, the temperature around the plants can, nevertheless, be influenced. Decreasing wind velocity is important and, for warmth as well as light, shade on plants should be kept at a minimum. Where there is sun, of course, there is probably warmth as well, and many of the northern gardener's schemes for increasing warmth depend upon solar power.

Clear plastic and glass are the gardener's best allies in making the most of the sun's heat in any unshaded location. Because of the "greenhouse effect," the sun's warmth is held and concentrated beneath such a transparent cover. We will discuss the uses of transparent or translucent materials as crop covers in "Gardening Under Glass" in Chapter III.

Because cold air moves downward, any device

Because it is frost hardy, easy to cultivate and unlikely to bolt to seed, Swiss chard is popular among Northerners

that raises plants above the surrounding soil surface also helps enhance and prolong the warming power of the sun; raising beds, gardening on a slightly sloping site and avoiding low spots or "frost pockets" can all make quite a difference. According to Alberta Agriculture, "On a small scale, the effects of cold air drainage may be visible in the widely variable frost damage observed within a medium-sized garden. The lowest areas are hardest hit while higher portions may escape all frost damage." Those gardeners who cannot avoid low-lying spots should plant only frost-hardy crops: Jerusalem artichokes, kale, Brussels sprouts, Swiss chard.

One of the most reliable ways to suit the garden to the available warmth is to grow only those plants that are frost-hardy or whose maturation time is less than the length of the growing season (the time from the last spring frost to the first fall frost). Sweet potatoes and okra can be expected to mature in few northern gardens, where sufficiently warm temperatures are simply not maintained for long enough. Many more gardens will not see watermelons, bell peppers or eggplants through to fruition, even if the plants are covered on frosty

nights. You can discover the approximate length of your growing season by calling the closest horticultural society, state agriculture extension service or office of the provincial department of agriculture. As well, frost date maps are included in this book in Chapters III and IX. Taking into consideration the microclimate of your own garden and annual variations, you can expect that the duration of warm weather will vary from the norm by two or three weeks in any particular year.

Garden Plans

A cleared patch of ground is now needed. How large an area you prepare depends not only on the amount you wish to grow but also on the way you garden; some methods make far more efficient use of space than others. In Chapter II we discuss the best methods of clearing and improving soil on the garden site, but before any clearing begins you should have a good idea of your space requirements. And remember, start small.

There are four basic garden types: the single-row garden, the temporary wide-row garden, the permanent wide-row garden and the container garden. A gardener can use only one or, more likely, will make use of a combination of two or more types, as each one has its own advantages and drawbacks.

The Single-Row Garden This has been the traditional Western garden plan for years, a small-scale derivative of large-scale farming that calls for planting vegetables in single rows, like lines of soldiers, with a pathway beside every row. Gardening this way takes a lot of space: Paths are usually 2 or 3 feet wide, while the crop may take up only a few inches in width.

This is the system best suited to extensive use of mechanization and as such is popular with market gardeners and others who tend very large plots which would otherwise demand an overwhelming amount of mulching or hand-weeding. If the paths are wide enough to accommodate a tiller, weeds will only appear in the space directly around and between each plant, so that weeding may not be necessary at all. Periodic tilling turns all other weeds under. After the harvest the entire garden can be cultivated, and next season's pathways may or may not fall where this season's vegetables grew.

Some crops are best suited to a single-row system. Asparagus, raspberries, corn and potatoes, for instance, need at least a foot between rows in any case, and ease of picking or digging necessitates much wider spacing. With other crops, such as leaf and root vegetables, however, the single-row system is as much as 30 times less space-efficient than a permanent wide-row garden. There are other disadvantages to the single-row system:

• It usually requires a monetary investment in mechanized garden equipment (or horse-drawn equipment) such as a tiller or cultivator

• Because it is seldom mulched, the garden is vulnerable to drought and does not receive the additional organic matter a mulch provides

• Despite cultivation, soil in growing areas becomes somewhat compacted because pathways change from year to year. This year's trampled pathway may support next year's plants

The Temporary Wide-Row Garden Instead of being sown in single lines, each separated from the next by a pathway, plants in the wide-row garden are sown in beds, usually 3 or 4 feet in width, narrow enough that the centre of each bed can be reached comfortably from the pathway on either side. Such plantings are far more space-efficient than single rows, but they also may be more labour-intensive: Once it has been sown, the entire bed must either be mulched or hand-weeded. Pathways should be wide enough, at least 1½ feet, to allow the gardener easy passage. Unless they are wide enough to allow passage of a tiller, they too must be hand-weeded or mulched.

After the harvest, all or part of the temporary wide-row garden is cultivated – both beds and pathways – so that the position of the pathways changes from year to year. Because this system, like the single-row garden, usually involves tiller use, it is most suitable for gardeners who must grow a great deal of food or who simply prefer mechanical over manual tending.

The Permanent Wide-Row Garden In this case, pathways are permanent. The same beds are used from year to year and may be either mechanically tilled or hand-spaded between crops. As with the temporary wide-row garden, space is used far more

efficiently than with single rows. Plants can be spaced much more closely, not only because there are fewer paths, but because the system improves the soil condition, which allows for closer plant spacing. Since pathways are permanent, they can be made attractive with some sort of paving. At the same time, all fertilizer and cultivation goes where it is most needed – in the beds – and no soil compaction need occur since beds are never stepped in. As a result, the soil in the beds should improve with time. Because the permanent wide-row garden is usually the most appealing in appearance and the most intensive in its use of space, it is often the choice of city gardeners, gardeners who are short of space or fertilizing materials, and gardeners who simply prefer its aesthetic attributes.

On the negative side, a great deal of work must be devoted at the outset to making the beds and laying the paths. This can be expensive, too, particularly if the gardener opts for buying materials such as framing lumber and paving stones. In succeeding years, the garden should be fairly easy and inexpensive to maintain, although a certain amount of hand labour will always be required in sowing, weeding, mulching and cultivating.

The growing beds of the permanent wide-row garden may or may not be raised, although elevation of the soil level in the beds is usually a natural part of establishing this type of garden. Topsoil is removed from the pathways, where it will not be needed, and added to the growing beds, effectively lowering the paths and raising the beds. Wide beds that are level with the paths are less susceptible to erosion than raised beds, which is a boon in very dry or windy areas, but raised beds are somewhat easier to tend since the soil surface is closer to the gardener's working level. This makes raised beds especially useful for handicapped and elderly gardeners. Also, a report from the University of Wisconsin notes: "Raising the soil level of the garden bed should be the first step taken to improve growing conditions on heavy soils. Better drainage can speed drying which in turn increases soil temperature and allows earlier working in the spring." Conversely, in dry areas and particularly where soil is sandy, raising the beds can worsen the effects of drought. Under these conditions, the beds should be at, or close to, path level, and should be well mulched (see pages 106 and 107).

Whether raised or level, the beds will usually be 3 or 4 feet wide and can extend for any length the gardener finds convenient, usually for the width of the garden. Paths should be at least 1½ feet wide to allow passage with a wheelbarrow. Leave 2 feet where the paths turn corners. A foot-wide path may look fine on paper but will not even be visible when bordered with full-grown bean and broccoli plants.

If beds are raised, the soil may or may not be contained within a framework. Many Chinese-Canadians use raised, unframed beds, which are popular in the Orient. These beds work well in areas that receive an overabundance of rainfall, such as on the Pacific coast. Unframed beds usually have a flat surface about 6 inches above the surrounding pathways, and their edges slope gradually to the path.

Alternatively, raised beds can be framed with such materials as brick, stone or, most commonly, lumber, in which case the gardener should use a decay-resistant wood such as cedar, buy wood that is pressure-treated, or treat the wood with copper naphthenate, a preservative that, when it dries, is not toxic to plants. Frames can be made quite simply from 2 by 4s, 2 by 6s, 2 by 8s or rough lumber, and can be constructed either outside the garden or *in situ*, after the soil has first been mounded into the shape of the bed. Surround the raised soil with the frame and later level the bed soil and fertilize it as described in Chapter II. Before the beds are constructed, deep digging, also described in Chapter II, will help ensure that the soil is in good condition.

While framed beds are attractive, they do require more work and possibly more expense than unframed beds. In addition, frost may cause frames to heave in some gardens, and wooden frames will eventually need to be replaced.

The Container Garden In Chapter VIII, we deal fully with container growing. At this point, suffice it to say that while all gardeners may choose to grow a few plants in containers, taking advantage of the compactness and portability of the system, it is of greatest value to gardeners with no real garden at all. Those with only an apartment balcony or an office rooftop, for instance, may have little alternative to keeping their horticultural adventures confined within the boundaries of a few apple crates.

A Small Raised-Bed Garden
providing most summer vegetables for a family of two adults and two children

This garden plan requires a gardening season of at least 100 frost-free days. Where the season is shorter (around 90 days), the following alterations are suggested: Plant kale instead of peppers; plant short-season tomatoes such as Sub-Arctics and include provision for covering plants; substitute broad beans for all bush and pole beans; and finally, with a shorter growing season, there will not be time to plant cucumbers after the peas.

Tomatoes

Broccoli

Chives

Spring order for the garden illustrated

Basil *1 packet seed or 6 transplants*

Beets *1 packet seed*

Beans, bush *1 packet of green, wax or broad*

Broccoli *1 packet seed or 4 transplants*

Brussels sprouts *1 packet seed or 2 transplants*

Cabbage *1 packet seed or 6 transplants*

Carrots *1 packet seed*

Cauliflower *1 packet seed or 3 transplants*

Celery *1 packet seed or 4 transplants*

Chives *1 packet seed or 1 transplant (perennial, should not need replanting next season)*

Cucumbers *1 packet seed or 6 transplants (vining, not bush variety)*

Dill *1 packet seed*

Kale *1 packet seed*

Lettuce *1 packet early (i.e. cos, romaine) and 1 packet late (i.e. Oakleaf)*

Onions *1 packet seed, 1 flat transplants or about 50 sets*

Parsley *1 packet seed or 2 transplants (replace every year)*

Peas *1 packet or 1 ounce (whichever is more) seed such as Sugar Snap, snow peas or shelling peas. If support can be constructed, order a tall type that requires staking. If not, order a non-staking variety such as Novella*

Peppers *1 packet seed or 3 transplants*

Radishes *1 packet seed*

Swiss chard *1 packet seed*

Tomatoes *1 packet seed or 5 transplants. Bush types should be supported by cages; vining types on stakes*

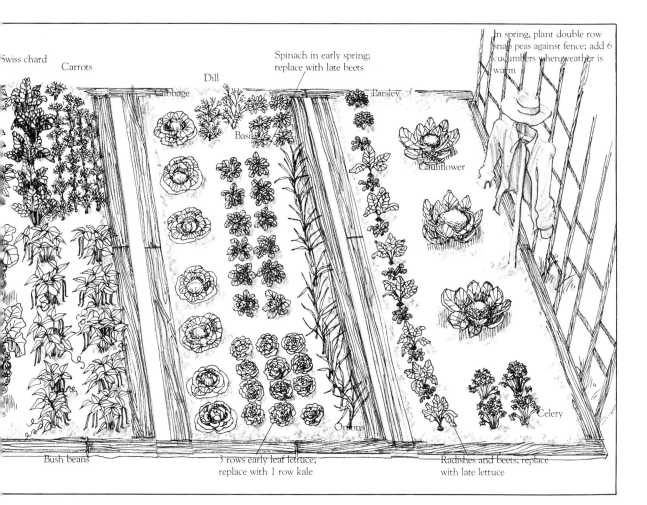

Swiss chard Carrots Dill Cabbage Basil Spinach in early spring; replace with late beets Parsley Cauliflower Celery Onions

In spring, plant double row snap peas against fence; add 6 cucumbers when weather is warm

Bush beans 3 rows early leaf lettuce; replace with 1 row kale Radishes and beets; replace with late lettuce

Using Space Efficiently

Vertical gardening This is not really a system unto itself, but rather a space-saving enhancement of any of the methods already described. Vertical gardening takes advantage of the fact that some plants will grow upward if offered support, thereby occupy-

A gourd plant demonstrates its skills as a climber on fish netting fastened up against a sunny outbuilding wall

ing less surface area, while keeping fruit clean, relatively free of pests and high enough to provide easy picking. Vertical gardening, then, is likely to play some part in all but the most spacious gardens.

Plants that grow upward on supports include clingers and climbers or twiners. The latter category includes pole or runner beans, asparagus beans (not related to asparagus, but actually a cow pea) and most flowering vines – plants that, given a chance, will wind around a stake. Clingers are those plants that support themselves with tendrils, and include peas – shelling, snow and snap – gourds and cucumbers. Vining vegetables with heavy fruit, such as most cantaloupes, watermelons, winter squash and pumpkins, have few tendrils to support their large fruit, so buttressing is necessary to prevent the fruit from pulling the vine down or breaking off and falling. Encourage such plants to grow upward by draping their vines over the trellis, and support their fruit with slings made of fabric tied at each end to the trellis, so that the fabric and trellis, not the vine, take the weight of the growing melons or squash. "Bush" varieties of cucumber, melon, squash and pumpkin will not

climb, but are ideal for gardens where vertical growing is not needed or not convenient.

Good vertical supports include wire fencing, a lean-to or wooden arch 6 or 7 feet high, and tripods or quadripods (teepee-shaped frames). In the last case, make the legs 8 feet long, using 1-by-2-inch

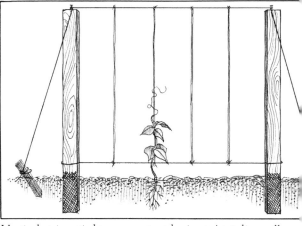

Vertical strings tied to a very taut horizontal top line will support twining plants or even trained tomato vines

lumber or fairly straight poles. Paint the bottom two feet of the legs with wood preservative, bury the painted ends 1 foot deep in the garden, and then tie the tops together.

Climbing or twining plants can also be encouraged to climb guy wires and apartment balcony railings, or to run up a trellis or fish netting fastened against the sunny wall of a house, garage or outbuilding. Scarlet runner beans, appreciated for their deep red blossoms as well as for their edible pods, are particularly decorative climbers, but cucumbers, gourds and melons also produce beautiful blossoms as well as attractive foliage and, of course, edible fruit.

Although tomatoes do not climb naturally, they are among the most popular candidates for vertical gardening. Again, this saves space, keeps fruit clean and allows for easy picking. Tomato plants can be tied to 5-foot stakes, trained to twine around vertical strings hanging from a supported cross-member, or held up in cylindrical cages made of wire fencing.

Fencing

A garden fence can serve many functions. It can be used to support vertical crops, as long as it does not shade crops within, and, as we have seen, it can lessen wind damage. Moreover, as Thomas McCulloch wrote in *The Stepsure Letters*, "good fences make good friends and safe crops." One's "friends" in this case may be chickens, cows, a raccoon eyeing the ripening corn, or a neighbour's child antici-

Tomato stakes should be driven in while the plants are small. Wire cages are about 18 inches tall and 18 inches wide

pating a "snowball" fight with those big, red tomatoes. Although even the best fence will not keep all unwanted visitors away — city squirrels and country crows find their way through, over or around almost anything — a good fence is certainly one of the best defences a gardener has.

Fencing materials include hedge plants, chicken wire and neat rows of white pickets, each material having its own expense and degree of usefulness. Chicken wire will resist chickens, but unless it is buried about a foot deep, ground hogs can tunnel under it. A single line of electric fencing around the perimeter should discourage raccoons. Bush-country gardeners who are really troubled by deer may want to try sloping the fence inward about 2 feet, so that the entire fence is inclined — deer are said to be unable to make the long jump necessary to clear such a barrier, which may deter wandering cows as well. Catharine Parr Traill wrote that she erected "an unsightly fence of split rails to keep cattle from destroying the vegetables." When designing a fence, don't forget to leave a gate wide enough to accommodate a wheelbarrow or, if necessary, cultivation equipment.

Paper Plans

All of the elements already described — the fence, the growing beds or rows, the vertical plantings, the pathways — should be plotted on paper as you, the prospective gardener, formulate your plans, taking into consideration the climate, your needs,

Vegetable Space Efficiency

The National Garden Bureau, a nonprofit American organization, has estimated the space efficiency of common garden vegetables. The theoretical maximum rating is 10, but no vegetable reaches 10 because no single item performs well under all soil conditions. In preparing these results, three dozen researchers across the U.S. considered total yield per square foot, average value per pound harvested, and seed-to-harvest time; some plants may produce more than one crop in a year.

Space efficiency will change as one moves further north. Hardier plants such as onions and peas will move upward on the scale, while tender selections such as tomatoes and summer squash decline in productivity, until finally, in the shortest-season gardens, they become totally unproductive unless grown under cover.

This chart is most useful for gardeners whose growing space is very limited. The highest-rated vegetables are those that, all things considered, such gardeners will find most productive or valuable.

Vegetable	Rating
Tomatoes, grown up supports to save space	9.0
Green bunching onions	8.2
Leaf lettuce	7.4
Summer squash: zucchini, scallop & yellow	7.2
Edible-podded (snow or snap) peas	6.9
Onion bulbs for storage	6.9
Beans, pole or runner (green or wax)	6.8
Beets, grown for greens and roots	6.6
Beans, bush (green or wax, snap)	6.5
Carrots	6.5

Cucumbers, grown on supports to save space	6.5
Peppers, sweet green or yellow	6.4
Broccoli	6.3
Kohlrabi	6.3
Swiss chard	6.3
Mustard greens	6.2
Spinach	6.2
Radishes	6.1
Cabbage	6.0
Leeks	5.9
Collards	5.8
Kale	5.6
Cauliflower	5.3
Eggplant	5.3
Peas, green shelled	5.2
Brussels sprouts	4.3
Celery	4.3
Corn, sweet	4.1
Squash, winter (not bush types)	3.8
Melons: musk, honeydew and water	3.8
Pumpkins	1.9

your skill and willingness to work, your tastes and the space to which you must confine yourself.

The article in this chapter, "The Greenhorn's Sneak Preview," will give the novice a rough idea how much of what to plant. In addition, the table "Quick Reference for Vegetable Yield" on pages 25 and 26 tells approximately how large a crop to expect from 100 feet of row and how much to plant in order to harvest an entire year's supply of that vegetable. More specific details can be found in the vegetable descriptions in Chapter IV.

Using graph paper and a convenient scale, say one square to 1 foot, mark the beds and rows of various vegetables. When deciding what to plant, remember each vegetable presents a different set of considerations. For example, would you like to

devote half the garden to potatoes? In that case, raised beds may be a nuisance when it comes time to hill and dig them — or they may not be, if you have a good supply of mulching materials. If you'd like to take a vacation in July, you should avoid planting early beans that will mature then. Or per-

haps you have an ideal spot for growing cucumbers, which you suspect will be a good barter item at pickling time. Take all your own preferences and conditions into consideration. Undoubtedly, you will make a few changes during the season, but this drawing-board preparation will keep overwhelming miscalculations, such as a half-ton harvest of zucchini, to a minimum.

Tools

And now you are ready to make your first monetary investment. The tools you require may be as expensive as a rotary tiller or as inexpensive as a spade or trowel, often available cheap at country auctions. Do not overinvest at the outset. Tillers can often be rented from garden stores or tool rental outlets, while lumber, poles, fencing and pathway paving materials may be available secondhand or free for the taking. Often rustic materials such as tree branches, stones and bark chips help create a very attractive garden.

A good spade, one with the blade nailed to the handle, will be necessary for digging beds and pathways, mixing compost and preparing hills for squash and melons. A small trowel is likewise almost indispensible from spring seeding through summer weeding and fall digging of garlic bulbs and carrots. A hoe is a wonderful levelling and weeding device. Scraped over the soil surface (in pathways, for instance) every few days, it can help keep weeds in check.

A soil thermometer is not a necessity, but it is a help to the beginner. Soil temperatures will be noted frequently in this book, particularly the ideal soil temperature for seed germination of individual vegetables listed in Chapter IV. Good quality soil thermometers are available from several mail-order seed houses, such as W.H. Perron, Johnny's Selected Seeds or Stokes (see Sources, beginning on page 185), as well as from some nurseries. A standard metal thermometer, inserted 2 or 3 inches into the soil, can also be used.

Buckets are useful for carting transplants to the garden, for watering, for bringing produce indoors, for preparing manure teas and as temporary resting places for perennial weeds. A bucket, in fact, performs many of the duties of a wheelbarrow but on a smaller scale. A wheelbarrow (or better yet, for those who can afford one, a garden cart) is good for transporting mulching materials, compost, soil, and harvested vegetables.

A manure fork (which has five tines, while a pitchfork has only three) is useful for turning compost, especially when the pile is newly made, and is also good for digging potatoes, Jerusalem artichokes and parsnips, although a potato fork, which has rounded tines, will do a better job with underground crops.

Some watering equipment is needed for most gardens. The system may entail a bucket to catch rainwater dripping from the house roof, a hose and sprinkler, a "drip" system involving perforated hoses, or even an irrigation network. Take into consideration your water pressure, the distance from water source to garden, the water supply and your own desire to use "elbow grease."

As you progress, you will probably add to your collection of tools and equipment, but it is best to do so gradually. Later, you may want to buy containers for home-grown transplants, row markers, a rake (useful for gathering compost and mulch materials), pruning shears, a watering can, plastic pump-type spray bottles, a gardening fork (for searching out weedy grass roots), plant pots, plastic mulches and hot caps (see Chapter III). Keep any hand tools under cover when they are not in use, and clean rusted metal blades with steel wool or sandpaper, wiping the blades with an oily rag at the end of the season.

Quick Reference for Vegetable Yields

The following chart lists "typical crop yields in northern home gardens of average fertility" according to estimates by Johnny's Selected Seeds of Maine; in other words, the yields are typical of the northeastern United States, about zone 5 in Canada (see climatic zone map in Chapter X). Gardeners with higher zone numbers may experience greater average yields (especially with fruiting crops), just as those with lower zone numbers may have lower yields. But, under any conditions, yields can and will vary greatly.

The planting recommendations apply to gardeners who wish to grow a full year's supply of that item for fresh use, storage, canning or freezing.

Vegetable	Average crop per 100 feet	Recommended planting per person
Beans, bush snap	120 pounds	20-30 feet
Beans, pole snap	150 pounds	20-25 feet
Beans, dry	10 pounds	100 feet

Vegetable	Average crop per 100 feet	Recommended planting per person
Beets, greens	40 pounds	15 feet
Beets, roots	100 pounds	10-20 feet
Broccoli	75 pounds	10-15 plants
Brussels sprouts	60 pounds	10-15 plants
Cabbage	150 pounds	10-20 plants
Carrots	100 pounds	25-30 feet
Cauliflower	100 pounds	10-15 plants
Celery	75 heads	5-10 plants
Corn, sweet	10 dozen ears	50-100 feet
Cucumbers	120 pounds	15-25 feet
Jerusalem artichokes	150 pounds	10-20 feet
Kale	75 pounds	10-20 feet
Kohlrabi	50 pounds	10-15 feet
Leeks	150 leeks	10 feet
Lettuce, head	80 heads	10-15 plants
Lettuce, leaf	50 pounds	10-15 feet
Muskmelon	75 fruits	10-15 feet
Onions, bulb	80 pounds	50-100 feet
Parsley	30 pounds	5-10 feet
Parsnips	100 pounds	10 feet
Peas, shelled	15 pounds	50-100 feet
Peppers, bell	50 pounds	5-10 plants
Potatoes	100 pounds	30-50 feet
Pumpkins	200 pounds	5-10 feet
Radishes	100 bunches	15-25 feet
Rutabagas	150 pounds	10-20 feet
Spinach	30 pounds	30-50 feet
Squash, summer	150 pounds	5-10 feet
Squash, winter	125 pounds	25-30 feet
Tomatoes	100 pounds	10-20 plants
Watermelon	50 fruits	10-15 feet

The Greenhorn's Sneak Preview

Although Chapter IV is devoted entirely to detailed descriptions of all the common vegetables, such specifics are not the concern of the beginner who should have a nodding acquaintance with the possible residents of the garden before pen is laid to paper or seed-buying cash changes hands. The following very general considerations will ensure that the novice gardener is forewarned and forearmed, and thus less likely to be discouraged by an unwieldy first effort. The harvest quantities noted are, of necessity, estimates only. Picking can vary from nil or negligible to enormous, depending on vegetable variety, your gardening experience, the garden itself and the weather.

Asparagus It is delicious, indeed an expensive delicacy for those who must buy it, and although it is easy to tend once established, asparagus is a perennial that can take up to three years to bear shoots large enough to harvest. After this, however, it may continue for a couple of generations. Consider growing asparagus if you have patience, space — each plant needs at least a foot in all directions, and can grow 4 to 5 feet tall — and if you don't expect to be transferred out of the country in a couple of years. About ten plants per person will yield only enough asparagus for spring and early summer dining and twice that much will be sufficient for the family to dine occasionally on frozen shoots for the rest of the year.

Beans, Snap Home-grown snap beans, yellow (wax) or green, often become a staple of the self-suffi-ciency garden. The plants are very frost tender, but if they are covered or the season is frost free, they are prolific, nutritious and much tastier than their supermarket counterparts. Bush beans grow about 1½ feet high and bear about ½ pint of beans per plant. Pole beans, which take longer to bear but produce slightly more pods per plant, are good for tight spaces, since they will cling unassisted to poles, guy wires and balcony railings. Plan on about ¼ pound of seed per person, to produce enough for dining on fresh, frozen or canned beans about once a week all year.

Beans, Shell Soybeans, baking beans, lima beans all take about the same amount of space as bush snap beans for a smaller harvest: only ¼ cup or so of shelled beans per plant. Broad beans are as frost hardy as peas and deserve a spot in very short-season gardens.

Beets Both greens and roots are edible and the latter are easy to store in a root cellar. Beets are quite easy to grow and provide well for the amount of space they need, which makes them good candidates for very small gardens and containers. Plan to harvest about a pound of roots and less than ¼ pound of greens per foot of row, with the plants thinned to one every 4 or 5 inches.

Broccoli Even the "mini" varieties are big and bushy, so allow about 1½ feet around each plant, and expect it to grow about 2 feet high. Broccoli is quite fussy about soil and moisture and, therefore, is not the best bet for the beginner. Once the large central head is har-vested, about nine weeks after planting, most varieties will produce smaller side shoots for the next couple of weeks. A packet of seeds will more than supply a family of four; allow about five plants per person for a year-round supply. Broccoli can be direct-seeded in most gardens, or the gardener can use home-grown or purchased transplants.

Brussels Sprouts This vegetable's hardiness is its strength — its harvest is just beginning when many other vegetables have already been killed by fall frost. But sprouts take up at least as much room as broccoli, and their lateness means they have nothing to show for themselves until the end of summer. If you have space and love sprouts, you should buy a packet of seeds and plant as for broccoli.

Cabbage Available with crinkle-leaf (savoy) or familiar smooth-leaved green or red heads, cabbages require as much space as broccoli, but the plants are quite easy to grow and the smallest-headed varieties require only a foot around each plant. If the plant is left to continue growing after the head has been removed, new smaller heads will form and mature in about a month. Plant just a few cabbage seeds or transplants every couple of weeks until mid-summer, so that all heads do not mature at the same time.

Carrots Nutritious, popular vegetables that are quite easy to grow and can be accommodated even in shady corners or balcony pots, carrots will produce about a pound of roots per foot of row, one plant every 4 inches. Estimate about 25 to 30 pounds per person for year-round consumption.

Cauliflower This is the most fragile member of the cabbage family, requiring particular soil and moisture conditions to head properly, and usually needing blanching (having its leaves tied over the head to prevent discoloration). It takes as much space as broccoli for just one head per plant. Gardeners who have space and don't mind fussing should buy a packet of seeds for four people, allowing about five plants per person for year-round dining. Beginners should try self-blanching cultivars. As cauliflower is usually started indoors, the beginner's best bet is nursery-grown transplants.

Celery It is easy to grow strong-tasting, stringy celery, but difficult to grow mild, tender celery without fertile soil or a good supply of compost. Beginners who don't mind taking chances can plant purchased transplants, while more advanced gardeners will start their own indoors. Grow about six plants per person, allowing 6 inches between each plant.

Corn Fresh home-grown corn is a summer delight, but is not recommended for gardeners short of space unless they wish to grow little else. Corn is not only hard on the soil and sometimes over 6 feet tall, but it returns very little vegetable for the amount of space used. Because it is wind pollinated, it is best grown in a block of plants at least 4½ feet by 4 feet (four rows 1½ feet apart and eight plants per row). Each plant should yield one to three cobs.

Cucumbers This vegetable is quite versatile. Without support it will sprawl for several feet, but vining varieties happily climb upward if given the chance and can be

Even children find potatoes an easy crop to plant and tend, but the returns are small compared to the amount of space they require, about 1½ feet around each plant

adapted to vertical growing in tight situations. Cucumbers can be planted from seed in the garden in areas with at least 90 frost-free days; where the season is short, cover a hill of three or four seeds with a hot cap or crop cover (see Chapter III). A single plant can produce from 10 to 50 fruits during the season, depending on how regularly they are picked.

Lettuce Head lettuce dominates the supermarket produce shelves, but is more difficult and time-consuming to grow than leaf lettuce, the better bet for beginning gardeners. Those who insist upon heads should allow 12 inches of space around each plant. A packet of seeds supplies summer salads

for a family of four. Most varieties of lettuce bolt to seed in summer, leaving the foliage tough and bitter, but some cultivars such as Oakleaf withstand hot weather better. Buy transplants or sow seeds of leaf lettuce in spring and thin the plants until each one has 4 to 6 inches of space all around it. Leaf lettuce is ideal for containers, window boxes and small gardens.

Melons Muskmelons, watermelons and honeydews are wonderful treats for gardeners with at least 100 frost-free days (or a large greenhouse), but they do require plenty of space; left to ramble, a vine will extend about 6 feet and may produce only two or three fruits. The seeds must be started early indoors or the gardener must purchase nusery-grown transplants and treat them with great care in planting outdoors. Vining cultivars can be trained to grow vertically if the fruits are supported.

Onions Easy to grow, easy to fit into out-of-the-way corners and good companion plants, onions of some sort should find a place in every garden. Bunching onions, from which the gardener can harvest both tender greens and small bulbs, are the most space-efficient choice and may be sown outdoors in early spring. One packet of bunching onion seed will cover 5 or 6 square feet of bed, producing 20 to 25 bunches of 10 onions each. Seeds for storage onions can be started indoors, or the gardener can buy transplants or sets (small bulbs). For a year-round supply of storage onions, plant 40 to 80 onions per person. Purchase one packet of seed for two people.

Parsley Sow a few seeds at the end of a garden bed or in a large pot in early spring for a summer-long supply of this nutritious garnish and potherb.

Parsnips This vegetable is not overly popular but is very hardy, easy to grow and almost as space-efficient as a carrot. Allow 4 inches around each plant after thinning. Plan to harvest about 1 pound of roots per foot of row.

Peas Shelled peas are very easy to grow if planted in early spring, allowing an inch between each seed alongside a fence, but they are poor producers. Plan to harvest only about ¼ cup of peas per plant. Edible-podded peas are twice as space-efficient as shelled peas and just as easy to grow. They are almost a must for the northern gardener. Snap or snow peas – peas that are eaten with pods intact – do best

with some support, so grow them near a fence or let them climb up a trellis of twigs. Plan to harvest about ½ cup of pods per plant. Buy ¼ pound of seed per person for a year-round supply.

Peppers Lovers of warm soil and warm weather, peppers, hot or mild, come to the northern garden only as transplants. The gardener can grow his own or buy them, planting around late May or early June in areas with at least 90 frost-free days. Plan to harvest about two to ten fruits per plant.

Potatoes Easy to grow, especially where the growing season is somewhat cool and damp, potatoes nevertheless do not present the gardener much in the way of economic return for the space they take. A pound of seed potatoes will produce approximately three plants, each one providing three to eight tubers. Allow about 1½ feet of space around each plant. Easy to store in winter, this vegetable may account for one-third of the space of a large self-sufficiency garden but is best omitted from a very small one.

Rutabagas These big roots are almost as space-consuming as broccoli; leave a foot around each plant. They are easy to plant and grow, but their space requirements make them best suited to large gardens.

Spinach As soon as the ground can be worked in spring, sow spinach in window boxes, flower beds or the vegetable garden for nutritious early greens. Plan on 30 to 50 feet of row per person, which will produce about 10 pounds of spinach. One packet should supply two people.

Squash, Summer The first time around, almost everyone plants too much zucchini. A single plant

can produce 16 to 36 fruits averaging ½ pound each. Allow a maximum of three plants for two people and select one each of three different types, perhaps a crookneck, a zucchini and a pattypan. A hill of three summer squash needs about 3 feet in all directions. To save space, select the "bush" varieties which are a little more compact than the others, or train vining cultivars to climb up a support.

Squash, Winter Like the melon, winter squash is a space glutton. Do not plant in rows – unless there is abundant room on both sides – but in hills, allowing 6 to 8 feet around each plant or each hill of three plants. It is best to plant them where they can sprawl on the lawn or on unused space by the garden. Plan to harvest about six fruits per plant.

Swiss Chard Gratifying for the beginner, chard produces large, spinach-like leaves. It will not bolt to seed in hot weather as spinach does. Chard, in fact, can be picked from spring through fall. It's a space-efficient leaf crop with an upright habit and requires about 6 inches of space all around.

Tomatoes Practically everyone who gardens in areas with at least 90 frost-free days grows tomatoes from transplants, and almost nobody has enough. Plan on harvesting six to 24 tomatoes per plant; with cherry tomatoes, the harvest may go as high as 150. Paste (elongated) tomatoes are best for sauces. The number of plants per person depends entirely on your garden space, climate, soil and appetite. For a family of four, 20 to 30 plants should provide enough fruit for fresh eating, sauces, stewed tomatoes and tomato paste for a year. For salads only, two plants per person should suffice.

Digging & Delving

"... this fertility must be maintained by rational, judicious cultural methods, or the excellent results obtained when these soils are first tilled will more or less rapidly disappear"

– Frank T. Shutt
Central Experimental Farm, Ottawa, 1908

Initially it's a little difficult for most of us to really enjoy working with soil. Ever since we could crawl through it, we've been warned to keep out of the mud, to keep clean. Reputations, we've since learned, can be "soiled," thoughts and books can be "dirty." No wonder we don rubber boots and gardening gloves before tackling the stuff that has suffered so much bad press.

But habits must change. Any gardener who truly wants a successful, satisfying garden will have to get used to working "hands-on" with the fingernail-clogging salmagundi that supports all vegetables and fruits, a goodly number of earthworms and, less directly, all the land-bound life of the planet. Gardening gloves do have their uses – in pulling stinging nettles, for instance – but otherwise they get in the way of that portentous handshake between gardener and garden.

Breaking New Ground

Will the garden soil be sandy, loamy or principally clay or silt? Little will be known until the land is cleared, a sometimes back-breaking task that should take place as far as possible in advance of the first gardening season. In this way, soil conditioning will have a few months' head start and the plot will be warm and ready for planting as early as possible in spring. No matter what the time of year, however, the gardener should not work very wet soil – soil that oozes water if a handful of it is squeezed – the situation immediately after a heavy rain or spring thaw. After being worked, wet soil will harden into rock-like, unmanageable clumps. Wait until the soil is slightly dry and crumbly.

Before any new garden plot can be worked, it must be cleared of stones, trash, bushes and trees. While debris can be removed right away, clearing of bushland is so time-consuming that it generally necessitates only a gradual expansion of the garden plot. If extensive bush-clearing is required, horse-power or mechanical power should be considered.

Once surface debris has been removed, power implements can be used to plow the plot several times, incorporating the surface vegetation. Most plots, however, are far too small for a tractor and plow even if the gardener has access to them, and a tiller will make little headway in sod. Sod can be smothered if it is blanketed for several months with a non-translucent cover such as black plastic or a deep mulch of compost or straw. Otherwise it must be removed by hand, a tedious job but one that makes the most long-lasting dent in weed growth. The sod can be removed all at once, or in strips by a process known as trenching.

If the soil under the sod is in fairly good condition, trenching may not be necessary. Simply pry up the sod a chunk at a time — most easily accomplished in spring when it is soft and wet — shaking free as much soil as possible and then piling the sod at one end of the garden where it will slowly compost. If it is occasionally turned and sprouting grass is removed, the compost can eventually be returned to the garden. When the surface is clear, work through it with a rake or pitchfork, removing stones, trash and weed roots. Thereafter, dig or till weeds as they appear. Twitch grass or quack grass is especially persistent, spreading both by seed and underground rhizomes, so it must be combated with diligence — roots should be dug up and tossed free of the garden, not into the compost pile.

Fertilize newly cleared ground by mixing as much compost as possible into the surface of the soil along with well-rotted animal manure at the rate of 5 pounds per square yard. If no compost or manure is available, use a synthetic fertilizer: 5 - 10 - 10 at 2 pounds per 100 square feet on sandy soil, or 3 - 18 - 9 at 1 pound per 100 square feet on heavier soil (see "Chemical Fertilizers," page 34). If you have decided on a garden plan using permanent beds (as described on page 19), they should be plotted out as soon as the land is cleared. Fertilizer then only need be applied to the beds. It may be necessary at this time to purchase topsoil for the beds if little is available on the site. The planting of a green manure crop, described later in this chapter, will also help get the new plot off to a good start and is an ideal way for city gardeners with no ready supply of animal manure or compost to add nutrients and organic matter to their soil.

Trenching This is a thorough method of soil preparation but so laborious that it is usually confined to gardens where the soil is very poor or where cultivation will be intensive. Proceed as follows:

• Remove the sod from a patch about 2 feet wide and the width or length of the garden, shaking free as much dirt as possible, and pile the sod at one end of the garden

• Dig a further 6 inches of soil from the cleared rectangle, piling it beside the sod and tossing any stones or trash into a different pile or into path areas

• Remove the sod from a 2-foot-wide strip parallel to and bordering the first trench, placing these chunks upside down on the bottom of the first

Always in too-short supply, compost can be used as both fertilizer and soil conditioner any time after the land is first cleared

trench and breaking them up with the spade

• Remove 6 inches of soil from the second trench and spread it over the sod in the first

• Proceed along the garden in this fashion, finally placing the sod and soil from the first trench in the last trench

• Fertilize the entire plot as described above

Deep Digging Where sod is not involved, trenching is easier and is known as deep digging. It is a useful way to rejuvenate an older garden or condition a new one. Its deep working of the soil allows plant roots, many of which descend several feet in well-worked soil, to grow unimpeded. Dig about 6 inches of soil from a long, narrow trench and pile the soil alongside it, removing stones, trash and weed roots. Break up the bottom of the trench with a spade and mix in 1 pound of manure per square foot. Then replace the topsoil, incorporating the topsoil from pathways as well if you are building raised beds (described on pages 19 and 20).

Once the soil has been cleared, future cultivation can be done by hand or with machinery as large as a tractor or horse-drawn cultivator or as small as a rotary tiller, depending upon the gardener's preference and scale of operation. However, horticulturist Bob Fleming of the Ontario Ministry of Agriculture and Food points out that the overuse of a rototiller can damage soil structure, since it reaches only to a depth of about 4 inches in heavy soils, which ideally should be cultivated to a depth of 8 to 10

on the Prairies or where excessive amounts of salt-rich additives such as gypsum have been used.

In the garden, organic matter is provided by animal manures, compost, fallen leaves, plant refuse, dead insects and organic mulches such as straw or grass clippings, peat moss or seaweed. The best gar-

Trenching, described on the previous page, is a labour-intensive method of conditioning a new plot of land or revitalizing an older garden. Because it involves very heavy work, most gardeners confine trenching to small gardens or to only part of a larger garden

inches. Fleming encourages trenching followed by hand-spading. "An easy way to make sure that you incorporate an even amount of organic material," Fleming says, "is to spread it evenly over the garden surface before you begin the spading process."

Organic Material By "organic material" Fleming means animal or vegetable materials that will improve the soil's fibre content and increase its content of humus. All soil contains organic matter, formed by the decomposition of animal and plant cells. Organic matter is the very life of the soil, binding particles together, providing a spongy texture that protects soil from erosion and drought, holding moisture for plant roots, feeding earthworms and containing more than half the nutrients needed by plants. A report from the University of Wisconsin illustrates this point. In a test plot provided with organic material (peat moss and sawdust) but no fertilizer, "the yield of beets and onions on heavy soils was increased 47 and 77 per cent respectively, and petunias produced 32 per cent more blooms where soil drainage and tilth were improved." Also, adding organic matter is one of the best ways of improving saline soils, most often found

dening practices focus on maintaining, or better still, increasing the levels of organic matter in the soil, thus automatically sustaining soil fertility and quality as well. By returning all crop, livestock and even human wastes to the soil, some Eastern cultures have managed to grow intensively planted crops on the same land for thousands of years without deterioration of soil quality.

Whatever the constitution of the soil, it will benefit from the addition of organic matter. Garden soil may be sandy or loamy, or principally composed of clay or silt. If *sandy*, it will feel gritty and will allow water to percolate through easily. Because sandy soil is well aerated, many crops appreciate it, but it does dry out quickly and thus requires mulching in most circumstances. Soils with high *clay* or *silt* content have particles so fine that the soil feels slippery or gluey. Rain stands in puddles, and the soil becomes hard and cracks as it dries. Such soils usually require the incorporation of a great deal of organic matter in the form of mulches or composts to make them really workable and porous. *Loam* is a mixture described by Agriculture Canada as "soil material that contains 7 to

27 per cent clay, 28 to 50 per cent silt and less than 52 per cent sand." Gardeners blessed with loamy soil have the very best starting point, but even it can be vastly improved with organic matter.

Fertility

If organic material is so essential for plant growth, what, then, is the role of fertilizer? The word fertility suggests the soil's nutrient content, which makes it capable of supporting plants. Just as people require various vitamins and minerals to remain healthy, so plants require a diet containing many elements: the macronutrients such as carbon, hydrogen, oxygen, nitrogen, phosphorus, potassium, calcium, magnesium and sulphur; and the micronutrients such as boron, copper, iron, manganese, molybdenum, zinc and chlorine. The macronutrients must be present in much larger quantities than the micronutrients, but all must be in the soil if the garden is to be productive.

Fortunately, providing such a complex diet is not as difficult as it appears. Plants, like people, can obtain all the nutrients they require from a very simple menu. Unfortunately, encouraged by the agricultural chemical industry, home gardeners sometimes wrongly take their cues from commercial growers for whom fertilizer use really is quite complex because of the scale of their operations and their use of methods that deplete soil organic matter and specific nutrients. The home gardener, on the other hand, grows a great variety of crops on a relatively small plot of soil, an ideal situation for the use of soil-amending measures such as crop rotations, mulching and composting. Also, because the home grower is much more willing to accept misshapen or blemished produce than the commercial grower, nutrient levels need not be precisely the best for each crop, an extravagant ambition under any circumstances.

Chemical Fertilizers There are a few situations in which chemical fertilizers are valuable: for quick correction of a severe soil deficiency (indicated by a soil test); as compost starters for far Northerners; to provide sufficient nutrients for a small garden that must produce a very large crop; and as all-round fertilizers for gardeners who cannot or will not devote the time or labour necessary for collecting or-

ganic fertilizers and adding them to the soil. In all cases, however, the use of chemical fertilizers should be balanced by the use of some organic ones, and no gardener should depend utterly on synthetic or chemical fertilizers for several reasons:
• They are expensive, nonrenewable and, since

they are petroleum-based, anyone who comes to rely on them will find gardening increasingly costly and may eventually be unable to purchase the additives at all
• Most synthetic fertilizers are fast-acting and powerful. They can easily be overapplied, in which case they will do more harm than good, killing plants, upsetting the soil balance and contributing to water pollution
• Synthetic fertilizers add nothing to the tilth or quality of the soil, the lack of which may be the basis for presuming fertilizer is required
• Synthetic fertilizers are truly necessary in very few instances. Gardeners often become involved in a routine of using these substances every year, whether or not they know fertilizer is required

Those who do wish to buy synthetic fertilizers should know that the numbers on the package (called the analysis) refer to the percentage, by weight, of nitrogen, phosphorus and potassium, in that order; so 11 - 48 - 0 (superphosphate) contains 11 per cent nitrogen, 48 per cent phosphorus and no potassium. The other 41 per cent of the mixture is composed of other chemicals or fillers. Compared with organic fertilizers, the analysis looks impressive. Poultry manure, for instance, if it were

The small amount of work involved in building and turning a compost pile pays dividends in healthy soil and productive plants

sold in the same fashion (and if such a low analysis were legal) would be labelled something like .9 - .7 - .4. But that doesn't tell the whole story. The other 98 per cent of poultry manure is all nutrients, water and organic matter; it is 100 per cent useful.

Acidic or Alkaline Whether they are organic or synthetic, fertilizers have the greatest effect on plants when the soil is close to neutral, the mid-point between acidic and alkaline. Chemists express acidity or alkalinity in terms of pH, a scale that varies from 0 to 14, with 7 indicating neutral. Values below 7 indicate increasing acidity; values between 7 and 14, increasing alkalinity. Values between 6 and 7, slightly acidic, are the best for most garden plants. (Other plants, however, may have quite different pH preferences.) The pH scale is logarithmic, so a pH of 6 is 10 times as acidic as pH7, a pH of 5 is 10 times as acidic as pH6, and so on.

As the soil pH approaches neutral, more nutrients become available to plants. Thus soil may be rich in nutrients, but if it is too acidic or alkaline the plants will nevertheless exhibit the same symptoms of nutrient deficiency that they would if the nutrients were not there at all. This also happens in cold soil, a frequent problem in the North where unhealthy looking plants often begin to grow vigorously as soon as the soil warms. Adding chemical fertilizer is no help in either situation because it simply upsets the soil balance. If the problem is an incorrect pH, however, adding organic matter may help, because it tends to urge the soil toward neutral. There are a number of additives that have a dramatic effect upon pH, but they should be avoided until the pH of the garden soil is known.

The precise soil pH is most easily determined by having a soil test done by the appropriate provincial ministry of agriculture or state extension department (see "Sources of Soil Tests," at the end of this chapter). Ask for soil test information, and the office will let you know the price and best method of obtaining a soil sample. For gardeners, this test is usually done inexpensively and may even be free. The soil test report will indicate to the gardener his soil pH and what should be done to adjust it.

Lime is usually recommended for raising pH in acidic soil. If the report calls for the application of lime, twice the amount of wood ashes may be substituted. There are two types of agricultural limestone available for this purpose: calcitic and dolomitic. Calcitic, the most common, is mostly calcium carbonate ($CaCO_3$), while dolomitic limestone contains a high proportion of magnesium carbonate ($MgCO_3$) and should be used if the soil test also indicates a magnesium deficiency.

If the soil is really off-balance, correcting its pH may have a dramatic effect upon yields. A report from the University of Pennsylvania notes: "Using sweet corn, snap beans, tomatoes and cabbage, when the best lime and fertilizer treatments were compared, the lime had nearly as great an effect on the total yield in tons per acre as the fertilizer treatment." The effect of liming is most dramatic on finely textured (clay or silt) soils.

Most acidic soils are found on the east and west coasts and, to a lesser degree, throughout the mideastern and northern regions.

Sulphur compounds are the prescription for helping to neutralize alkaline soils, those usually found in areas of low rainfall such as the Prairies or the interior of British Columbia and the North, as well as where the bedrock is composed of calcitic rocks. Peat, which is somewhat acidic, will also help neutralize alkaline soils.

The other most common nonorganic additives are natural deposit fertilizers such as rock phosphate. These substances, which should be used with caution, contain nutrients that are no different qualitatively from those in synthetic fertilizers, but they do contain micronutrients, involve fairly benign methods of manufacture and are generally quite slow-acting in their effect on soil and plants. For an analysis, see the accompanying table "Analysis of Organic Fertilizers" on page 41.

The Soil-Building Program It is not really necessary for most gardeners to have a soil test done, nor is it necessary to follow the soil test's recommendations. Since they are based on only one tiny sample, they may be quite inconsistent with the garden's productivity. It is important, however, to avoid the use of pH-altering soil amendments and even wood ashes if you are not sure whether your soil is acidic or alkaline, or to what degree. The soil can be badly damaged by the improper use of such amendments.

Ultimately, the best proof of the garden's soil will be the health of the garden. If it is reasonably productive, be patient and continue using organic soil-building techniques. If, despite adequate weeding and watering, plants are stunted, leaves are discoloured or splotchy and vegetables are discoloured or misshapen, a soil test should be done.

Green Manures Whether or not the gardener orders a soil test, mulches, compost and green manures can be used freely and safely. Green manures are crops that are not harvested but turned back into the soil. They can be used to increase soil quality in garden areas not in use (as part of the crop rotation plan) or they can be useful in the off-season for gardeners who find organic matter hard to come by.

Green manure plants bring nutrients from deep in the soil to the topsoil, convert sunlight and rainfall into organic matter and may even incorporate or "fix" atmospheric nitrogen into the soil. Plants that can fix nitrogen are members of the Leguminosae family and called legumes; they include alfalfa, clover and vetch. In an experiment in Charlottetown, Prince Edward Island, the yield of potatoes was 248 bushels per acre after fallow (no crop) and 294 bushels per acre after a green manure crop of clover was plowed under.

Legumes are a uniquely valuable plant family because of their ability to fix nitrogen, some of which remains in the soil for the use of following plants. This ability comes from a symbiotic (mutually beneficial) relationship between the legume and soil organisms of the *Rhizobium* genus. Different species of legume work with different species of *Rhizobium*. If

Tiny nodules on the root of a soybean indicate to the gardener that nitrogen fixation has taken place in the legume

in most of Canada, while winter wheat, another overwintering crop, can be planted in areas of Canada where temperatures are not likely to go much lower than 19 degrees F (-7 degrees C), although hardier varieties are now being released. Broadcast fall rye or wheat seed about two weeks before the first fall frost at the rate of 2 or 3 pounds per 1,000 square feet. Seeds can be lightly raked to cover them. Spade or plow the crop under as soon as the soil is dry enough to work in spring and then wait two weeks before planting vegetables, allowing the green manure time to begin decomposing. In the case of grains, be sure they do not go to seed before harvesting – or else "volunteer" seedlings will sprout in the garden. The object is to turn the crop under when it is young and juicy – 4 or 5 inches high – not mature and dry. (You may, however, elect to let a patch of grain mature for harvesting and use in breads or cereals.)

Hardier crops without culinary value include Russian wild rye grass, crested wheat grass, creeping red fescue, timothy and smooth brome grass. Green manure crops suitable for your area should be stocked by local feed and grain outlets. In the far North, where green manure crops are not hardy enough to survive the winter, sow part of the garden each spring to field peas, fall rye, barley or buckwheat, to be dug down in fall.

Crop Rotation Green manuring can form part of a crop rotation routine. The gardener who has plenty of space may be able to grow a legume on one side of the garden and vegetables on the other, rotating every year. Or the green manure crop may temporarily fill a bed or a section of the garden.

With or without green manures, the best crop rotation plans take into consideration the types of plants grown in the garden. Each plant is affected by different pests and diseases, reaches to different depths in pursuit of nutrients and requires different nutrients, with the legumes actually contributing to soil nitrogen levels. Anyone who has grown potatoes in one spot for several years will usually notice a rise in the number of Colorado potato beetles. Moving the potato patch to the other end of the garden will cause a sudden drop in beetle population. Clubroot can be kept in check if brassicas

the correct microorganisms are not present in the garden, little or no fixation will occur, so some gardeners inoculate the seeds with bacteria before planting them. This makes fixation more likely but still not certain – bacteria differ slightly with soil conditions and area – but those who wish to make fixation more likely can order an all-purpose garden inoculant mix from a garden seed house. The inoculant comes with directions for application. Once an area of the garden has been treated, it should not require any further inoculation. While thinning leguminous plants or during harvesting, the gardener can check for fixation by examining the roots for tiny nodules, the evidence that fixation has occurred.

Unfortunately, legume seed is expensive and legumes take some time to become established. While they are best sown in spring or fall and left at least a year before plowdown – often a forage crop is taken off in the meantime – legumes are not as hardy as some grasses. The gardener who has just cleared a new piece of ground might be better off planting a hardy overwintering crop such as fall rye, which germinates in fall, remains dormant over the winter and, if conditions are favourable, grows again the next spring. Fall rye should survive the winter

Common Food Garden Plant Families and How to Rotate Them

Family name	Family members	Rotation
Chenopodiaceae *(the beet family)*	Vegetables: beets, Swiss chard, spinach, Malabar spinach and tampala	Of medium height, these plants will rotate with others in the garden's mid-range: Cruciferae, Leguminosae, Liliaceae, Solanaceae
Compositae *(the sunflower family)*	Vegetables: globe and Jerusalem artichokes, sunflowers, endive, cardoon, escarole, lettuce, salsify, chicory, dandelion Flowers: daisies, zinnias, dahlias, marigolds, asters, chrysanthemums Herbs: yarrow, camomile, tarragon (perennial)	Jerusalem artichokes are perennial and so will not be rotated. Rotate sunflowers with staked peas or pole beans. Leafy Compositae are best rotated with Cucurbitaceae, Leguminosae, Liliaceae, Solanaceae, Umbelliferae. Interplant and rotate marigolds with tomatoes
Convolvulaceae *(the morning glory family)*	Vegetables: sweet pototoes Flowers: morning glories	Sweet potatoes are grown only as a novelty in most areas. Plant in full sun. Morning glories may be interplanted with climbing peas, beans, Cucurbitaceae
Cruciferae *(the mustard family)*	Vegetables: broccoli, Brussels sprouts, cabbage, Chinese cabbage, cauliflower, kale, kohlrabi, mustard greens, radish, rutabaga, turnip, cress, watercress Flowers: alyssum Herbs: horseradish (perennial)	Watercress needs a very wet spot where it will grow every year. Rotate all others with members of other families that grow to about the same size (mid-range) — bush beans and onions, for example
Cucurbitaceae *(the gourd family)*	Vegetables: summer and winter squash, pumpkins, melons, cucumbers, gourds	If staked, rotate with staked tomatoes, pole beans, sunflowers, peas. If allowed to sprawl, rotate with other space-demanding crops, such as potatoes, or other low-growing crops such as leafy Compositae
Graminae *(the corn family)*	Vegetables: corn	One of the garden's hungriest crops, corn should be rotated with legumes whenever possible
Leguminosae *(the pea family)*	Vegetables: beans, peas, lentils, peanuts Flowers: sweet peas, lupines	Although they will grow happily in the same spot for several years in succession, their nitrogen-adding properties make them valuable in rotation with all other families
Liliaceae *(the lily family)*	Vegetables: asparagus (perennial), onions, garlic, leeks, shallots Flowers: lilies (perennial) Herbs: chives (perennial)	Asparagus is perennial and so does not rotate as is also true of perennial onions. All others are valuable in rotations and interplantings with all other families (as long as they are not overly shaded) as they have few pests and may help repel pests from other plants
Solanaceae *(the nightshade family)*	Vegetables: eggplant, peppers, tomatoes, garden huckleberries, ground cherries, tomatillos, potatoes Flowers: nicotiana, petunia	Quite susceptible to fungus diseases and nematodes, members should not be next-door neighbours and should follow other families of similar mid-range height in rotations
Umbelliferae *(the parsley family)*	Vegetables: carrot, celery, celeriac, parsnips Herbs: parsley, dill, fennel, lovage (perennial), chervil, caraway, anise, coriander	Deep-rooted plants that help break up soil; interplant and rotate with leafy or fruiting crops of other families, lettuce and tomatoes, for example

such as cabbage and turnip, which are vulnerable to the disease, are rotated with other plants.

In crop rotation, the gardener must consider not only the plant itself but also its family. All plants belong to families, which are then further divided into genera, species and varieties. Beets, for example, belong to the family Chenopodiaceae. Their botanical name (which can be likened to the Chinese system of listing the surname first) is *Beta vulgaris*; *Beta* is the genus, *vulgaris* the species. Swiss chard has the same botanical name but includes the variety *cicla*; it is *Beta vulgaris cicla*. There is lit-

tle benefit, then, in exchanging beets with Swiss chard in a rotation, as they are virtually identical botanically. Replacing any crop with another in its family is far less valuable than replacing it with one in another family. The table "Common Food Garden Plant Families and How to Rotate Them" on the opposite page indicates which rotations will be of the greatest benefit.

Livestock manures Besides legumes, another common source of soil nitrogen is livestock manure. While all livestock manure is valuable, it varies in nutrient content according to the type of live-

stock and is best allowed to compost before use, even though some nutrient loss will occur. Agriculture Canada notes that "weight for weight, rotted manure is more valuable than fresh manure, because it contains a larger percentage of plant food elements in more readily available form." For in-

same time ensures that the plants are not overfed.

Side-dressing schedule

Root crops – four to six weeks after planting

Vine crops (melons, squash, cucumbers) – when vines begin to "run"

Fruiting crops (tomatoes, peppers) – when the

Composition of Fresh Manure
produced by animals that have been provided with ample bedding. All figures are *for the total combination of feces, urine and bedding, and all values are approximate*

Animal	Amount of manure produced annually in tons	Percentage of Nitrogen (as N)	Percentage of Phosphorus (as P_2O_5)	Percentage of Potassium (as K_2O)
Horse	9	.66	.23	.68
Cow	11.7	.57	.15	.53
Pig	1.6	.56	.32	.52
Sheep	.9	.90	.34	1.00
Chicken	.04 (90 lbs.)	.97	.77	.41

stance, there are approximately 12 pounds of nitrogen in a ton of fresh cow manure and 17 pounds in a ton of well-rotted manure. Gardeners who keep rabbits are well advised to situate worm beds directly under the rabbit cages, as does Rene Clark, secretary of the Dominion Rabbit and Cavy Breeders Association. The worms ingest the droppings to produce what amounts to instant compost. "That was the loam we used for our garden and the neighbour's, too," says Clark.

Those who keep livestock, or have a neighbour who does, have a ready supply of manure; or it can be bought packaged from garden supply stores. Dig manure into newly cleared soil at the rate of 5 pounds per square yard. It can also be used more sparingly in manure teas, or as a side-dressing.

To make manure tea, place about 1 pound of manure in a bucket and fill it with water. Let the mixture sit for a day, then use the liquid on all plants, following about the same schedule as that for side-dressing. Side-dressing is done by applying a line of fertilizer evenly under the edge of the foliage of a row of plants; this conserves fertilizer and at the

first few fruits are set

Cabbage family – two to three weeks after transplanting into the garden, and every week thereafter

Leafy crops – three to four weeks after thinning, and every week thereafter

Corn – when knee-high, and every week thereafter

Legumes (beans, peas) – do not side-dress

Do not use pet or human feces as fertilizers. Both may contain parasites or pathogens that can be transmitted to the gardener. While either can be made safe through proper composting (and indeed sewage sludge is available commercially as a garden fertilizer), northern temperatures and the randomness of most home composting make their use unwise. Human urine, however, is nitrogen-rich (about 2.5 per cent) and safe, as long as the donor does not have a bladder or kidney infection.

Earthworms No discussion of fertilizers would be complete without mentioning the humblest of manure-producing "livestock," the earthworm, literally worth its weight in fertilizer every day. They may be the plainest of creatures, but earthworms are a gardener's friends, aerating and perforating

Analysis of Organic Fertilizers

This chart shows how the content of a fertilizer is analyzed to determine the percentage of three major soil nutrients: nitrogen (N), phosphorus (P) and potassium (K), listed in the formula N - P - K. In fertilizer, phosphorus is present in the compound P_2O_5 and potassium in the compound K_2O

Organic materials	Analysis	Applications
Livestock manure & bedding	.5 to 2 - .1 to .8 - .4 to 1.0	Excellent fertilizer and soil conditioner. See chart on specific values from different animals. Apply rotted manure to good soil at 5 pounds per square yard (12 tons per acre), double that as an initial application on poor soil. Use as manure tea throughout the season
Sewage sludge (dry) (i.e. Milorganite)	.7 to 5.1 - 1.1 to 6.1 - .2 to 1.1	Human wastes treated to kill pathogens and commercially prepared sewage sludge may still contain harmful amounts of heavy metals. If certified safe in this respect, use in place of any high-nitrogen fertilizer. Otherwise, use only on lawns and flowers
Compost	.5 to 3.5 - .5 to 1 - 1 to 2	Apply freely where most needed, year-round
Bone meal (steamed)	0 to 4 - 11 to 26 - 0	Apply sparingly to compost pile or as side-dressing if soil test indicates lack of phosphorus. One pound of bone meal per 100 square feet is usually adequate
Cottonseed meal (dry)	6 - 2.5 - 1.7	Expensive, seldom available in Canada. Apply sparingly as side-dressing
Dried blood	12 - 1.5 - .57	Expensive and very rich in nitrogen. Use sparingly in compost or as side-dressing
Fish emulsion	5 - 2 - 2	Rich in micronutrients. Dilute and apply as foliar (leaf) spray or fertilizer throughout season according to need
Sawdust & wood shavings	.4 - .3 - .7	Use in garden pathways or sparingly in the compost pile
Straw	.5 - .2 - .1	Use as mulch or as an ingredient in the compost pile
Natural Deposits		
Wood ashes	0 - 1 to 2 - 3 to 7	Use only if soil test indicates acidic soil, lack of calcium. Substitute double the rate recommended for crushed limestone
Colloidal phosphate	0 - 25 - 0	Use only if soil test indicates lack of phosphorus
Rock phosphate	0 - 20 to 30 - 0	Use only if soil test indicates lack of phosphorus
Granite meal or dust	0 - 0 - 3.5	Apply only where soil test indicates lack of potassium. Also contains trace minerals
Greensand	0 - 1.35 - 4 to 9.5	Sea floor deposit containing many trace minerals. Mix with high-nitrogen fertilizer as compost additive

the soil with their tunnels, bringing up nutrients from deep in the soil and digesting organic matter to produce nutrient-rich castings. Tests at the Connecticut Agricultural Experiment Station have indicated that earthworm castings contain five times the nitrogen, seven times the available phosphorus, three times the magnesium, 11 times the potash and one and a half times the calcium of the surrounding soil. And the earthworm excretes its weight in castings every day.

Unfortunately, not every garden has earthworms; it takes some time for them to invade newly cleared northern land. They can be introduced, however, and will thrive if they are given a diet high in organic matter — kitchen scraps, grass clippings, manure, fallen leaves. The same soil conditions that otherwise promote healthy plants encourage earthworms: a pH near neutral, plenty of organic matter, adequate moisture. Under an organic garden mulch, earthworms breed prolifically. On the other hand, soil that is very low in organic matter, especially if fine in texture, seems to suffer from the presence of earthworms, and their tunnels dry rock-hard. Gardeners have been known to apply pesticides to the soil to kill earthworms, compounding their problems. The best answer to this sticky situation is organic matter. What keeps the worms happy keeps plants and gardeners happy too.

That Old Black Magic Compost

Compost, a stable humus material that promotes both healthy soil and healthy plants, is the most valuable free soil conditioner available to the gardener. Agriculture Canada's "Manures and Compost" booklet notes that compost "improves the physical and biological condition of the soil and supplies major and minor plant nutrients." Could you ask for more?

Compost also happens to be very easy to prepare. In fact, it practically makes itself, given only a little cooperation from a gardener who has plenty of patience and organic refuse. The patience is kept on hand while the organic matter is piled up and kept warm and moist. The pile heats spontaneously and decomposes with the help of air and microorganisms to produce a crumbly, rich humus. Some common compost ingredients include kitchen scraps, grass clippings (but not from a lawn recently sprayed with a herbicide), fallen leaves (avoid those of walnut trees), livestock manures, spoiled hay, straw and seaweed. Avoid in-

gredients that are not biodegradable: plastic wrapping, foil, glass and such.

City gardeners may be worried about the unsightliness and smell of a compost pile. Small amounts of compost can be made quickly and easily if the gardener pours kitchen garbage and other moist biodegradable materials into black plastic bags which are then tied and placed in a sunny spot. Composting should be complete in two weeks to a month during warm weather. Larger amounts of compost can be prepared inoffensively in an attractive compost container. Most odours can be avoided by turning the pile occasionally to keep it well aerated — that "rotten egg" smell comes from oxygen-free (anhydrous) decomposition that results when a pile is overly wet or compacted.

The gardener also should steer away from using meat scraps and bones, which will attract cats and dogs from miles around — undesirable for both the compost pile and the garden. Birds and squirrels might be attracted to vegetable

peels and seeds in the compost pile, but these visitors are hardly objectionable — indeed, they are often welcome since they will likely barter a few droppings for their compost meal. Any compost pile can be unobtrusive and odour and pest free if it is properly tended within the garden fence and covered with wooden slats or chicken wire. Locate the pile at the edge of the garden and, if possible, in full sun where composting will take place as rapidly as ambient temperatures permit.

Containers A compost pile can be just that, a pile exposed on all sides. Albert Howard, a British agronomist who first systematized the composting procedures he observed in India, recommended a compost pile 6 to 7 feet wide, 3 to 5 feet high, and 7 to 30 feet long — a massive construction that required a great deal of biodegradable matter, all at once. Ingredients were layered, and the completed pile was watered and then covered with a layer of soil, hay or burlap.

Such a gargantuan project is fine for gardeners or farmers with

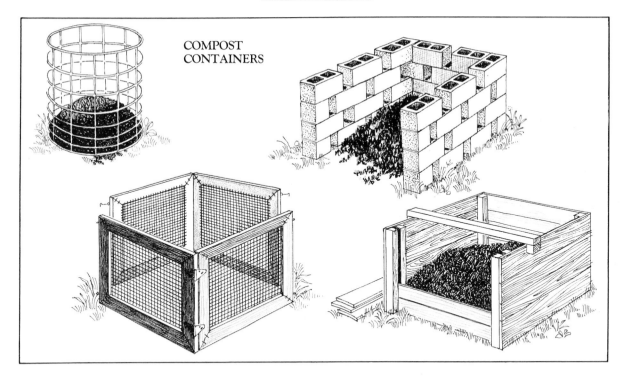

COMPOST
CONTAINERS

plenty of manure, straw and space, but most gardeners work on a far smaller scale. For them it is best to have a container or enclosure into which ingredients can be piled as they become available, creating the same effect as layering. If the container is of sufficient size to keep about a cubic yard of material moist and well aerated, composting can be almost as satisfactory as Albert Howard found it.

The container should be rot resistant, fairly large, permeable to air and easy to work with. Try a perforated oil drum or barrel, or cylinders made of chicken wire or snow fencing; they are lifted off when it is time to turn the pile, which is then shovelled or forked back into the cylinder. Three-sided boxes of rough or used lumber are permanent, attractive and easy to use. Four-foot-square boxes will hold about a ton of compost and can be constructed in rows of three or four boxes, each

holding a pile in a different stage of decomposition. In 1940, J.J. Woods, an agronomist working at the federal agricultural experimental station in Agassiz, British Columbia, reported his success using this type of box: "The writer, in his own garden, produces about 2 cubic yards of compost soil each year in a bin approximately 4 feet square and 4 feet deep built alongside a garage, from the roof of which, during rainy weather, adequate moisture is supplied through the use of an eaves trough and drain pipe."

Inner Workings The size of the compost pile (and therefore of the container) determines both the amount of "fuel" available for composting and the amount of insulation available to contain the heat, since both fuel and insulation are provided by the organic matter. Optimally, temperatures of 158 degrees F (70 degrees C) are reached in the centre of the pile, killing

pathogens and weed seeds. This high temperature can be reached only if conditions are just right, which is not likely to be the case with a small garden compost pile where potentially pathogenic matter (human or pet feces, diseased plant material) and weed seeds should therefore be scrupulously avoided. This does not mean that composting will not occur in a cooler, smaller pile, but it will be slower and less thorough.

In any pile, occasional turning is necessary so that cooler outside material is incorporated into the warm interior for composting. The frequency of turning depends upon how quickly the pile works, and that, in turn, depends upon the size of the pile, the type and coarseness of ingredients and the ambient temperature. Most northern compost piles will cease working in fall, freeze solid in winter and begin working again after thawing in spring. Covering the pile with a sheet of clear polyethylene will speed warming. But a summer pile can be thoroughly composted in less than a month if ingredients are finely ground, damp and fairly high in nitrogen.

The efficiency with which the material composts depends upon its average carbon-to-nitrogen (C:N) ratio. The more nitrogenous matter it contains, the faster it decomposes. Urine, livestock manures, grass clippings, seaweed, hay and kitchen wastes (especially coffee grounds and egg shells) are relatively high in nitrogen. Straw, paper and sawdust are lower. If possible, use one part of high-nitrogen ingredients to two or three parts of carbonaceous (low-nitrogen) ones. A very carbonaceous pile – a truckload of sawdust, for instance – will eventually compost, but it could take years. A very nitrogen-rich pile, on the other hand, will probably smell of ammonia, a sign that precious nitrogen is being lost to the air. Ingredients that fall into the middle range, such as grass clippings and fallen leaves, are more successful on their own. A gardener with little else to add can pile these ingredients alone, adding about an inch of garden soil on every foot or so of leaves or grass.

Chopped or shredded materials decompose faster than those left whole. Thus, a small amount of sawdust could be added to a compost pile while wood chips or twigs would greatly slow the composting. Bone meal can go on the pile, but not discarded soup bones. Shredded paper will compost better than whole sheets, although both should be used sparingly, if at all. And cardboard is taboo – it is just too high in carbon. Material for composting can be run through

a lawn mower or through a specially designed compost shredder. These shredders can render tree roots, branches, leather, bones, whole fish and sea shells into a "meal" so pervious to air, moisture and microbes that it decomposes very quickly even under adverse conditions. The Berkeley compost method, devised in California, uses shredded material for its 14-day beginning-to-end processing.

The Berkeley method calls for turning the moistened pile on the 4th, 7th and 10th days after at least a cubic yard of material has been collected and shredded. Albert Howard's method, on the other hand, called for turning those huge compost piles two or three weeks after piling and again two or three weeks later, with the compost ready for use about three warm months after piling. A garden compost pile requires turning whenever the pile shrinks noticeably in size – by the end of composting, the pile will be about one-third its original size – but no more frequently than twice a week. It is ready to use when it is cool and fairly dark and crumbly but some shape of the original matter is still evident.

Where summers are very short, the use of a chemical "starter" will help speed heating and decomposition. A starter can be bought ready-made from some garden supply outlets or concocted at home. Agriculture Canada offers the following recipe:

40 pounds (18 kilograms) sulfate of ammonia (21 - 0 - 0)

20 pounds (9 kilograms) superphosphate (11 - 48 - 0)

10 pounds (4.5 kilograms) muriate of potash (0 - 0 - 60)

20 pounds (9 kilograms) ground limestone *or*

40 pounds (18 kilograms) wood ashes

Thoroughly mix the ingredients and spread 4 to 6 pounds (2 to 3 kilograms) over each 100 pounds (45 kilograms) of organic matter.

One shovel of fresh manure per 100 pounds of organic matter is a good substitute starter, where it is available.

Compost Applications Compost is an all-round soil conditioner and mild fertilizer that can be used wherever it is most needed; for houseplants, potting vegetable transplants, in hills for squash and melons, as a side-dressing for all vegetables or small fruits in summer. It is almost impossible to overuse compost because it is a gentle, slow-acting fertilizer that is always in short supply. In fact, plants that grow in the compost pile itself are often the healthiest, most productive vegetables you will see.

Compost-Making Points

• Keep the pile as warm and as sheltered from wind as possible

• If pets or predators are a problem, do not include meat scraps

• Use only biodegradable ingredients, 2 or 3 parts carbonaceous to 1 part nitrogenous

• Collect at least a square yard of material before letting it compost

• Include a sprinkling of garden soil throughout the pile. This can also be used to cover the pile and keep lightweight ingredients like fallen leaves from blowing away

• Where the growing season is very short or cool cover the pile with a sheet of clear polyethylene

• Keep the pile moist, neither sodden nor dry

• Bring some compost indoors in fall for use as potting soil and for next spring's transplants (described in Chapter III)

Sources of Soil Tests

Write to the appropriate address to request prices and instructions on gathering soil for testing. All departments offer a graduated system of tests; the least expensive generally measures phosphorus (P), potassium (K), magnesium (Mg) and pH; additional elements will cost more. The returned reports will include fertilizer recommendations. Some offices will also test composts and manures.

British Columbia and the Yukon
Griffin Laboratories
1875 Spall Road
Kelowna, British Columbia V1Y 4R2

Alberta
Soils and Animal Nutrition Laboratory
O.S. Longman Building
905, 6909-116 Street
Edmonton, Alberta T6H 4P2

Saskatchewan
Plains Innovative Laboratory Services
Saskatchewan Soil Testing Laboratory
118 General Purpose Building
University of Saskatchewan
Saskatoon, Saskatchewan S7N 0W0

Manitoba
Norwest Labs
Agricultural Services Complex
203-545 University Crescent
Winnipeg, Manitoba R3T 5S6

Ontario
Ministry of Agriculture and Food
Legislative Buildings
Queen's Park
Toronto, Ontario M7A 2B2

Québec
Tests available to farmers only.

New Brunswick
Land Resource Branch
Department of Agriculture, Soil Laboratory
Box 6000
Fredericton, New Brunswick E3B 5H1

Nova Scotia
Department of Agriculture and Marketing
Box 190
Halifax, Nova Scotia B3J 2M4

Prince Edward Island
Soil and Feed Testing Laboratory
Box 1600
Charlottetown, Prince Edward Island C1A 7N3

Newfoundland and Labrador
Soil and Land Management Division
Provincial Agriculture Building
Box 8700
St. John's, Newfoundland A1B 4J6

United States
Contact the extension service of the appropriate state agricultural college listed in the telephone directory or in Chapter X. For a modest sum, the extension service will conduct and interpret a garden-soil test.

Wood's End Research Laboratory Inc.
Old Rome Road, Box 1850
Mount Vernon, Maine 04352
Wood's End offers a detailed analysis of the soil as well as recommendations for nonsynthetic additives. Write for prices and Customs information if you are ordering from Canada.

A Movable Spring

"Snow lingers in secluded corners and frost is still in the ground, but spring is awaiting a welcome"

— Samuel Thomas Wood
Rambles of a Canadian Naturalist, 1916

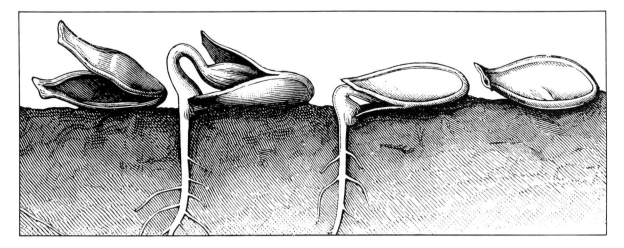

Spring comes earliest to gardeners. Long before the possibility of another blizzard has disappeared with the last snowy owl, gardeners are ordering seeds, mapping out their paper gardens and then sowing seeds indoors. The tail end of winter is immeasurably cheered by a window ledge full of tiny lettuce, cabbage and tomato plants.

Growing your own transplants – that is, sowing seeds indoors for plants that will grow outdoors – can be much more economical than buying commercial transplants, and offers the gardener a far wider variety than can be found in any corner store. It also gives you a satisfying feeling of being involved in the entire life cycle of your plants, from germination to harvest. But home-grown transplants may not be for everyone. They require space, care and, as we shall see, light. The beginning gardener is wise to delay growing transplants for at least a season; your first garden is usually challenging enough.

In Chapter I, some consideration was given to the type and amount of seed a gardener requires. (See "The Greenhorn's Sneak Preview," page 27, the "Quick Reference for Vegetable Yields," page 25, and the sample garden plan, pages 20 and 21.)

Now we will add one simple rule: You will need only one packet of seed for any vegetable that would normally be started indoors. This is so because big seeds such as those of corn, beans, peas and sunflowers, all vegetables that are sown directly into the garden, are also those usually bought in multiple packets or in larger package sizes.

Now that we have established a rule, we will qualify it. The "one packet" rule is true only if the gardener is not growing a great deal of food; market gardeners or self-sufficient families may need more. And it does not take into consideration the gardener's preference for more than one variety; one packet of tomato seeds will be more than enough, but if you'd like to grow cherry tomatoes, paste tomatoes and beefsteaks, you'll need three packets. Also, some expensive hybrid varieties are sold in very small amounts, 20 or 30 seeds per packet (the measure "packet" is unfortunately an imprecise one). When this is the case, it should be mentioned in the seed catalogue or on the packet.

You will note, as you scan the seed catalogues, that there are both "treated" and "untreated" seeds. Companies such as Stokes and Vesey's offer the gardener a choice. Others, such as Harris, sell only treated seeds, while Sanctuary and William Dam sell only untreated seed. Treated seed is brightly coloured, evidence that it has been coated with a fungicide such as captan or thiram, which in this instance helps prevent two fungal ailments, seed decay and damping off. Because the safety of these chemicals is in doubt, many gardeners avoid them. Both diseases can be minimized if the gardener uses sterile potting mix, avoids sowing seeds outdoors in soil too cool for the crop and ensures that the soil is well drained, perhaps in raised beds.

Indoor and Outdoor Planting

Once the seed order arrives in the mail or is bought at the store, between January and March, the gardener should separate the seeds into indoor and outdoor seeders. Then divide them according to planting dates, writing the best sowing date right on the packet or on a divider in a seed file box to ensure that all seeds are sown on time. If the packet contains more than enough seed for the season, write the year of purchase on it for reference in following years.

Vegetables are sown indoors for three reasons: because they have a longer maturation season than most northern gardens can provide (onions, globe artichokes); because they are frost tender and must mature while the weather is still warm (tomatoes, peppers); and because the gardener would prefer an early harvest (cabbage, lettuce). While most frost-tender vegetables (with the exception of cucum-

Approximate Dates of the Last Spring Frost – Canada

| Before April 1 | April 1 - April 15 | April 15 - May | May 1 - June 1 | June 1 - June 15 | June 15 - July 1 | After July 1 |

bers, squash and pumpkins in most areas) *must* be started indoors, many others depend upon your own choice and climate.

Indoor Planting Schedule

In most areas, indoor seeding begins in late February or early March. For a more precise date, check maps below for the approximate date of the last spring frost in your area. Because local conditions may vary, it is wise to double check with local gardeners, a nearby horticultural society or agricultural representative. *Before you read any further, do that.* Practically every planting calculation from now on depends on the estimated date of your last spring frost. Find out what it is and then record it in your garden notebook along with the approximate date of the first fall frost. Now you can estimate spring indoor planting dates by subtracting the following numbers of weeks from the last spring frost date. For example, Calgary's last spring frost usually occurs around May 20, so the first indoor seeding will occur 10 weeks earlier, about March 11.

10 weeks – onions, leeks, peppers, early celery, eggplant, asparagus

9 weeks – globe artichokes, parsley, celeriac

8 weeks – early lettuce

6 - 8 weeks – tomatoes, early basil

6 - 7 weeks – early cabbage, broccoli, Brussels sprouts, kohlrabi, kale, early head lettuce

5 - 6 weeks – late cabbage, late celery, early leaf lettuce, cauliflower

Approximate Dates of the Last Spring Frost – United States

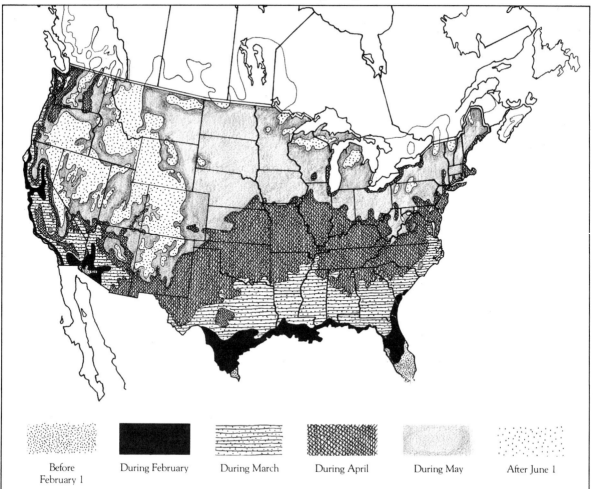

| Before February 1 | During February | During March | During April | During May | After June 1 |

4 - 5 weeks – cucumbers, melons, squash, pumpkins, gourds

It is not usually wise to start plants much earlier. Overly mature transplants become root bound and stunted, wilting easily and often displaying symptoms of nutrient deficiencies. When they are

transplanted outdoors, they suffer the change more acutely. They may produce a smaller harvest than those transplanted at a younger stage.

Outdoor Planting Schedule

Outdoor planting times are also calculated around the usual date of the last spring frost. As is apparent from the following list, many of the vegetables listed above can be sown outdoors in addition to or instead of indoors.

5 - 7 weeks before the last spring frost – seeds of leaf lettuce, carrots, peas, broad beans, spinach, turnips; onion sets and transplants; parsley seeds or transplants

3 - 4 weeks before the last spring frost – all items mentioned above; lettuce seeds; seeds or transplants of asparagus, beets, broccoli, Brussels sprouts, cabbage, collards, kale, potato eyes, radishes

2 - 3 weeks before the last spring frost – all items mentioned above, lettuce transplants, corn seeds

Around the last frost date – all items mentioned above; seeds of beans, peanuts, sunflowers; seeds or transplants of cauliflower, cucumbers, summer squash; transplants of globe artichokes, tomatoes, peppers. Cover all tender plants on cold nights

1 - 2 weeks after the last frost date – seeds of lima beans, soybeans; seeds or transplants of winter squash, pumpkins; transplants of celery, muskmelon, watermelon; sweet potato roots

Sometimes sowing or transplanting earlier than these dates will be successful, especially if hot caps or row covers are used. It all depends on the garden site and the weather in any particular season. Ex-

Window greenhouses (top left and right) and attached greenhouses extend the indoor light available to sun-hungry plants

perimentation is definitely worthwhile, as long as some seeds or transplants are saved for insurance in case of early crop failure.

Light Requirements

Seedlings that will grow indoors need a dependable supply of bright light. Leaf and root crops require at least four hours of direct sunlight daily, while fruiting crops such as tomatoes need a minimum of eight, preferably more in both cases. A south-facing window ledge, therefore, is required by any plants that will not receive artificial light. Or the plants must be moved from window to window with the sunlight. The window ledge itself may have to be extended in order to accommodate the plants.

Besides providing natural light, window ledges allow plants to use household heat while keeping them within easy reach. Unfortunately, space on window ledges is severely limited in most homes. By the time all the seedlings have been transplanted into larger containers, some are far from the glass. This situation can be relieved by the use of attached or free-standing growing shelters, described in "Gardening Under Glass" on page 57. As well, fluorescent or incandescent fixtures can be used to boost the light supply.

Basing your calculations on the plant requirements stated above, supply two hours of artificial light for every hour of natural light missed. This artificial light may be provided in any of several ways:
• Commercial grow-light fluorescents, used according to the manufacturer's directions
• Household incandescent bulbs and cool white fluorescents, at the rate of 1 watt of the former to 3 to 5 of the latter. Keep incandescent bulbs about a foot above plant tops, as they produce a considerable amount of heat. Fluorescents may be 6 inches above the plants
• 40-watt fluorescents, in a one-to-one ratio of cool white to warm white tubes. Two tubes should supply an area of about 4 feet by 6 feet
• Where there is a good supply of natural light, cool white fluorescents can be used alone

In all cases, bulbs should be set in reflectors that will direct the light downward, and all units should be installed by a window. All should be shut off for a rest period of about eight hours at night.

Gardeners using window ledges for seedlings should note that the night temperature by the glazing may be very low. Prepare to move all the plants to a warmer spot at night, putting them by the window again in the morning. Give the container a half-turn every morning to ensure that stems grow straight.

Containers

Gardeners who have been starting seeds indoors for a few seasons become quite ingenious at recycling containers suitable for seedlings. As long as a

container is reasonably sturdy, 2 or 3 inches deep, will drain water, and can be expected to release the root ball easily, it should be adequate. Egg carton indentations are too small to be really useful, while large plant pots take too much space and soil to be practical. Paper or Styrofoam beverage cups or cottage cheese containers, their bottoms perforated, are ideal, and even allow the gardener to write the variety name on the rim – use crayon on plastic containers, ballpoint on others. Litre-sized milk cartons are good for large transplants such as melons and tomatoes, while a 2-litre container will hold four young tomato or pepper seedlings. Peat pots and peat pellets are both intended to be planted directly in the garden. As such, they involve no harmful root disturbance. They are quite expensive, however, and peat pellets are too small to allow you to take many transplants right to the garden.

Flats can be filled with growing medium and used for some seedlings, or they can hold several smaller containers. A shoe box cut down to 3 inches high, a foil baking pan, fibre flats (the sort that come with purchased plants) and wooden flats are all fine. To make a wooden flat, cut end pieces of ⅝-inch lumber 12 inches long, side and bottom pieces of ¼-inch wood 22 inches long. Nail the side pieces into a rectangle, and then nail on the bottom board or boards, leaving narrow spaces between them for drainage. Containers with large drainage holes such as these flats have should be lined with a single sheet of newspaper before they are filled with growing medium.

The container that is best for any particular seed or seedling depends in part upon the sensitivity of that plant to transplanting. Some seeds must be sown in the pots in which they will remain until they are planted in the garden; others are usually transplanted once or even twice, each time receiving more growing room.

Beets, Swiss chard, spinach, broccoli, Brussels sprouts, cabbage, lettuce and tomatoes are easy to transplant, and so can first be sown thickly in rows or broadcast evenly in flats. Later they can be transplanted into larger containers before finally being moved into the garden.

Cauliflower, celery, eggplant, onions and peppers need more care when transplanted. Either plant them initially in the containers that will hold them until they are moved into the garden, or try to retain as much of the root ball as possible when transplanting them.

Cucumbers, melons, squash and gourds are extremely sensitive to root disturbance. Those that cannot be sown directly in the garden must be sown in containers large enough to hold them until they are transplanted into the garden. The container should either be the type that can be planted (a peat pot or peat pellet), or one that will easily release the entire root ball intact. Cardboard or Styrofoam containers are suitable, as they can be torn away from the root ball.

Soil Mixes

From the time that seeds first germinate until the true leaves begin to form, they live on nutrients stored within the seed itself. This is why commercial growers often start their seedlings in a fairly infertile growing medium, moving the plants into a more fertile medium at greater spacing when their true leaves form. (The seedling leaves, or cotyledons, the first leaves the young plant produces, are usually very simple, either elongated or rounded, lacking the indentations and wrinkles of the "true" leaves that come next.) A medium for germination alone can be provided by any of the following ingredients, usually in a mixture containing some peat:

Perlite – volcanic rock that has been heated to about 990 degrees C, expanding it and making it porous. Although nonnutritive and not able to hold water as well as vermiculite, it is lightweight and sterile.

Vermiculite – a mica compound heated to about 765 degrees C, which causes it to expand and become porous. It holds water well, contains some potassium and magnesium, and is lightweight and sterile. Zonalite, vermiculite packaged for use as insulation, costs less than horticultural vermiculite.

Sand – Blowsand or builder's sand (but not ocean beach sand, which is salty) is heavier but less expensive than perlite or vermiculite. It too promotes drainage and aeration. It is not sterile.

Peat moss – Peat, partially decomposed sphagnum moss, has a great ability to hold water when damp, but will shed water if allowed to dry out thoroughly. Initially, knead water into it and thereafter do not let it dry out. It has little or no nutritive value, but is often quite acidic.

Sphagnum moss – is sold both milled and unmilled. Milled is easier to handle but more expensive than unmilled. Both have water-holding properties similar to those of peat moss. Because it is slightly antiseptic, sphagnum helps the gardener avoid soil-borne diseases. A quarter of an inch of sphagnum on top of any other soil mix will help prevent damping off (a common fungus disease).

Many other growing media composed of paper, polystyrene and minerals are similarly sterile and low or absent in nutrients.

For the home gardener, such ingredients are usually used in combination with more fertile ones capable of feeding the seedling for some time. Often, in fact, it is most convenient to use the same growing mix throughout the indoor growing

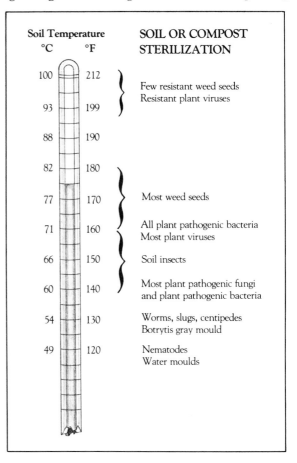

Soil Temperature		SOIL OR COMPOST STERILIZATION
°C	°F	
100	212	Few resistant weed seeds
93	199	Resistant plant viruses
88	190	
82	180	
77	170	Most weed seeds
71	160	All plant pathogenic bacteria
		Most plant viruses
66	150	Soil insects
60	140	Most plant pathogenic fungi and plant pathogenic bacteria
54	130	Worms, slugs, centipedes Botrytis gray mould
49	120	Nematodes Water moulds

schedule. Because topsoil alone becomes too compact indoors for best root growth, it must be combined with one of the above ingredients so that the mix is aerated and drains well. Tender young roots can best make their way through a lightweight medium. Suitable mixes can be purchased or made at home. Some good mixes that can take the gardener right from seed germination to outdoor planting include:

• 1 part potting soil or topsoil – 1 part peat – 1 part perlite or sand
• 1 part compost, garden soil or potting soil – 1 part perlite, vermiculite or sand
• 7 parts by weight of fertile soil – 3 parts peat – 2 parts sand
• 1 part compost – 1 part soil

Gardeners who have compost shredders can substitute shredded pine cones for peat. If compost or garden soil is to be used in the mix it should be brought indoors in fall, before freeze-up. Left in bags in the porch or basement it may freeze before use, so should be brought into a warm room to thaw for about a week before it is needed.

Compost or garden soil must be sterilized before it can be used for seeding indoors. In its natural state it contains weed seeds, fungi, bacteria and viruses that can compete with or harm seedlings, but that the gardener can destroy easily although malodorously by spreading the soil no more than 4 inches deep in baking trays and baking it in an oven at 300 degrees F (148 degrees C) for about 90 minutes. If you have a meat or candy thermometer, cover the trays with foil pierced to admit the thermometer into the soil. After the temperature reaches 180 degrees F, bake 30 minutes more. Then allow it to cool, and it will be ready for use.

Sowing Seeds

Sort the containers, deciding which are appropriate for which plants according to their tolerance to transplanting. Mix the soil with the other ingredients and fill containers to within ¼ inch of the top, tamping the soil down lightly. If necessary, water it with a warm spray – the soil should be just damp.

As a general rule, seeds are planted at a depth from one to three times their diameter both indoors and outdoors. Very fine seeds such as those of celery, lettuce and some herbs, are just lightly pressed into the soil surface, while those as large as pumpkin seeds go about ½ inch under. The soil surface should not be allowed to dry out before the seeds sprout. Either spray the surface regularly, cover the containers with plastic, or place the flats or containers in a bath of lukewarm water ½ inch deep until the seedlings emerge. Seeds germinating in sunlight under glass – in a window greenhouse, for instance – should not be covered with plastic, which creates a "double greenhouse" effect that can bake the soil and kill the seedlings.

As we have noted, some seeds will go immediately into the container that will hold them until transplanting. In this case, allow each seed about 1 square inch of soil surface, pinching off all but the strongest seedling at the soil level after the true leaves have formed.

Other seeds can be planted quite thickly in rows or evenly broadcast over the soil surface and then covered to the proper depth. Later, it is usual to transplant all the healthiest seedlings into larger, perhaps even individual containers. This is the case with lettuce, spinach, beets, chard, and the cabbage family. Onions and celery are exceptions. They are sown thickly – seeds can be spaced a few millimetres apart in rows 1 inch apart – but they are often left in the original flats until they are planted in the garden, celery thinned to ½ inch between seedlings. Onions need not be thinned.

Pregermination

The fact that seeds germinate best at higher temperatures than those preferred by the plants themselves presents gardeners with a problem in logistics. Newly sown flats or containers should be placed in a spot warm enough to promote fairly speedy germination – 60 to 90 degrees F (16 to 32 degrees C) is a satisfactory temperature range. Under a heat lamp or on the warm top of a refrigerator or wood stove are suitable locations. In a cooler spot, seeds will germinate very slowly or simply die and rot. Fortunately, most seeds do not require light for germination, so the containers can go into a warm place inside the home until the seeds sprout, when they must immediately be moved into the light.

The germination problem can be further circumvented if the gardener sprouts his seeds before sowing them. This simplifies the provision of ideal germination conditions, and also ensures that the gardener plants only viable seeds — wasteful thinning of healthy seedlings is avoided.

Pregermination should be done with large seeds only, as the handling of tiny seeds is very difficult. Tomato or eggplant seeds are the smallest to be pregerminated. Other seeds that can be handled this way are those of peppers, okra, cucumbers, squash, melons, beans and peas. Pregermination can precede either indoor or outdoor planting.

To germinate seeds, collect a few containers that can be securely lidded. Container size will depend on the quantity of seeds in question — cottage cheese or yogurt containers are usually suitable. Place a paper towel or piece of finely woven cotton on the bottom, wet it with lukewarm water and, to allow for germination failures, spread on it a single layer of about 25 per cent more seeds than you want plants. Several cultivars can be put in a single container if you draw sections on the towel with a ballpoint pen and then record the variety name on each section.

Lid the containers and place them in a warm spot, preferably 80 to 90 degrees F (26 to 32 degrees C), no hotter. Check every day to ensure that the towel is still wet. Germination will take from a couple of days to two or three weeks, depending on the type of seed, its freshness and the temperature. As soon as its tiny root or radicle appears, the seed is ready for planting at the usual depth — one to three times the diameter of the seed. Plant it very carefully so that the radicle is not damaged and lies sideways or points downward. Cover the seed and tamp the soil down gently. Pregerminated seeds may be placed at the final transplant spacing best for that vegetable. Water with lukewarm water, place the seeded containers in a warm spot and make sure the soil remains warm and damp until the sprouts appear.

One of the most common disorders of seedlings is damping off, a fungus disease that may attack the tiny shoots before or after they emerge from the soil. Damping off is usually manifest either as "germination failure" or as a pinching of the stem at the soil line, which causes the seedling to bend over and die. The gardener can best avoid damping off by using sterilized soil, by keeping seedlings warm and by ensuring that the soil is well drained and never sodden. The use of peat in the mix or sprinkled on the soil surface also helps discourage the disease. Do not sow seeds too thickly or too deep. If damping off does infect plants, try applying a spray of crushed garlic cloves and water.

Transplanting

From the time the seedlings appear, they must be allowed sufficient light and enough water so that the soil never entirely dries out. Always use slightly warm water — never hot or icy cold. As soon as the true leaves form, those plants that have been sown in rows or broadcast in flats should be transplanted into larger containers. Use the tip of a knife to obtain as much of a root ball as possible and, holding the seedling by its cotyledon (first leaf), plant it

All seedlings should be transplanted gently so that root damage is minimal. Tamp soil down lightly after transplanting

slightly deeper than its original soil level in the new container, allowing 1 to 1½ inches around each seedling. Onions and celery can be left in their original flats; members of the melon family should not be transplanted.

Every couple of weeks, water the transplants with manure tea or a dilute solution of fish fertilizer according to the directions on the bottle. If plants become pale, discoloured or cease growing, they should be transplanted into larger containers. Tomatoes may need a further transplanting about two weeks before they go into the garden. Again, plant them deeper than they were before, setting them into individual containers about 5 inches deep. During *any* transplanting operation, disturb the roots as little as possible.

Cold Treatment
The early yield of tomatoes and peppers may be increased by a cold treatment, a sort of premature hardening off that may be included as a matter of

---

After the soil has been weeded and raked level, seeds are then sown at a depth of one to three times their diameter

course by gardeners who cannot avoid the low temperatures involved. In the treatment, tomatoes are grown at a minimum night temperature of 50 to 55 degrees F (10 to 13 degrees C) for three weeks from the time the first true leaves appear. After three weeks, the temperature is maintained at 60 to 65 degrees F (16 to 18 degrees C) day and night. Similarly, when the third true leaves of peppers appear, they are subjected to a night temperature range of 53 to 55 degrees F (12 to 13 degrees C) for four weeks, after which they are kept at around 70 degrees F (21 degrees C) day and night. Although cold treatment will not increase overall yield in most cases, it will encourage the development of those important first fruits.

Hardening Off
About a week before plants are ready to go into the garden they must be hardened off, made ready for the harsh environment that awaits them outdoors. Hardening off involves dropping the air temperature, withholding moisture, or both. For home gardeners, the best way to harden plants is to take them outdoors on a calm, warm day (at least 60

degrees F, 16 degrees C) about a week before the planting out date, leave them in a shady spot for about an hour and bring them in again. The next day leave them in the shade for two hours, and the next day give them an hour in full sun and a couple of hours in the shade. By the end of the week they will remain outdoors all day and, if there is no danger of frost, all night as well. Be sure that they do not dry out enough to wilt, but do not keep them constantly moist. Hardening off can be done in a cold frame, whose construction is described on pages 59 and 60. Plant all vegetables outdoors according to the schedule.

Transplanting Outdoors

As we have seen, some plants are sown or transplanted into the garden before the last frost in spring, some around the time of the last frost, and the most tender plants after the soil is warm and nights are mild. Before the garden is ready to receive seeds or transplants, however, you should weed and rake the seeding area flat and work the soil to a crumb-like texture as you remove stones and break up clods.

The best day for setting out transplants is a calm and overcast one. Laying down plastic mulch or protecting transplants under shelters will help get them off to a good start. See "Gardening Under Glass" on the facing page.

Because cutworms can make quick work of tender seedlings, emerging from underground to sever the stems at the soil line, surround all transplants with a collar made of cardboard or a tin can with both ends removed. The collar must extend above and below the soil line about 1½ inches.

Outdoor Transplant Spacing

Space transplants approximately as follows (all of the measurements indicate the minimum amount of surface area left around each plant):

Plant	Inches
Asparagus	18
Beets*	2
Broccoli, Brussels sprouts, Cabbage	18
Cantaloupe	In hills of 2 or 3 plants, each hill with at least 3 feet all around. Or plant vining varieties 1 foot apart against a fence, and support fruit
Carrots*	2
Cauliflower	18
Celery	6
Cucumbers	As cantaloupe, but vining varieties may be spaced 6 inches apart against a fence. Fruit support unnecessary
Eggplant	18
Globe artichokes	36
Kale	12
Kohlrabi	8
Leeks	6
Lettuce, leaf	4
Lettuce, head	12
Onion sets or transplants	4
Parsley, Parsnips*	4
Peppers	12
Potatoes	One piece of seed potato needs 18 inches all around
Radishes*	1
Spinach	4
Squash, summer	As cantaloupe, but fruit may not need support
Squash, winter & Pumpkins	As cantaloupe, but hills at least 6 feet apart
Swiss chard	6
Tomatoes, staked	18
Tomatoes, unstaked	2-3 feet
Watermelon	As cantaloupe, but hills 4 feet apart

*Usually sown in the garden, not transplanted

Seeding Outdoors

To sow seeds directly outdoors, follow the same rule that applied indoors – they go at a depth about two or three times the diameter of the seed. As is the case indoors, pregerminated seeds sprout faster. For most seeds, dig a furrow in the soil with the point of a stick or trowel to the correct depth for planting each particular seed, spaced at the rate recommended in Chapter IV (or on the packet). Very fine seeds such as lettuce, however, may be broadcast on the soil surface and lightly pressed down. Later, all seedlings are thinned to the rate for transplants listed on the opposite page.

Others, notably melon, squash and cucumber seeds, are usually planted in hills in groups of two or three seeds. To make a hill, dig a hole where the hill will be, about the depth of the blade of a spade, and about 1 foot in diameter. Fill the hole with compost or well-rotted manure and cover it with the removed topsoil, then shape it like a shallow volcano, making an indentation in the centre where the seeds will go. Space the seeds or transplants evenly around the indentation.

After all the seeds are sown, water the beds or rows if the soil is dry. Covering the seeds with damp compost rather than soil may hasten their germination, which depends largely upon soil temperature. If soil is heavy, water the furrow before sowing the seeds, then cover with compost or soil but do not rewater. Heavy wet soil may form a crust impenetrable to tender seedlings.

The identity of the seeds in each row or bed can be marked with a seed packet or with plastic or wooden markers that can be purchased from garden outlets. Or you may prefer to identify them only in the appropriate spaces of the paper garden plan in your gardener's notebook. Mark down also the date of planting and the weather on that date. Those who have a soil thermometer should also note the soil temperature at seeding time, and the length of time it takes for sprouts to appear.

Gardening Under Glass

Fashions in gardening are usually subtle and often influenced by changes in technology. A couple of generations ago, gardeners made extensive use of a device heated with decomposing horse manure. Known as a hot bed, it was deemed once by a Canadian horticulturist as "desirable wherever vegetables or flowers are grown in Canada. . . . With a hot bed it is possible to mature certain vegetables in parts of Canada where, if started in the open, they would not ripen before being killed by frost." Since then, a shortage of horse manure along with a plentiful supply of new plastics and electric grow lights has almost eclipsed the use of the hot bed. Now, rather than being "started in the open," seeds are sown under lights or inside any of several types of plant shelter.

All fall into one of two general categories: There are attached shelters and there are detached or free-standing shelters. While hot beds are included in the latter category, attached shelters such as window greenhouses are directly connected to the house or another building. Although both types extend indoor growing space and increase the amount of sunlight

available to plants, it is how each type of shelter uses the heat from sunlight that distinguishes most clearly between them.

When the sun shines through glass or plastic into an enclosed space, heat is absorbed by objects in the shelter but does not pass out easily through the glazing. Instead it collects, causing the tem-

perature in the shelter to rise, a gain that may be spectacular and even deadly to plants. Any type of shelter, then, requires ventilation to allow excess heat to escape while supplying plants with fresh air. With detached structures, this heat is vented to the outdoors. With attached ones, it enters the neighbouring building for further use. In spring and fall, a northern home can receive heat on clear days from an attached greenhouse. Attached structures have another big advantage. They are easily accessible from indoors, which is a real boon at all times, since plants in shelters require daily and sometimes hourly maintenance, and is especially convenient when icy weather makes the trip outdoors an unpleasant ritual.

Attached structures are, however, less versatile in their location than detached ones. Also, they usually demand more sophisticated carpentry and thus a greater initial investment of time and money than free-standing shelters, most of which can be easily constructed and placed in almost any sunny spot.

The Passive Solar Greenhouse
If fashion has taken the hot bed almost into obscurity, it has likewise brought the passive solar greenhouse to the forefront of today's gardening scene. Modern insulation and glazing materials have made this large, energy-efficient plant shelter a practical tool for many gardeners.

Attached to the south, southwest or southeast side of a building, it is among the most sophisticated of growing spaces, a well-insulated, permanent structure large enough to allow the gardener to stand inside it. It has growing beds

or benches all along the south wall and, above them, glazing that slopes upward to meet either the greenhouse roof or the house wall. The back (north) wall often contains thermal mass – usually stones or containers of water – to store

Easily accessible from indoors, the attached passive solar greenhouse collects heat that encourages plant growth and helps warm the building behind the north wall

the solar heat. A doorway customarily leads from the greenhouse into the house, and another may lead outdoors.

Although it requires a suitable location, often a building permit, and usually the expenditure of considerable time and money, the solar greenhouse is very useful for anyone who wishes to garden beyond the growing season and whose home can accommodate it. As well as growing all garden transplants it can, in most areas, produce frost-hardy vegetables economically throughout much of the winter. Numerous books have been published on the construction and use of solar greenhouses; any bookstore will carry at least one. As well, *Harrowsmith* magazine has published a number of articles on the attached greenhouse, most notably in issue number 39.

Window Greenhouses A window greenhouse is a small version

of an attached solar greenhouse. As such, it shares many of its advantages – easy access for the gardener, air exchange between house and greenhouse – but has a few unique qualities of its own. Compared with a full-sized green-house, it requires less time and money, can be built onto most homes, and needs little maintenance. Its growing space is, however, far more limited – the arm's-length space that can be reached through a standard-sized window can hold just enough transplants to supply a regular-sized garden.

This addition is built on the outside of any sunny window that slides open or can be opened inward. Extending to the outside from the bottom of the window frame, its floor is a shelf, often insulated, that may go beyond the window on both sides but is small enough that all corners can easily be reached from inside the house. Plastic or glass is supported and attached to the shelf and to the outside of the window frame in such a way that a tent-like shelter is formed. Window greenhouses can be temporary, made of plastic stapled to the growing shelf and window frame, or they can be permanent, a wooden framework supporting panes of glass, the whole structure supported on a foundation with footings below the frost line. Opening the window provides enough ventilation in cool weather, but any unit used in summer will require ventilation to the outdoors as well (see photograph, page 50).

Detached Growing Spaces A free-standing greenhouse is the best-known and largest type of detached shelter, and is favoured by commercial growers. On a smaller scale, where the growing season demands a large structure for summer protection of tender plants, or where the gardener cannot provide a suitable location for an attached greenhouse, this is a useful and sometimes indispensable aid for growing plants. Built of plastic stapled to a wooden frame with an A-frame or Quonset (semi-circular) shape, it can be constructed quickly and quite cheaply. Double-glazed, metal-framed commercial units, on the other hand, can be very expensive.

The detached unit has the disadvantages of being separate from the house and therefore relatively inaccessible, and of requiring a good deal of supplementary heating if it is to be used in winter, spring or fall – temperatures in the greenhouse may be as cold as outdoors at night or on cold, windy or overcast days. Any solar heat that is collected is ventilated to the outdoors.

Hot Beds, Cold Frames Hot beds and cold frames are small versions of the detached greenhouse. One, obviously, is heated and the other is not. Consequently, hot beds receive plants earlier in the season than do cold frames. Hot

beds are usually put to work as soon as seedlings started indoors have their first true leaves. The units can even be used for germination, but in the North that is risky, demanding frequent temperature checking and insulation adjustments. The cold frame, however, usually receives tender plants only in time for hardening off. While frost-hardy plants may be sown there, they are more often transplanted into the bed after the first true leaves have developed. A cold frame is, after all, as cold as the outdoors at night and on overcast days. As the weather warms, the top of the frame is left open for increasingly long periods, so that the plants in the frame gradually become acclimatized or hardened off and ready to face life in the outdoors.

Both the hot bed and the cold frame are enclosed by a ground-level frame with the southernmost wall about 8 inches high, and the back wall about 13 inches high. The frame is made of corner-braced lumber treated with copper naphthenate, or of logs, stones or cement blocks. If the structure is heavy and permanent, the footing must extend below the frost line to prevent damage from soil heaving. The frame must be big enough to support whatever glazing will be used, often recycled 3-by-6-foot storm windows. Two such windows, supplying 36 square feet of growing space, are sufficient for most home gardens. The windows rest on the frame, angled toward the south. The glazing can be hinged to the frame, but need not be; instead, it can be turned slightly when ventilation is required. The outside of the frame is bermed all around to the rim with soil.

Both structures can overheat

quickly on sunny days because of the relatively limited amount of contained air space. The temperature in the bed should always be between 50 and 85 degrees F (10 and 30 degrees C). Leave a thermometer inside where it can be seen through the glazing. On frosty nights, both structures should be covered with straw, old carpets, blankets or burlap bags.

Venting is necessary when the outdoor temperature rises above 45 degrees F (7 degrees C), but take care that icy winds do not blow on the young plants – a narrow crack is often all the venting needed. The proper care and maintenance of a cold frame or hot bed is a skill that comes with practice. Checking is needed at least twice daily.

To harden off plants before transplanting them into the garden, open the glazing for a few hours when the air is warm and the sky is overcast, and continue leaving it open a bit longer each day until the frame is open all day and, if possible, all night just before transplanting. A few plants can be left in the open frame to mature. In fact, frames with very high walls can be covered on frosty nights until the plants are mature, which is a good idea where summer frosts are possible.

Cold Frame Installation In autumn, choose a sunny, well-sheltered spot, clear the sod and make a 6-inch-high pile of light, fertile topsoil, slightly wider all around than the frame. Mulch the pile with 2 feet of fallen leaves or straw. About a week before the frame is to be used in spring, remove the mulch and place the frame and glazing over the soil, allowing it a few days to warm. Hardy seeds can then be sown directly into the soil in the frame, or transplants planted at the spacing recommended for transplanting into containers. Alternatively, plants can be left in their individual containers, which are buried to the rim in soil. If you do this, be sure to water *inside* the containers.

Insulated Cold Frames By insulating a cold frame that extends into the soil below the frost line, the duration of usefulness of the unit can be lengthened, often by weeks. Such insulated frames, like attached solar greenhouses, have attained popularity quite recently thanks to new insulation and glazing materials that make good use of solar heat. The north wall is high and insulated, with the south-facing double glazing angled to accept the perpendicular rays of the sun in spring and fall. In mild areas of the North, it is actually possible to garden throughout the winter with such a device. Researchers at Prince Edward Island's Ark project (which, until it was disbanded in 1981, conducted research in alternative agriculture under the sponsorship of the provincial and federal governments), wrote in the Ark's final year that "in two years of trials. . . selected cold-tolerant greens have produced well in winter and very early spring inside the insulated frames, and have survived even the coldest winter weather, although with lowered yields."

The Ark frames were used for germinating hardy seedlings that would later be transplanted into the garden, and for transplants that were started indoors and took up temporary residence in the insulated cold frame before moving outside. In summer, heat-loving vegetables could be left to mature in the frame, its glazing open. To make an Ark frame:

• Find a sunny sheltered spot and dig a pit 2 feet deep and of suitable size to accommodate the chosen glazing. The frame in the diagram requires a pit approximately 4 feet by 8 feet. The long axis of the pit runs east-west. Place topsoil in one

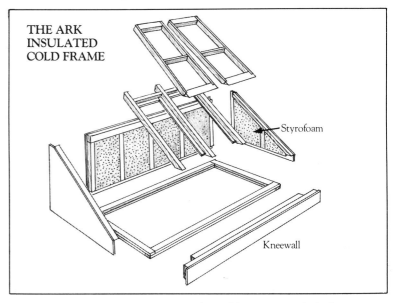

THE ARK INSULATED COLD FRAME

Styrofoam

Kneewall

pile, subsoil in another
• Insulate the bottom and sides of the pit with slabs of 2-inch Styrofoam, letting it extend about 2 inches above ground level
• Refill the pit, first with subsoil, then topsoil mixed with compost
• Complete the structure as the diagram above indicates, glazing with plastic or glass, and hinging the doors to open sideways

Hot Beds As we have noted, traditional hot beds were warmed with decomposing horse manure, which creates heat in the same manner that composting produces heat. This keeps plants warm and also supplies them with carbon dioxide, which enhances growth. To make a manure-heated bed, build the same type of frame as for a cold frame and then proceed as follows:

• In a sheltered sunny spot, before the ground freezes in the fall, dig a pit 2 feet deep which extends 1 foot beyond the edge of the frame on all sides. Its long axis should run east-west (the manure can be piled on the ground in spring, but this is not as effective)

• About two weeks before it is time to use the hot bed, pile beside the pit enough fresh cattle or horse manure to more than fill the pit
• Five or six days later, fork the manure into the pit, tramping it down a layer at a time before adding more. When you are finished, it should be heaped above the edges of the pit. Set the frame and glazing on top of the pile
• In two or three days remove the glazing, tramp down the manure, and add 5 or 6 inches of good topsoil. Insert a soil thermometer, or any thermometer without a wooden base (wood will warp), into the soil. When its temperature has dropped to 80 or 90 degrees F (26 to 32 degrees C), sowing or transplanting can begin

Electric Hot Beds It is now more common to heat hot beds with electricity. One system, described in the booklet, "The Home Vegetable Garden," from the British Columbia Ministry of Agriculture and Food, uses a buried electric cable, available from any hardware or building supply store, its thermostat set at 65 degrees F

the seeds or plants in the garden. They speed soil warming and plant development, often encouraging maturation one to three weeks sooner than otherwise. They also provide some protection against frost; a single layer of plastic will

mercially and many others can be made at home. Waxed paper hot caps are sold in 6- to 12-inch heights and must be perforated for ventilation. They can be quite easily made at home out of waxed paper circles stapled into a teepee

A COLD FRAME CONSTRUCTED TO USE FOUR STORM WINDOWS

(18 degrees C). To contain the cable, this frame must be set 6 inches into the ground so that, in total, it is 14 inches deep in front, and 19 inches deep at the back. Since the electrically heated bed dries out rather quickly, moisture levels should be checked daily.

Electric heating can also be provided with a cable hung around the inside of the frame walls above the ground, or, for a 3-by-6-foot unit, with eight 25-watt incandescent bulbs in porcelain sockets mounted on a board which is attached under the glazing or to the back wall. Use a weatherproof extension cord between the house and shelter.

Row Covers, Cloches and Plant Protectors These are devices that bring the mountain to Mohammed; all are portable structures that are built or set directly over

protect plants from very light frost, while a double layer will keep plants from harm to about 27 degrees F (-2.8 degrees C). If the temperature is expected to drop further that that, cover the plastic with blankets.

The original cloche, French for "bell," was just that, a glass bell jar used by French market gardeners as a plant protector. Now, however, the term encompasses almost as many sizes and shapes of plant cover as there are sizes and shapes of gardener. They may cover entire rows or individual plants. All are fastened to the ground so that they will not blow away and all are designed to shed water. As is the case with other plant shelters, they must include some provision for ventilation.

For individual plants, several styles of cover are available com-

shape. Plastic, capless bleach bottles, their bottoms removed, are a recycled substitute.

Wall o' Water teepees are plastic protectors that incorporate water to provide heat-storage capability. Even newer are bonded row-cover fabrics such as Reemay, which retain heat, resist light frost and keep insects off crops. These fabrics have enabled gardeners to mature tender crops in marginal areas and to raise vegetables free of damage from pests that resisted other organic methods of control.

Some of these shelters are designed only to get the crop off to a good start. Others may see a crop of tender vegetables through to maturity, but in gardens where summers are quite dependably frost free this is not recommended, as temperatures in the shelters are likely to rise too high. Remove the covers when the plants outgrow them or as soon as all danger of frost has passed.

Slitted Row Covers   In 1980, Ortho S. Wells and J. Brent Loy of the University of New Hampshire published a pamphlet, "Slitted Row Covers for Intensive Vegetable Production." The pamphlet explained that slitted row covers have a series of short, crosswise slits which provide ventilation on sunny days. Without these slits, the covers would have to be manually opened and closed daily to provide ventilation during the day and protection from the cold at night. These slits, which are 5 inches long and ¾ inch apart along two rows, can be made before or after installation. It is also possible to make the slits in other configurations.

While bonded row covers such as Reemay have now replaced plastics in many situations, the following covers are inexpensive and have been used successfully at the University of New Hampshire and on several commercial farms.

Plastic Clear polyethylene, 5 feet wide and 1½ to 2 mils thick, is the most convenient material, although it can only be used once. Heavier plastic, such as 4- or 6-mil, can be used but it is more difficult to work with because it sags between hoops and usually comes folded in the roll. This makes it hard to unroll as one sheet. The heavier plastic has an advantage since it can be reused, but the extra labour requirement for installation, removal and storage could prove prohibitive.

Hoops Hoops made of number 8 or 9 wire are cut 63 inches long, the optimum length for 5-foot-wide plastic. When the hoops are cut from a coil of wire, they are already preshaped and are very easy to manage.

Installation of Row Covers Because row covers are being recommended primarily for warm-season, frost-tender vegetables (although other crops should be tried), it is advisable to use row covers in conjunction with black plastic. There are two reasons for this:

• Black plastic generally results in increased yields

• Black plastic mulch provides for weed control under the cover

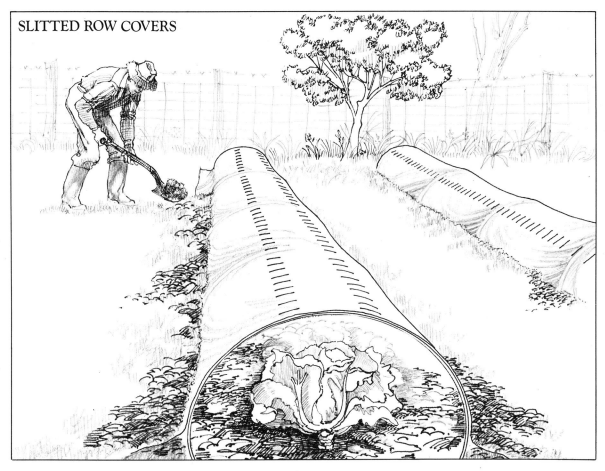

SLITTED ROW COVERS

If commercially slitted material is not used, growers can make their own slits during installation using a simple slitting device made by mounting double-edged razor blades at a 45-degree angle to the end of a block of wood.

The row cover is now in place and needs no further maintenance except to check for possible wind damage. When properly secured, as outlined above, the row cover is very resistant to wind, even strong gusts. If necessary, the gardener can replace plants by reaching through the slits. Since the crosswise slits in the cover provide ventilation, nothing else need be done for this purpose. Depending on the crop and growing conditions, the cover can be removed in four to six weeks.

Frost Protection Frost protection with slitted covers is not as good as with solid covers. Only 28 to 29 degrees F (about -2 degrees C) can be endured under a double row of slits, whereas greater frost protection has been attained under solid covers. Therefore, do not attempt to plant extra early and hope to be protected against heavy frosts. Crops can be planted out only 10 days to two weeks earlier than usual. Because of the better ventilation of the slitted row cover, it provides a reasonable compromise between maximum frost protection and a saving in labour. Row covers should not be viewed merely as a frost protection system but as a growth-intensifying system during cool spring weather.

Late spring frosts are probably not the biggest limiting factor in the early culture of muskmelon and other vine crops. Cool soil in the spring tends to inhibit growth and the water and nutrient uptake by young seedlings and trans-plants. Row covers, in combination with black plastic mulch, will usually increase soil temperatures by 6 to 8 degrees F (3.3 to 4.5 degrees C). Unfortunately, row covers will not protect vine crops (especially muskmelon and watermelon) against the effects of extended periods (5 or more days) of cloudy, cool weather. With this weather pattern, the soil temperature drops, preventing the uptake of water by the plants. Consequently, when sunny weather returns, the young transplants tend to wither.

Excessively high temperatures under the cover during hot days can also be a potential danger. With the double row of slits, the temperature under the cover can reach 120 degrees F (48 degrees C) when the outside temperature rises as high as 95 degrees F (35 degrees C), although this is somewhat unusual for springtime temperatures. No apparent damage has been observed at these high temperatures if the flower buds are not actually open.

Precautions

• Weeds will germinate just inside the cover between the cover and the black plastic, but they generally will cause no problems and can be easily hand pulled when the cover is removed

• Under experimental conditions, insects and diseases have caused no problems beneath the covers. Be prepared to control these disorders when covers are removed

• Tomato blossoms (open flowers) will burn if they touch or nearly touch the cover on hot days

Plastic Mulch Although it is not really a plant cover, plastic mulch is included here since it also makes use of the greenhouse effect to encourage plant growth. Clear plas-tic warms the soil, often by as much as 12 degrees F (6.7 degrees C). To help the growth of early crops, spread sheets of 2-mil clear plastic along the rows or on the beds after a rain and about a week before sowing seeds or setting out transplants, weighing down the edges of the plastic with soil to keep it in place. Slits or Xs are then cut into the plastic where the seeds or transplants will go. (Or the plastic is removed, seeds – pregerminated or not – are sown and the plastic is laid down again and then slit as soon as the seeds sprout. Leaving the plastic unslit after sprouting will eventually kill the seedlings.)

Plastic mulches also retain soil moisture, one of the reasons that a 47-per-cent increase in carrot yields was charted by Canadian scientist G.H. Gubbels in his experiments with mulched and un-mulched beds in the Yukon. Cabbage growth, too, was enhanced by plastic mulch. In the *Canadian Journal of Plant Science*, Gubbels noted, "The important point demonstrated is that clear poly can be used to increase soil temperature while making maximum use of water in northern latitudes where low soil temperature and moisture often limit plant growth."

Black plastic is less effective than clear plastic in providing warmth, but it controls weed growth better. Among dark plastics are photodegradable plastic mulches that decompose in sunlight, an advantage because leftover plastic mulch is usually a mess of tatters by the end of the season – all plastic is made brittle by sunlight. Unfortunately, photodegradable mulch does not decompose in the shade of plant foliage and is thus only partially successful.

Alphabetical Vegetables

"In these pages will be found some hints that will help the Canadian farmer to an acquaintance with requisites essential to success in the cultivation of the garden. . . "

– D.W. Beadle
The Canadian Fruit, Flower and Kitchen Gardener, 1872

What is a vegetable? In customary or culinary terms, the question is easily answered. Vegetables are those edible plants, often annuals, that are usually eaten with the main course at dinner, perhaps *au gratin* or lightly buttered. Savoury foods high in vitamins, they may be stems, leaves, roots, seeds, flowers or tubers, but all of them complement the ingredients in a stir-fry dish or partner the inevitable potato beside the T-bone. Fruit, on the other hand, is that sweet stuff often borne by perennial plants and regularly eaten raw or as dessert. A chef finds no problem with the fruit-or-vegetable quandary, being as unlikely to serve an entrée of grapes with cheese sauce as to present the guests with a dessert of tomatoes *belle Hélène*.

For the botanist the answer is equally clear, though different. Again, a vegetable is any edible plant that is not a fruit, but in botanical terms fruit has a more precise definition. It is the ripened ovary and accessory parts of a plant, usually containing seeds. Corn is an aggregate fruit. Beans, peppers, tomatoes, cucumbers, squash and eggplant are all botanical fruits, as are the foods we usually consider fruit, except rhubarb, which is a vegetable.

For our purposes, we shall use the customary,

not the botanical, definitions of fruits and vegetables; the "dessert plants" are omitted while we include such fruits as muskmelon, watermelon, garden huckleberry and ground cherry because they usually inhabit the vegetable garden.

In most cases, we will not recommend specific cultivars of these fruits or vegetables – both because new and often faster-maturing cultivars appear every year and because each seed company includes only a limited selection. When in doubt, look for the quickest-maturing selection from a company that specializes in seeds for the North. Also, the following vegetable listing is not exhaustive. The seed industry introduces entirely new vegetables quite regularly, thanks both to importation and to the work of breeders who have brought out such remarkable plants as the snap pea and the "colbaga," a combination of turnip, rutabaga and Chinese cabbage developed at the University of New Hampshire. Search the seed catalogues every year to keep up to date on the best selections available to Northerners.

Directions indicating that a vegetable can or must be started indoors do not imply that you must necessarily grow your own transplants. Greenhouses, nurseries, even grocery and department stores often carry a selection of transplants in spring. Gardeners buying these plants can ignore the indoor planting directions and pick up the instructions with outdoor timing and spacing. Do, however, harden off commercial transplants in the same way as home-grown transplants by following the instructions on page 55.

Artichokes, Globe
(Compositae, *Cynara scolymus*)
French artichoke

Description *Cynara scolymus* was described in 1754 as "very like the thistle but hath large scaley heads which are shaped somewhat like the cone of the pine-tree. The bottom of each scale as also at the bottom of the florets, is a thick fleshy eatable substance." Native of the humid, warm climes of the southern Mediterranean, the globe artichoke is not usually considered a resident of the northern garden, but where the season is 100 days long it will survive if started early indoors. The large, bushy, prickly plant grows tall, about 3 feet (though heights of 10 feet have been reported in very mild areas), and so should be planted where it will not shade other vegetables but will itself receive full sun. Grown from seed, some plants will be nonproductive, but others may produce three or four heads during the season.

Culture Nine weeks before the last spring frost date, plant two or three seeds to a 3-inch container. The seed germinates in 10 to 15 days at a soil temperature of 70 to 75 degrees F (21 to 24 degrees C). After the first true leaves form, thin to one plant per container. Four weeks before the last frost, transplant into 5-inch pots. Harden off for a week before planting outdoors in fertile, well-drained soil, allowing at least 3 feet around each plant.

Harvest Cut the central head while it is still compact and almost entirely edible – as the flower head opens, it becomes tough. Cut through the stem about 1 inch below the head, then remove and discard the rest of the stem. Smaller, lateral heads will form later in a manner similar to broccoli. The plant will survive light fall frost. Before the soil freezes, cut the plant to the ground. In mild areas, the roots may overwinter successfully in the garden if they are hilled over and heavily mulched. Covering the crown first with a box will help shed moisture – plants that stand in water will not survive. In spring, dig down to the roots and remove suckers to use for propagating the plants. (In warm regions where artichokes are grown commercially, they are propagated only by sucker, not by seed, which produces a high percentage of nonflowering plants.) In colder areas, dig the roots after the last frost and plant them indoors, keeping them cool and watered. Set outdoors the following spring around the last frost date. Plants should be renewed by seed or sucker every four years.

Pests & Diseases Grown beyond its usual range, the plant suffers little infestation. If flea beetles are troublesome, use rotenone or diatomaceous earth regularly. The artichoke plume moth can be combated with plant rotations and garden cleanliness.

Artichokes, Jerusalem
(Compositae, *Helianthus tuberosus*)
Sunchoke

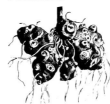

Description A perennial sunflower grown for its sweet, tender tubers, *Helianthus tuberosus* is one of only a few vegetables native to the northern part of North America. Champlain, in 1603, wrote that the Algonquin Indians served cultivated roots that tasted like artichokes. The misnomer "Jerusalem" probably originates from an English version of its Italian name, *girasol*, which refers to the flower's habit of facing the sun. Because it is a native plant, it is exceedingly hardy and easy to grow. In fact, it is considered a weed in some areas. Tall enough, at 6 to 8 feet, to form an effective windbreak, it must be planted where it will not shade other vegetables. It should, in fact, be allotted a permanent, well-chosen spot, because it is very persistent and difficult to eradicate.

Culture *Helianthus tuberosus* does not breed true from seed, but is propagated by tubers which should be planted as soon as possible after they are

received – do not let them dry out. Plant as soon as the soil can be worked in spring, or any time thereafter until fall, cutting tubers to one or two eyes per piece, and planting them 4 inches deep and at 12- to 14-inch intervals in rows 24 to 40 inches apart.
Harvest Tubers are ready to dig from late summer until the soil freezes, or until spring if the plants are mulched. In fall, cut the stems down to the ground and mulch them heavily, so that tubers can be dug until they sprout in spring. Thin-skinned, they do not store well unless kept moist in a root cellar or bagged in the refrigerator. Tubers are eaten raw, or cooked like potatoes.
Pests & Diseases None of note.

Asparagus
(Liliaceae, *Asparagus officinalis*)

Description One of the earliest vegetables to appear in the spring is asparagus, a perennial native of Europe and North Africa, but hardy enough to overwinter almost everywhere south of the permafrost. The plants need a well-fertilized, well-drained permanent plot with a pH of about 6.6, where their 5-foot height and 4-foot root spread can be accommodated. They are dioecious – some plants are male and some female, producing berries. If your soil has a high salt content, asparagus will be one of the most successful vegetables in your garden.
Culture Asparagus can be grown from seed or transplants; the former is considerably less expensive, but does delay the first harvest by a year. If using seeds, soak them in lukewarm water for 48 hours before planting, then sow at ½-inch intervals in ½-inch-deep drills 1 foot apart as soon as the soil can be worked in spring. As the seeds are slow to sprout, rows can be marked with radish seeds. Alternatively, seeds can be sown indoors and transplanted at 2-inch intervals outdoors in early spring. A year later, they are planted in their permanent location in the same manner as purchased transplants. It is very important that perennial weeds, especially twitch or couch grass, be eliminated from the bed. Prepare the asparagus bed by turning the

soil and incorporating well-rotted manure and compost into it. The pH should be about 6.6. Dig trenches 6 inches deep and 2 to 4 feet apart. Lay a low ridge of manure along the centre of each trench and then spread the roots of each plant over the ridge at 18-inch intervals. Cover the roots and gradually fill in the trench as the shoots grow. When the trenches are filled, mulch the entire bed deeply with grass clippings, leaf mould, straw or hay to discourage weeds and retain moisture. Diligent weeding is otherwise mandatory. Manure and mulch should both be reapplied every spring. In marginal growing areas, mulch the roots heavily over the winter.
Harvest No picking at all is done either the year of transplanting or the following spring. The next year, spears may be picked for about five weeks; the following year and thereafter, for six to eight weeks. Cut the spears with a knife or break them off just below soil level. Shoots are cut when 6 to 8 inches long and before the tips begin to open – harvest may be daily in warm weather, twice weekly in cool. Do not cut spears less than ¼ inch thick, but allow the ferns to reach their full height in order to produce nutrients for the next crop. Asparagus loses its quality quickly after picking – eat or preserve it as soon as possible. Dead plants can be removed in late fall or early spring.
Pests & Diseases The worst pest is the black and white asparagus beetle and its small, greyish larva which can be dusted with lime or rotenone. Rust and fusarium wilt are easily combated by choosing a resistant variety – check the seed catalogue listing. Removing dead ferns will help prevent pest and disease infestations.

Beans, Broad
(Leguminosae, *Vicia faba*)
Fava bean, Horse bean,
Windsor bean, Tick bean

Description A Eurasian native, *Vicia faba* is far hardier than its New World relatives. It is, in fact, a blessing to gardeners of the high latitudes, bringing home-grown beans to their dinner plates and leaving a bonus of nitrogen in the gardens. The bean itself varies in size according to cultivar, but most, when mature, are larger than any other common bean. Five to eight beans are produced in each pod, which may be as long as 7 inches and is borne singly or in a cluster in the leaf axil. The pod, whose interior is white and fuzzy, is not usually eaten. The plants are upright, tall (about 3 feet) and slender, with heavy stems. There are two types of broad beans: field beans and garden beans, the former smaller and rounder than the latter. Broad beans were the only garden beans known to Europeans before the discovery of the New World, and were a common ensilage crop. Recently, their substitution for soybeans in livestock feed has been increasing.

Culture Consider *Vicia faba* more like a pea than a bean in its cold tolerance. It is generally seeded directly outdoors as soon as the soil can be worked in spring – light frost will not harm the young plants – but can be given a boost in a cold frame or cool, sunny window, planted four weeks before the last frost date. In very mild areas, it may be planted in late summer for a fall crop – allow the plants two to three months to mature before frost, which will damage the pods. As the bean requires cool, moist weather for best growth, spring planting should not be delayed past the last frost date. Plant seeds 1 inch deep at 4- to 6-inch intervals in rows or beds. If seeds are planted in beds, leave about 1 foot between crosswise rows to allow for cultivation with a hoe. Plants may require staking.

Harvest The beans should be ready to pick 65 to 90 days after planting. Immature beans may be bitter; pick the pods when they are almost full-grown but not ripe; the beans inside will be slightly visible as bumps. Shell them and then cook or preserve them like green peas, by freezing or pressure canning. Or allow the mature beans to dry on the plant or indoors and use as baking beans. The plants do not continue bearing for long.

Pests & Diseases Plants are fairly pest and disease resistant. Aphids can be controlled with insecticidal soap used according to the manufacturer's directions. Pinching off plant tops as soon as pods have formed will also help control aphids.

Beans, Kidney
(*Phaseolus vulgaris*)

Description A type of string bean, the kidney bean takes its name from the doctrine of signatures, a system of belief which held that the curative properties of vegetables were linked to the human organs they most closely resemble. The kidney bean requires a fairly long season – about 100 days – to mature, and does best where killing frosts do not occur before late September.

Culture Plant kidney beans at the same time and in the same way as bush snap beans. The plant produces large, flat green pods filled with red kidney-shaped beans.

Harvest The beans may be picked fresh and shelled, or left to dry on the vine, but do not let them freeze or become mouldy. If left too long, the pods will split and beans will be lost. If they are shelled when mature but not dry, the beans should be roasted on cookie sheets in a warm oven until dry and hard. Store in jars or paper bags in a cool, dry place.

Pest & Diseases As for snap beans.

Beans, Lima
(*Phaseolus limensis*)

Description Available in pole or bush varieties, limas' need a warmer soil than do snap beans and they also take longer to mature: 65 to 80 days for bush varieties, 85 to 100 for pole limas. All in all, limas are an unpredictable crop in most of Canada and the northern U.S. Choose the earliest varieties available or, for a better harvest, select one of the very early, lima-like beans such as Limelight or its predecessor, Princess of Artois. Although these beans are *Phaseolus vulgaris* cultivars, lacking the lima bean flavour, they do have the bean's colour and shape, and are ready to harvest at the green-shell stage about 70 days after sowing.

Culture Plant as snap beans, but not until two weeks after the last spring frost. The seeds will not germinate in cool soil, and will take 17 days to germinate even at a soil temperature of 68 degrees F (20 degrees C) – the coolest recommended. They germinate in six days at 77 degrees F (25 degrees C). To extend the season, start them indoors four weeks ahead of the planting-out date.

Harvest Pick beans before the pod shows any yellowing; it should be green and succulent, the beans swollen inside. Shell and serve fresh or preserve by freezing or drying.

Pests & Diseases As for snap beans.

Beans, Scarlet Runner

(*Phaseolus coccineus*)

Description This pole bean, whose vines may reach 10 feet in length, is widely grown just for its beautiful clusters of red blossoms and its large leaves, but the beans are also edible. The pods may be picked like snap beans when young and tender, or they may be shelled, and the black and scarlet beans eaten fresh or allowed to dry. The beans mature in about 70 days.

Culture, Harvest, Pests & Diseases As for pole snap beans.

Beans, Snap

(Leguminosae, *Phaseolus vulgaris*)
String beans

Description Thanks to the work of seed breeders, string beans are now snap beans, the fibres or strings having been bred out of the pods of all but the old, heirloom varieties, some of which were observed by Jacques Cartier in 1535 growing in native gardens of the St. Lawrence valley. Snap beans, whether of vining or bush-forming habit, whether green-, yellow- or purple-podded, whether with flat or round pods, are the only beans routinely eaten with pods intact. Bush beans will grow about 18 inches tall on sturdy plants, while pole beans need support and will grow to heights of 6 to 8 feet. All are tender plants that cannot withstand frost and require warm soil

to germinate and grow, ceasing growth if temperatures drop to 50 degrees F (10 degrees C). The blossoms may drop off if prevailing daytime temperatures are over 90 degrees F (32 degrees C). Given suitable growing conditions, however, they are so prolific and dependable that their first-place rank in seed purchases is understandable.

Culture Snap beans are usually seeded directly outdoors around the last frost date and at two- or three-week intervals until mid-summer; allow the plants at least two months to mature before frost. Seeds can be soaked for half an hour or even pregerminated before planting for speedier emergence. Treat with nitrogen-fixing inoculant, available from many seed outlets, if they are to be sown where beans have not grown before. Seeds will germinate in 16 days at the coolest recommended soil temperature of 60 degrees F (15 degrees C), in 11 days at 68 degrees F (20 degrees C), in eight days at 77 degrees F (25 degrees C), but will not germinate in very hot soil. Seed treated with fungicides will be less likely to rot at cool soil temperatures, but treatment is not needed at 68 degrees F (20 degrees C) or warmer. If using untreated seed, either delay planting or warm the soil with clear plastic before sowing. Plant seeds of bush beans 1 inch deep and 2 inches apart in rows or in beds. If in beds, plant in crosswise rows about 1 foot apart, far enough that weeding can be done with a hoe. Thin plants to stand 4 inches apart. The plants need full sun and well-drained soil that has been well worked. Plant pole beans at 2-inch intervals along a fence, thinning later to 6 inches apart, or plant four seeds around a 6-foot pole. Cover plants if frost threatens. Surrounding the plants with plastic mulch or growing bush beans in a cloche will help ensure maturation in cool-season areas.

Harvest Bush beans mature 45 to 60 days from planting, pole beans about 10 days later. Pick pods when they are at pencil thickness, or before the beans inside swell noticeably and the pods discolour. Continual picking will prolong the harvest, which usually recurs about every three or four days for about three weeks. To serve, remove the blossom end, pull off strings if any are present, then snap into pieces and cook or preserve. Left to mature further, the beans can be shelled and served as lima beans, or they may be left to dry on the vine or brought indoors to dry for use in soups and baking. Horticultural beans and navy beans are *Phaseolus vulgaris* cultivars meant primarily for shelling.

Pests & Diseases Do not tend wet plants, as this can spread disease. Remove plant debris at the end of the season and compost it. The Mexican bean beetle, a problem in some southern areas of Canada, can be controlled with a tea of cedar chips brewed in warm water, or with pyrethrum or rotenone. As this beetle looks much like the beneficial lady beetle, check with an expert before harming it. Deformed or curled bean pods may result from lack of moisture, from drought or from insect damage during blossoming. Fungus diseases are common on pods, especially in damp weather. Discard discoloured pods and beans.

Beans, Soya

(Leguminosae, *Glycine max*)
Soybean, Vegetable soybean, Mao du

Description Cultivated in the far East for centuries, strains of *Glycine max* are now among North America's most important forage crops, and their value as a food crop is also increasing. They are exceedingly high in protein – about 40 per cent on a dry weight basis – double that of lima beans. The soybean's range is moving steadily northward as breeders pare days from its maturation requirements. Now most Northerners can grow early cultivars, and may even have sufficient time before frost to allow the beans to dry on the plant. Select early-maturing cultivars carried by companies catering to Northerners. Plants grow about 14 inches tall; 3-inch fuzzy pods enclose two or three beans each.

Culture Sow soybeans directly in the garden at about the same time as limas, two weeks after the last frost date – the seeds germinate best at 86 degrees F (30 degrees C) – or start them indoors four weeks before the planting-out date. Pregermination of seed indoors will also speed emergence. Plant seeds 1 inch deep and 2 inches apart in rows

or in beds. If in beds, leave 1 foot between crosswise rows so that they can be cultivated with a hoe. Do not tend plants when they are wet.

Harvest Each plant produces about 50 pods, ready to be harvested 70 to 120 days after planting, depending on variety and soil temperature. For fresh beans, pick the pods when they are just beginning to change colour from green to yellow. Boil for one minute, then cool in ice water and shell by squeezing out beans. Serve or preserve as for green peas. Beans can be dried on the plants or roasted on cookie sheets in a warm oven until hard. Store in jars or in paper bags in a cool, dry cupboard and use as baking beans.

Pests & Diseases Seeds will rot before emergence if they are planted in too-cool soil. The bean leaf beetle may attack plants in eastern Canada. It is ¼ inch long, reddish-orange and shiny with a black head, and sometimes black spots. The larva is a small white grub. Hand picking is usually sufficient control but rotenone or pyrethrum can be used for severe outbreaks. Ground hogs are fond of young soybeans. Good fencing buried at least 1 foot below the soil surface will help control them.

Unusual Beans

As a look through the catalogue of a seed saver's exchange or the Vermont Bean Seed Company will confirm, there are hundreds of varieties and types of beans. Many are variations of string beans, snap beans or shelled beans meant to be eaten fresh or dried for later use. They appear in almost the full spectrum of colours and in many sizes and shapes. Unfortunately, many of these heirloom varieties, and some of the more unusual beans such as garbanzo beans (*Cicer arietinum*) or winged beans (*Psophocarpus tetragonolobus*), either produce so few beans per pod or require such a long season that they are impractical as northern garden crops. A few of the more popular novelty beans are:

Adzuki Beans

(*Phaseolus angularis*)
Description A small baking bean, the adzuki bean is found in many colours in Asia but dark red beans predominate in North America. It is high in

protein, cooks more quickly and is more easily digested than most other baking beans, but requires a very long, hot season: approximately 120 days from planting to maturity. It will not, therefore, mature successfully in most northern gardens. The bushy plants with yellow flowers produce pods up to 5 inches long.

Culture, Harvest, Pests & Diseases As for soybeans, used shelled and dried.

Asparagus Beans
(*Vigna unguiculata*)
Yard-long bean, Dow guak, Cheung kong tau
Description The asparagus bean is a runner (vining) bean that can grow 6 to 9 feet in length and needs to be supported on poles, a fence or trellis. Attractive, unusual and prized in the Orient, it unfortunately has the same drawback for Northerners as does the adzuki bean: It requires a long warm season for maturation. It bears yellowish flowers and an abundance of pods 2 feet long.
Culture Plant the asparagus bean in warm soil about two weeks after the last frost date and allow it a long, hot season of about three months to mature. Plant spacing as for pole snap beans.
Harvest Harvest pods when they are about 16 inches long, chop into small pieces and use like snap beans, or wait until the pods are just turning yellow and shell to use fresh.
Pests & Diseases None of note.

Mung Beans
(*Vigna radiata*)
Description This is another bean unusual in appearance, producing spoke-like clusters of thin, olive-green, fuzzy pods that turn black as the beans mature. The erect, 2-foot-tall bushes are grown more often as a novelty than as a space-efficient crop, as the beans, generally used for sprouting, are available inexpensively in natural food stores.
Culture Plant and tend as soybeans.
Harvest The small, olive-green beans can be cooked and eaten when fresh, but are usually left to dry on the plants or are picked when mature and dried indoors. Do not roast. When thoroughly dry, they are stored in paper bags in a cool, dry place and

used for sprouting. To make sprouts, place about ¼ cup of beans in a quart jar, cover with cool water and leave the beans about an hour. Pour off the water, cover the jar loosely and place it in a warm, dark cupboard, rinsing the beans occasionally.
Pests & Diseases As for soybeans.

The mung bean is the only member of the bean family (Leguminosae) whose seeds are grown primarily for sprouting

Beets
(Chenopodiaceae, *Beta vulgaris*)
Beetroot

Description Although it was originally prized more for its spinach-like greens than for its swollen root, the beet's priorities have been more or less reversed by North Americans. The plant, a biennial, produces a sweet, tender root that may be purple, white or golden and varies in shape from the usual globe, big or small, to cylindrical. A variation, the sugar beet is grown mostly for sugar production in temperate climates while another, the mangel, is chiefly a forage crop. Either can also be used for the table if harvested while young and tender. Beets love cool, moist conditions and are thus ideal crops for Northerners, producing crops even where the season is as short as 80 days. A beet "seed" is actually a dried fruit composed of several seeds.
Culture Beet seed can be sown as early as the soil can be worked in spring, and then every two weeks until early summer. A late storage crop such as

Winter Keeper should be sown about 10 weeks before the first fall frost. The crop prefers a deeply worked, loose soil high in organic matter with a pH above 6. The seed germinates in four to ten days within its preferred soil temperature range of 45 to 70 degrees F (7 to 21 degrees C). Sow seeds about 1 inch apart and ½ inch deep. Thinnings may be eaten whole, either cooked or raw. Keep the plants thinned sufficiently to maintain about 1 inch between each root. Plants need a steady supply of water and will tolerate light frost, but may bolt to seed in areas where the days are very long. In the far North, choose quick-maturing, small-rooted varieties. Bolting quickly reduces leaf and root quality. Mulch plants or keep them well weeded, as weed competition can produce tough roots.

Harvest The greens, high in vitamins and iron, are at their best until roots are 1 to 1½ inches in diameter. Pull only a few outer leaves at a time so that the roots continue to grow. Use greens fresh or cooked like spinach. Except for the large storage varieties, roots are best when 2½ to 3 inches across, and are woody when overmature. For winter storage, however, large, fully mature roots keep best. Pull them on a dry day after the first fall frost, cut tops to within 1 centimetre of the root and leave them outdoors on newspaper one sunny day to cure, turning roots occasionally and rubbing off loose soil. Store in moist sand, peat or perforated plastic bags at 32 to 40 degrees F (0 to 4 degrees C) and 95 per cent relative humidity. Roots may also keep in the garden over winter if heavily mulched before the soil freezes. Harvest before plants go to seed in spring.

Pests & Diseases White rings in the root are caused by growth checks – the best roots develop quickly and steadily. Internal browning of the root, often a problem in alkaline soil after a long hot period, is caused by soil low in boron. Apply boron according to soil test recommendations. Scab, raised brown spots, is also common in alkaline soils. However, none of the above conditions makes roots inedible and all can be countered with a high proportion of organic matter in the soil.

The green caterpillar of the beet armyworm can be controlled with hand picking or *Bacillus thuringi-*

ensis. The beet leafhopper, a tiny, greenish insect, can be controlled with diatomaceous earth.

Broccoli
(Cruciferae, *Brassica oleracea italica*)

Description A cabbage mutant but, unlike cabbage, an annual, broccoli was first described in the Middle East in the 12th century. The part eaten, the head, is actually a cluster of inflorescences, immature flowers harvested before they bloom. The word broccoli is Italian, and means tender stalks – an apt description of broccoli raab or sprouting broccoli, a European strain that does not form a central head, but produces small shoots throughout the season. Chinese broccoli or Chinese kale, guy lon, is similar to raab, producing no large central head. Broccoli plants grow about 2 feet tall and are quite wide and bushy. They do best in very fertile soil mulched with straw, grass clippings or leaf mould.

Culture To mature, broccoli needs about two months without a succession of hard frosts. Starting seeds indoors six or seven weeks before the last spring frost will ensure an early harvest, although in most areas seeds of early varieties may be sown directly in the garden from two weeks before until two weeks after the last frost. Seeds germinate in about seven days in soil 45 to 90 degrees F (7 to 32 degrees C). As very young plants are more frost hardy than mature ones, early planting is recommended in short-season areas. Plants mature 60 to 70 days from transplanting, 80 to 90 days from direct seeding. Sow seeds ½ inch deep in hills of three or four seeds spaced 1½ feet apart, or at 2-inch intervals in rows. Gradually thin plants to stand 18 inches apart or plant transplants at 18-inch intervals, deeply enough that the first true leaves are just above the soil level. Mulch with about 4 inches of organic material when the soil is warm and plants are growing well. Throughout the season, ensure that plants receive adequate moisture – about 1 inch a week – and fertilizer. Roots are close to the surface, so do not cultivate deeply. Watering with manure tea or fish fertilizer every two weeks will help maintain suitable soil nutrient levels.

Harvest When the flower buds are full but before they begin to open, cut the large central head at the stem. Smaller, lateral heads form later and should be harvested in the same manner. Serve fresh or freeze heads to preserve.

Pests & Diseases Flea beetles and root maggots are the worst pests when plants are young. Control the former with rotenone. For root maggots, which crawl down plant stems to the roots, encircle the stem with a tarpaper or cardboard disc flat against the soil. Later, various cabbage moth larvae are troublesome and best controlled with *Bacillus thuringiensis* used according to the manufacturer's directions. Light infestations can be controlled with hand picking or with rotenone – but do not use rotenone within a week of harvesting. Clubroot, a fungus disease, is best controlled by cleanliness, crop rotation, the use of resistant cultivars and by ensuring that the soil is well drained and near neutral in pH. Destroy any infected plants.

Brussels Sprouts

(Cruciferae, *Brassica oleracea gemmifera*)

Description Closely related to cabbage and broccoli, Brussels sprouts originated in Belgium, where *spruyten* were grown for about 400 years before they made their way into France in the 18th century and Britain in the 19th. The sprouts, tiny cabbage heads that form from the ground upward, grow in leaf axils along the stem. The plant is among the hardiest of the brassicas. It is an easy plant for Northerners to grow, and, like all brassicas, thrives in very fertile soil during cool, moist weather. Most sprouts are green but there are purple varieties as well.

Culture Plant and tend as for broccoli. Brussels sprouts take about three months to mature, and their plantings should be timed so that they are mature by the first fall frost. As the sprouts form, pull out the lower leaves, gradually removing them to about halfway up the stalk. To encourage sprout growth, pinch off the top of the plant about two weeks before the first frost date or when the lowest

sprouts are about 1 inch across.

Harvest Start to harvest the lowest sprouts when they are about 1½ inches across. Moving up the stem, continue to harvest them gradually until all are picked or until the plant is killed by frost. Light frost, however, improves the flavour. In the kitchen, remove the loose or discoloured outer leaves of the sprouts, which may be cooked and eaten fresh or frozen. Each plant produces about one pound of sprouts. Before the soil freezes, the entire plant can be pulled from the garden and hung upside down in a cool, moist cellar to prolong the harvest.

Pests & Diseases As for broccoli, but pest problems are less severe with Brussels sprouts because they mature after the worst pest infestations.

Cabbage

(Cruciferae, *Brassica oleracea capitata*)

Description Cabbage, introduced to the North by Jacques Cartier, is a native of the northern Mediterranean. An easy crop to grow and one that thrives in the cool northern growing season, it may have smooth or curly leaves (savoy), and may be purple or green. There are "mini" varieties with heads about 6 inches across, while others may produce heads more than twice that size. Like other leafy crops, cabbage is at its best when it grows steadily and quickly, which is most probable when the soil is moist, high in organic matter and very fertile. A Canadian scientist noted in 1917, "We have never heard of anyone using too much manure for cabbage."

Culture Plant and tend as for broccoli. If properly hardened before setting out in the garden, transplants will withstand a temperature of 20 degrees F (-6 degrees C), but otherwise will be quickly killed by such frosts. (Crops seeded outdoors harden themselves automatically.) Early varieties mature about 70 days after transplanting – the main crop in 75 to 80 days, storage varieties in 90 to 100 days. Add 10 or 20 days for direct seeding. Since heads may crack when overmature or after heavy rains, gardeners who wish to delay harvesting mature heads should twist the head slightly or thrust a spade into the soil on one side of the plant to break some of the roots. Time fall plantings so that heads are mature just before the first frost. Light frost will not harm them, but will slow or stop their growth.

Harvest Cut through the stem just below the head, leaving the surrounding leaves on the plant. After the first head is harvested, three to five small heads will grow on the central stem and be ready for harvest a month or two later. Cabbage can be made into sauerkraut or preserved by slicing and freezing, or entire heads can be stored for several weeks in a damp root cellar at a temperature near freezing. To store them this way, harvest the entire plants complete with roots, remove damaged leaves and hang the plant by the roots, or harvest the heads only and store them in perforated plastic bags in the root cellar or refrigerator.

Pests & Diseases As for broccoli.

Carrots

(Umbelliferae, *Daucus carota*)

Description The carrot is a highly refined version of a common weed, Queen Anne's lace, both of which originated in the Middle East. There are many sizes and shapes of carrot. Very small ones, either round or cylindrical, are best in shallow soil or where quick maturation (about 55 days) is desired. Fat carrots such as Chantenay and Oxheart are best in heavy soils and for storage. The long, thin commercial types need very loose, deeply worked soil and a steady water supply. Like any root crop, the best carrots of any type will grow in deeply worked, well-drained and aerated soil without clumps or stones. If the soil is heavy or compact, grow carrots in raised beds in which the soil has been mixed with peat, compost and sand. Carrot growth and colour develop best in moderate soil temperatures of 60 to 70 degrees F (15 to 20 degrees C). Because they prefer cool soil, carrots will mature in almost every northern garden.

Culture Seeds can be sown outdoors any time after the soil can be worked in spring, although faster growth will occur with those seeds planted around the last frost date. Plant carrots for winter storage about 100 days before the first fall frost. Carrot seed is very fine and difficult to sow evenly, but try to sow at ¼-inch intervals in a furrow about ½ inch deep. Cover with finely textured soil, pat firmly and, if dry, water with a fine spray. The seed is slow to germinate, taking six to 21 days at 45 to 86 degrees F (7 to 30 degrees C). Adequate watering is most important from the time seeds are sown until root swelling begins a couple of weeks after emergence; be sure that the soil never dries below the top ½ inch. As they grow, thin carrots regularly so that the roots are never closer together than 1 inch. Hill the soil over the crowns to prevent greening of roots, which causes bitterness. Keep the bed clear of weeds by mulching or diligent weeding.

Harvest Harvest and store as for beets. Eat the roots of young thinnings raw or cooked. Carrot tops may be used fresh or dried as a potherb, fed to livestock or used as compost or mulch.

Pests & Diseases Few present a real risk to garden carrots, most doing cosmetic damage only. The bluish-white, 1-inch larva of the carrot beetle, wireworms and the ½-inch-long yellow or white larva of the carrot rust fly chew holes in roots and are best controlled by crop rotation. The parsleyworm which is the larva of the black swallowtail butterfly, chews foliage but seldom requires more control than hand picking. Hairy carrots are caused by overfertilization with nitrogen, or by irregular weather conditions during early root formation. Splitting can be caused by heavy rain just as the roots are maturing. Forked carrots are the result of compact heavy soil or stones.

Cauliflower

(Cruciferae, *Brassica oleracea botrytis*)

Description The first part of its name comes from the Latin *caulis*, stem; the ending identifies the part of the plant eaten, the flower. Cauliflower is the most temperamental of the brassicas, the least frost hardy, the most likely to suffer damping off, to bolt to seed or to be attacked by root maggots; in short, the most likely to produce no crop. From seeding to harvest, it does best with little fluctuation in temperature or moisture, preferring cool, damp weather and fertile, moist soil high in organic matter. Purple-headed cauliflower is much less demanding, but its heads do not have the delicate flavour of the common white curds. "Mini" varieties, producing a central head about 4 inches across, are best where quicker maturation is required – about 50 days, compared with 55 to 85 for others. All plants grow to about 14 inches in height.

Culture Sow and transplant as for broccoli, but start the seeds indoors later (five or six weeks before the last spring frost), and do not move outdoors until the last spring frost date. The plants will not stand as much cold as other brassicas but are just as frost hardy when very young, so planting should not be left so late that maturation is checked by fall frost. Since overgrown transplants are likely to bolt to seed or become stunted, select the youngest available if purchasing them. Applying about 4 inches of mulch to plants at least that tall will help maintain adequate soil moisture. As soon as heads are teacup-sized, blanch them by gathering the leaves up over the head and tying them with string. Some new varieties are self-blanching – check the seed catalogue descriptions. Unblanched heads become greenish or purplish and may have a strong, bitter flavour, but their vitamin content will be enhanced. Do not blanch purple-headed varieties.

Harvest Heads are ready to cut when they are full and frothy but the flowers have not yet begun to open. Cut the stem just below the head, which may be cooked, served raw or frozen to preserve. (Purple heads turn light green in blanching or cooking.) After the heads have been harvested the rest of the plant should be removed from the garden and composted, as it will produce no more heads.

Pests & Diseases As for broccoli. Leafy curds are caused by high temperatures, by great fluctuations in temperature or by too much high-nitrogen fertilizer such as manure. This degree of overfertilization is uncommon, however, where only organic fertilizers are used. Browning of the heads may be caused by a boron deficiency. Apply boron at the rate recommended by a soil test report.

Celeriac
(Umbelliferae, *Apium graveolens rapaceum*)
Turnip-rooted celery

Description This relative of celery produces a turnip-like root that has the flavour of celery. Roots are mature in about four months, and the plants are as cold hardy as celery.

Culture Celeriac benefits from the same soil and planting schedule as celery, although the plants do not need blanching. Set them outdoors at 9-inch intervals.

Harvest Pull before the soil freezes. Roots may be stored as beets if they are at least 2 inches across. They may attain weights of 2 to 4 pounds. Serve them raw or cooked.

Pests & Diseases As for celery.

Celery
(Umbelliferae, *Apium graveolens dulce*)

Description The word "celery" comes from the Greek *selinon* meaning parsley, to which celery is related. Although few gardeners will produce stalks as succulent, long and blemishfree as those in grocery stores, celery's reputation for being a difficult crop to grow is undeserved. It is simply slow to germinate and grow, and must be nursed along in very fertile, moist soil if the stalks are to be top quality. Celery can withstand light frost but is likely to bolt to seed if the young transplants are exposed to temperatures under 55 degrees F (13 degrees C) for 10 days or longer. As well as the standard green varieties, there are golden strains of celery, and self-blanching varieties are now available.

Culture Celery is so slow to germinate that it is best started indoors. At a soil temperature of 60 to 70 degrees F (15 to 21 degrees C) it germinates in 10 to 21 days. Seeds should be lightly covered and kept moist throughout, with day temperatures around 75 degrees F (24 degrees C) and night temperatures of 65 degrees F (18 degrees C) until germination. When seedlings are 2 inches tall they can be transplanted, 2 inches apart, into new containers. If they become spindly, cut off the top half. Harden off seedlings by letting the soil dry slightly, but do not expose them to cold. Set them outside about a week after the last frost date, choosing a well-worked, sunny or partially sunny spot where manure or compost has been worked into the soil. Set plants 6 inches apart in the garden, in double rows or staggered in beds. Keep plants well watered. Blanching of the spears is not necessary but will produce a milder flavour. To blanch, dig trenches 1 foot deep and 1 foot wide, and fill with 8 inches of good soil mixed with 25 per cent manure or compost. Set transplants in this mixture 6 inches apart along the trench. As the plants grow, fill the trench with soil or a soil/manure mixture, holding the stalks together as the mixture is placed around them. In cold areas, celery can be left to mature in cold frames.

Harvest Stalks can be pulled singly from the outside of the plant while it continues to grow, or entire heads pulled, trimmed and stored in a cool, damp place — wrap in plastic and store in the refrigerator or a cold room. After the first fall frost, pull heads with roots, remove one-quarter of the tops and replant them in damp sand in the root cellar. With a temperature of about 45 degrees F (7 degrees C) and high humidity, the heads will keep for several weeks. Celery leaves may be used fresh or dried for use as a potherb.

Pests & Diseases The parsleyworm, larva of the black swallowtail butterfly, can be hand picked from foliage. Stem cracking may be caused by a boron deficiency; apply boron according to recommendations in a soil test report.

Chicory
(Compositae, *Cichorium intybus*)
Witloof, Magdeburg,
Italian dandelion, Radichetta

Description Like its wild, blue-flowered counterpart, cultivated chicory is a very hardy, vigorous plant whose foliage has a bitter taste unless it is blanched. There are several types. Asparagus chicory is grown for its thick, leafy stems. Heading types may be used for summer greens. Magdeburg produces large, parsnip-like roots usually used as a coffee substitute or extender (as roots of wild chicory can also be used). Witloof, or leaf chicory, may be eaten as a summer salad green but is grown primarily for forcing in winter (see below). Highly valued in Europe, the ability of all varieties of chicory to produce fresh greens in winter has not yet been fully appreciated in North America. Radichetta is a "looseleaf" type whose foliage becomes very sweet and tender in winter. Chicory is sometimes called French or Belgian endive, names that confuse it with true endive, *Cichorium endivia*.

Culture Plant all varieties after the last spring frost, sowing seeds about 1 inch apart and ½ inch deep in rows, or in groups of three or four seeds spaced at 6-inch intervals. Thin later so that the plants stand about 1 foot apart.

Harvest Foliage of all types can be eaten in summer, though it will be bitter unless blanched under inverted flower pots or boxes like endive. After the first fall frost, all are harvested. Magdeburg is dug up, the tops trimmed off and the long roots washed, ground or cut into small pieces, then spread on cookie sheets and roasted in a warm oven until coffee-brown. Use alone for brewing or blend with coffee. Wild chicory roots can be prepared in the same manner. For Witloof, cut stems and foliage back to within 1 inch of the soil, dig up the root and replant it upright in a box of wet sand. Place the box in a cool (50 to 65 degrees F, 10 to 18 degrees C) cupboard or root cellar. Absolute darkness is necessary: Any light will cause bitterness in the heads, or *chicons*, which are cut at the soil level after two or three weeks when they are 4 or 5 inches long. As with beets, roots can be stored horizontally until they are needed throughout the winter. One set of roots will produce two or three *chicons*, but each crop will be smaller than the former. Spent roots can be used as livestock feed. Radichetta, available in green and red cultivars, is used only as a leaf vegetable. Again, the plants are dug in fall, transplanted into boxes or pots of wet sand and placed in a cold frame or greenhouse where they can be kept at a temperature around the freezing mark. The plant produces new, mild-tasting, tender foliage until it freezes or goes to seed in spring. In very mild areas, radichetta will overwinter in the garden under burlap or straw.

Pests & Diseases As for dandelions.

Locally grown Chinese cabbage is sold in Vancouver's Chinatown, where it is one of the most popular vegetables

Chinese Cabbage

(Cruciferae, *Brassica pekinensis*)
Celery cabbage, Michihli, Wong bok,
Suey choy, Pe tsai

Description Because Orientals grow a variety of brassicas, there is more than one plant known as Chinese cabbage. The most common one produces loose, upright heads of somewhat wrinkled leaves closer in texture to lettuce than cabbage. A cool-weather crop, Chinese cabbage stands light frost but will bolt to seed very quickly, even before heading, in hot weather or where daylight is very extended. In 1980 variety trials in Alaska, all cultivars bolted to seed before harvest. Chinese cabbage is thus not recommended for far Northerners and others must plant it in early spring or late summer. The plant thrives in moist fertile soil high in organic matter and in a temperature range of 60 to 68 degrees F (15 to 20 degrees C). It will withstand light frost in the spring and fall. A steady water supply will produce lush heads like those pictured above.

Culture Sow as cabbage, but do not transplant unless a short season demands it, as the change in conditions is likely to cause it to bolt. Seeds germi-

nate best at a soil temperature between 68 and 77 degrees F (20 and 25 degrees C), but the plant will grow at temperatures as low as 40 degrees F (5 degrees C). Apply mulch when the plants are a few inches high to protect them from drought.

Harvest Use like lettuce or cabbage, pulling leaves as needed or harvesting the entire head. The plant is especially suited to stir-fry dishes. Trimmed and wrapped in newspaper or perforated plastic, the heads can be stored for several weeks in a root cellar or refrigerator at a temperature just above freezing and in high relative humidity.

Pests & Diseases As for broccoli.

Corn

(Graminae, *Zea mays*)

Description Bred into hundreds of variations by the Indians of North and South America, this annual member of the grass family has since been developed further, to produce ever sweeter kernels for gardeners ever further north. Because it is tall, 5 to 8 feet, and wind-pollinated, corn tends to dominate the garden. Several rows of each variety must be planted to ensure full ears. Pollen is produced on the tassels that form at the tops of plants; the female receptacle for the pollen is the silk at the top of each ear. Every strand of silk pollinates one kernel, so incomplete pollination results in poorly filled ears. Corn needs a great deal of nitrogen to grow well. Incorporating manure or compost into the corn bed before planting will help it along. Sweet corn is available with yellow, white or bicolour kernels. Very early varieties (53 to 60 days) such as Polar Vee, developed in Ontario, produce "mini" cobs 4 to 6 inches long, best for short-season areas. Buy them from companies specializing in seeds for Northerners. Mature corn will withstand light frost, but the kernel flavour will deteriorate.

Culture Corn may be started in flats four weeks before planting out, but because it germinates and grows quickly in warm soil it is usually sown directly in the garden. Plastic mulch will help warm the soil in marginal areas, and has been found to speed maturation by 10 to 12 days in experiments in Atlantic Canada. Sow the seeds around the last frost date, or early enough to allow it to mature at least two weeks before the first fall frost, spacing seeds at 2-inch intervals in rows about 2 feet apart, later thinning plants to stand 6 inches apart. Or sow in hills of two or three seeds, each hill 12 inches from the next in the row, with rows at least 2 feet apart. Seeds germinate in four to seven days at 60 to 90 degrees F (16 to 32 degrees C). Allow four rows of each variety. Varieties that mature at the same time should be separated by a tall crop such as sunflowers or kept at least 10 feet apart to prevent cross-pollination which can drastically reduce kernel quality. Keep the bed well weeded until plants are tall enough to compete. Thereafter, a mulch will help control weeds. Do not cultivate deeply because roots are shallow.

Harvest Plan to harvest about two ears per plant. When corn is ripe, the silks appear dry and the cobs full. To check for ripeness, pull back the husk on one ear; the top kernels should be full. Standard sweet corn loses its sweetness quickly after it is picked. Serve or preserve as soon as possible, or put it into cold storage immediately — conversion of sugar to starch is five times faster at 80 degrees F (26 degrees C) than at 30 degrees F (-1 degree C). New "super-sweet" or "EH" corn varieties retain their sweetness after picking.

Pests & Diseases Incomplete filling of ears is usually the result of too few plants in a patch, but may also result from poor weather during pollination. Corn smut, which causes an immense swelling of kernels, comes from a wind-borne fungus. Cut off affected cobs and burn them — if the kernels burst, spores will be spread throughout the garden where they will survive for four to five years. To combat corn ear worms, squirt mineral oil down into the silks four or five days after they wilt. Corn borers overwinter on stubble left in the garden; discourage them by removing corn refuse after the harvest. Larger predators must be fended off with larger means. Catharine Parr Traill wrote that corn "has many enemies; bears, raccoons, squirrels, mice and birds, and is a great temptation to breachy cattle who, to come at it, will even toss down a fence." A wire or even an electric fence will deter most predators, while birds and squirrels can be foiled with paper bags placed over the ears after pollination. Planting vining crops such as pumpkins around the patch is something of a deterrent to small animals, as is cayenne pepper applied to the ears after every rain.

Ornamental Corn, Indian Corn, Dry Corn

Description, Culture & Harvest These are long-season (over 100 days) types of corn that usually grow about 8 feet tall. Plant like sweet corn. Harvest ornamental corn as for popcorn but leave the kernels on the cobs for use in decoration. This is an enjoyable crop for children to grow, but be sure to keep it separate from other cultivars that mature at the same time. Varieties of dry corn suitable for grinding are available from a few companies such as Johnny's Selected Seeds. Harvest as popcorn and grind as needed.

Popcorn

Description, Culture & Harvest Available with large or small, white, yellow, blue, red or black kernels, popcorn is planted and grown like sweet corn, but harvested when the stalks and leaves are completely dry, even if this means waiting past the first few light frosts. Do choose early varieties, however, as many require a long hot season of more than 100 days. Bring the ears indoors, husk them and hang them in a warm, dry place to dry further, popping a sample from time to time to test it. As soon as they pop well, remove the kernels by twisting them off the cobs, and store in airtight containers so they do not dry further.

Pests & Diseases As for corn.

Corn Salad

(Valerianaceae, *Valerianella locusta*)
Lamb's lettuce, Feldsalat, Doucette

Description Corn salad matures fairly quickly, producing spoon-shaped leaves during cool spring or fall weather. Plants are easy to grow and frost hardy. Because they are small, only about 3½ inches tall at maturity, they are useful in interplantings and in small gardens.

Culture Sow two weeks before the last spring frost and continue through late summer, thinning seedlings to 6 inches apart when they are about 2 inches tall. In very mild areas, late plantings will bear all winter and go to seed in spring, or will remain dormant during the winter and produce early greens in spring. Heavy mulching will enable crops to overwinter in cooler areas.

Harvest As leaf lettuce. Begin harvesting the outer leaves after three or four true leaves have developed, and until the plant bolts.

Pests & Diseases As for dandelions.

Cress

(Cruciferae, *Lepidum sativum*)
Peppergrass

Description A native of the Middle East, cress is the garden's fastest maturing crop, ready to harvest only 10 days after sowing in damp, cool soil. Familiar as the mossy vegetable that grows on terra cotta lambs and pigs from specialty stores, cress does equally well outdoors or indoors on a sunny window sill. Plants go to seed very quickly in hot weather, and produce small white flowers.

Culture Seed may be sown outdoors or indoors in pots, or even on a wet brick or sponge set in a pan of water. Sow seeds by broadcasting them evenly on the surface; if on soil, press them in and water with a fine spray. The seed germinates in about a day at 49 to 59 degrees F (10 to 15 degrees C). Resow every two or three weeks. During hot, dry weather, sow in a moist, shaded place for the tenderest leaves.

Harvest Begin to harvest cress when its leaves are 1 to 1½ inches long, by holding the tops in one hand and "mowing" them with a sharp knife held in the other. Use fresh in salads or sandwiches. Cress has a pungent, peppery flavour similar to that of watercress.

Pests & Diseases As for dandelions.

Cucumbers

(Cucurbitaceae, *Cucumis sativus*)

Description The cucumber is an Old World plant popular with North America's early settlers, who found that it suited their new situation well. One, Thomas McGrath, wrote from Toronto in 1832, "Melons, cucumbers and pumpkins grow freely and very abundantly in the open air, and require less attention than any crop we have." Had McGrath been living further north, he'd have given his cucumbers more thought. The plant is very frost sensitive, so in most far northern gardens it should be protected for at least part of the season. Vining cucumber varieties can be allowed to sprawl in the garden or can be grown against a trellis or fence about 5 feet high, which they will climb readily. Bush varieties do not climb, but take less garden space than do unsupported vining cucumbers – some require as little as 18 to 20 square inches. As the cucumber is monoecious, producing separate male and female flowers, it must be pollinated by insects or by hand. Some varieties produce mostly female, fruit-producing flowers. Marked "male" seeds are included in the packet; plant one for every one to six females. Seedless "all female" varieties are meant for greenhouse culture only, as pollination will lower the fruit quality. There are also lemon-shaped cucumbers, low-acid "burpless" fruits, and some that are long, thin and snake-like. Pickling varieties produce a large crop of 3- to 4-inch-long fruit almost simultaneously, often about 48 days after planting. Slicing varieties produce longer, 9- to 10-inch fruits one at a time over a longer period.

Culture All of the cucurbits have very delicate roots that must not be damaged in transplanting. Sow cucumbers directly in the garden around the last frost date or transplant them in peat pots, peat pellets or containers that can be removed without disturbing the roots. Seeds germinate in three to seven days in the preferred soil temperature range of 68 to 95 degrees F (20 to 35 degrees C), but will not germinate below 50 degrees F (10 degrees C). Choose a sunny, sheltered place for cucumbers –

excessive winds will damage plants and slow growth. If they are to be supported, sow two or three seeds ½ inch deep, or set transplants at 6-inch intervals along the fence or trellis; or give each plant its own pole, slanted to form a teepee or A-frame structure. As plants grow, thin to one every 6 inches. Vining or bush varieties may be planted in hills of two or three plants (six to nine seeds, thinned later), the hills 3 feet apart — or less if small bush varieties are grown. Covering plants with commercial or homemade shelters will help start them off well, as will a black or clear plastic mulch (see the instructions for building a row cover on pages 62 and 63). Hand pollination will be necessary if the plants are unlikely to be visited by bees (see the instructions on page 111). If pollination does not take place, no fruit will form. Wet plants should not be touched, because they are susceptible to fungus diseases.

Harvest Continual picking will prolong the harvest. Most plants will produce only 10 to 12 fruits if they are allowed to remain on the vine, but may produce 40 to 50 if they are picked while young. Pinch or cut the fruits off with a knife because pulling hard may damage the plant. Pick all fruits before they turn yellow. Often, however, overmature fruits will appear under leaves in late summer — or the harvest will simply get ahead of the gardener. These cucumbers are consumed by most livestock.

Pests & Diseases Many gardeners have no pest or disease problems. Squash bugs can be controlled with a tea of cedar bark chips or by placing boards on the ground around the plant. At night the bugs congregate under the boards and can be killed in the morning. Earlier in the season, destroy their clusters of yellow to brown eggs usually found between two main veins on the underside of the leaf. Striped cucumber beetles do little damage themselves but may spread bacterial wilt. Control them with pyrethrum or rotenone. If a single vine suddenly wilts, the culprit is likely the squash vine borer. Search along the vine to find a hole. Slit the stem, remove the borer, hill soil over the damaged vine and water. If bacterial or fungal diseases do occur, destroy all plant refuse at the end of the season and choose a resistant variety the next spring.

Dandelions
(Compositae, *Taraxacum officinale*)

Description, Culture & Harvest This plant needs little introduction, so thoroughly has it become adapted to life in North America. It is, however, not only a weed but also a salad vegetable or potherb, with leaves that are very rich in vitamin A and iron, and roots that may be prepared as a coffee substitute in the same way as for chicory. While the weedy dandelion may be used in these ways, the more cultivated strain carried by some seed houses has milder-tasting foliage. Young leaves may be used fresh in salads, while more mature ones take the place of spinach. Even the commercial strains, however, have foliage more bitter than that preferred by the average North American palate, and are best blanched like endive. In *Roughing It In the Bush*, Susanna Moodie's 19th-century journal of life in rural Canada, the author notes, "The dandelion planted in trenches and blanched to a beautiful cream colour with straw makes an excellent salad, quite equal to endive, and is more hardy and requires less care." Sow seeds in spring for a fall crop, or sow later for harvest the following season, mulching the roots over winter. Allow each plant 1 foot all around. Roots can be dug up in fall and forced like chicory.

Pests & Diseases Slugs can be troublesome, especially during damp weather or in deeply mulched gardens. Depress saucers or jar lids of beer around the plants, or dust plants and the surrounding soil with diatomaceous earth, reapplying it after every rain. Flea beetles may attack young plants and, although they seldom kill them, the beetles can be controlled with rotenone or diatomaceous earth.

Eggplant
(Solanaceae, *Solanum melongena esculentum*)

Description Eggplant, an annual from South America, is a luxury crop for Northerners. It loves heat and is extremely sensitive to cold weather, so much so that any thoughts of growing it in the North have arisen only recently with the development of quick-maturing cultivars. Fruits may be elongated or globe shaped, the former tending to be the short-season varieties, maturing in about 60 days as opposed to 70 to 75 days for the larger globe fruits. White-fruited varieties are also available and sometimes promoted as "egg trees."

Culture Eggplant must be started indoors at least 10 weeks before the last spring frost, as it grows very slowly. Seeds will not germinate in a soil temperature below 60 degrees F (16 degrees C) and prefer 85 degrees F (29 degrees C). The plant grows best around 70 to 75 degrees F (23 degrees C). Transplant outdoors about two weeks after the last frost date or when night temperatures are consistently warmer than 45 degrees F (7 degrees C). Choose a sunny, sheltered place where the soil is well worked and perhaps prewarmed with plastic mulch, setting plants 1½ feet apart. In most northern gardens, hot caps or cloches are recommended for at least the first two weeks.

Harvest With a knife or pruning shears, cut fruit off when it is firm and glossy. Each plant should produce one to 10 fruits. As the fruit does not store well, it should be cooked soon after picking.

Pests & Diseases Eggplant transplants are very attractive to flea beetles which can be controlled with rotenone or pyrethrum. Colorado potato beetles and their larvae can be hand picked or dusted with rotenone. To avoid verticillium wilt, do not plant eggplant where relatives (see page 38) or strawberries grew the previous season. Protect transplants from cutworms by encircling them with paper collars that extend 1½ inches above and below the soil surface.

Endive & Escarole
(Compositae, *Cichorium endivia*)

Description Endive and escarole are closely related to chicory, and the three are sometimes confused. Endive and escarole are more cold sensitive than chicory but, like chicory, produce foliage that may be bitter if not blanched. The lettuce-like plants produce large, bright heads that go to seed in hot weather, but they are more frost hardy than lettuce and thus stand longer in the garden in fall. Green endive has deeply serrated, curly leaves, while escarole or Batavian endive has upright, broad leaves and a self-blanched heart.

Culture Both plants may be sown in a partially shady spot in furrows ½ inch deep with the seeds ½ inch apart in rows 18 inches apart. Thin plants to stand 12 inches apart. For a fall crop, sow in mid-season, early enough to allow the crop to mature around the last frost date, about 90 to 100 days after sowing. To blanch, tie outer leaves around the head, invert a flower pot over each head, or cover rows with cloches for about three weeks before harvesting. Plants grown in a cold frame or under cover are less bitter than those grown in the open air. Prolonged hot weather increases bitterness, while cool fall weather produces the sweetest greens.

Harvest Cut the entire head and use as lettuce.

Pests & Diseases As for dandelions.

Garden Huckleberries
(Solanaceae, *Solanum nigrum*)

Description Unrelated to the sweet, red, wild huckleberry, *Solanum nigrum* is also quite unlike it. Related to peppers and eggplants, the bushes are similar in appearance, but larger and more spreading, growing about 30 inches tall. The purple-black berries are tart and pulpy when eaten fresh. They are used only after cooking with sugar or honey, after which they lend a blueberry-like flavour to desserts and preserves. The plants are prolific enough that most families will want only two to six plants.

Culture Start plants indoors about six weeks before the last spring frost, in flats or individual containers, allowing each seedling 1 inch of space all around. Set outdoors a week after the last frost date, leaving 2 feet around each plant. In cool-season areas, grow this frost-tender plant under cover or cover it when frost threatens. It requires about three months of frost-free growing.

Harvest Pick berries when they are very black and ripe — they may contain toxins when green — to use in desserts or preserves, mixed with enough sweetener to bring out the fruity flavour.

Pests & Diseases Garden huckleberries are remarkably vigorous and have few problems as long as the soil is sufficiently warm, though flea beetles may attack the young seedlings. If necessary, control with pyrethrum or rotenone. Colorado potato beetles and their larvae can be hand picked. Remove leaves bearing their bright orange egg clusters.

Unrelated to the wild huckleberry, the garden huckleberry is actually a first cousin of the potato, also of the Solanum genus

Garlic

(Liliaceae, *Allium sativum*)

Description Garlic has been highly esteemed as both a seasoning and a medicine for thousands of years. It is very easy to grow, although large bulbs do not always result from home plantings. As it does not reproduce true from seed, garlic is propagated with cloves, the divisions into which the bulb easily separates. Supermarket garlic can be used for planting, but seed companies often sell larger-bulbed varieties such as elephant garlic, each clove of which may weigh an ounce.

Culture Garlic cloves may be planted in very early spring for fall harvest but, as they require a long season (three or four months) to mature, they are better planted in fall for harvest the next year. This also ensures that the bulbs' dormancy is broken; plants never exposed to temperatures below 64 degrees F (18 degrees C) may fail to form bulbs. Break the bulb into cloves, discarding the long, slender ones at the middle of the bulb, and plant, if possible, in fertile soil high in organic matter, each clove

with its pointed end up and about ½ inch below the soil surface. Allow each clove 3 to 6 inches all around. Cloves may also be interplanted with other crops as long as they are not crowded out or overshadowed. Garlic is shallow rooted, so avoid deep cultivation. In the far North, mulch the cloves over the winter or plant in early spring in a cold frame, moving them into the garden later.

Harvest Bulbs are ready to pull when the tops die back. Cure and store as onions.

Pests & Diseases None in most areas, which makes garlic an ideal companion plant in the vegetable garden.

Ground Cherries

(Solanaceae, *Physalis pruinosa*)

Description This bushy, medium-sized plant produces golden, ¾-inch-diameter berries enclosed in papery husks similar to the ornamental "Chinese lanterns" to which they are related. The fruit is used for desserts and preserves, although it is sweet enough to be eaten out of hand. The bushes are frost tender and so should be grown in cloches in short-season areas or covered when frost threatens.

Culture Sow seed indoors in flats or individual containers about six weeks before the last frost date, allowing each seedling 1 inch all around. About a week after the last frost, transplants can be placed outdoors as with garden huckleberries. Gardeners in very mild growing areas can seed directly outdoors around the last frost date. Volunteer plants are likely to appear the following year if some mature fruit has been allowed to remain in the garden.

Harvest The berries are ready to pick when the husks are straw coloured and the fruits golden, about 70 days after transplanting. The papery lantern is quite easily removed, but leave it on if fruit is to be stored. It will keep for a few weeks placed in a single layer in a box in any cool dry place. Fruit may be eaten fresh, frozen or made into preserves.

Pests & Diseases Flea beetles may attack young transplants, while the striped blister beetle may attack ripe fruit in some gardens. Neither is likely to inflict severe damage, but rotenone or pyrethrum can be applied if infestations are severe. Hand pick tomato hornworms, Colorado potato beetles and their larvae. Ground cherries are not the first dietary choice of these pests, but they will spread onto most members of the Solanaceae family in a year of severe outbreaks. Do not plant ground cherries next to other Solanaceae, and rotate with other families.

Ground cherries are decorative, easily grown and can be eaten fresh, or they may be used in preserves and desserts

Kale

(Cruciferae, *Brassica oleracea acephala*)
Borecole

Description Kale is a standby in short-season gardens, an easy crop to grow and one that matures even on permafrost. In fact, it does not grow well in hot weather, preferring cool, damp days for the best development of its curly, dark green leaves, rich in vitamins A and C and iron. Kale is grown primarily as a fall green, as it is very frost resistant, usually the last leafy green standing in the garden as winter approaches. All types of kale grow about a foot tall and spread a foot or two in width. Siberian kale has fairly smooth leaves, while Scotch kale has very curly leaves. Ornamental kale is also edible. Chinese kale or Chinese broccoli, *gai lohn* or *gai lan*, is also frost hardy, yielding smooth kale-like leaves and small broccoli-like buds.

Culture In short-season areas, kale can be started indoors six weeks before the last frost date and grown in a cold frame, but it is generally seeded directly in the garden about two weeks before the last frost. Sow seeds ½ inch deep and at ½-inch intervals or in groups of three or four seeds, each group 1 foot from all others. Thin seedlings or set transplants so that each plant has 1 foot all around. Seeding may continue until mid-summer, as long as the gardener allows the plant about two months to mature before the first fall frost, though leaves may be harvested before then. If the garden is very hot, plant kale in a shady spot and keep it watered. Watering with manure tea once a month will help produce large leaves.

Harvest The most tender leaves grow at the centre of the plant. Pull leaves singly as needed, using them in the same manner as cabbage.

Pests & Diseases As for broccoli.

Kohlrabi

(Cruciferae, *Brassica oleracea caulorapa*)
Stem turnip

Description This odd member of the *Brassica* genus takes its name from the Latin *caulis*, stem, and *rapum*, turnip. The part eaten is a turnip-like swelling partway up the stem. Kohlrabi is easy to grow, and good vegetables are produced if the plants are given plenty of water and harvested young; otherwise they are likely to be woody. Green and purple varieties, both white under the skin, are available. Kohlrabi will stand light frost throughout the season.

Culture Plant like kale, with a final spacing of 8 inches all around. Kohlrabi does best in well-worked, fertile soil that is kept moist.

Harvest Pull the entire plant when the swelling is about 1½ to 3 inches across, about 50 days after seeding or 40 days after transplanting. Peel the vegetable and use fresh or cooked, as cabbage. It can be stored for a few weeks in a cool, damp root cellar. Cut off leaves, stem and root, and spread the vegetables between layers of straw or newspaper in a box.

Pests & Diseases As for broccoli. Because kohlrabi is planted early in the season and harvested early, and because the stem is not easily damaged, kohlrabi usually requires no protection from pests.

Leeks
(Liliaceae, *Allium porrum*)

Description A thickened, sweet, nonbulbing onion, the leek was one of the most popular of European medieval vegetables, and has retained a favoured position among *cordon bleu* chefs. Though not strictly necessary, the best leeks are blanched; unblanched leeks are stronger in flavour and darker in colour. Leeks do best in very fertile, finely worked soil, and will not tolerate weed competition. Although frost tolerant, they require about a three-month growing season, and so should be started indoors or purchased as transplants.

Culture Sow seeds thickly indoors in flats or containers, as for onions. Keep seedlings clipped to a 4-inch height before planting outdoors from four weeks before until two weeks after the last spring frost date, allowing each plant 6 inches all around. To blanch, set transplants in a 6-inch-deep trench at 6-inch intervals, in the same manner as asparagus, filling the trench with rich soil or a soil/manure mixture as they grow. Then mulch with organic matter.

Harvest Pull plants as needed until the soil freezes. In mild areas they may overwinter successfully in the garden, especially if trenched and mulched; the harvest then resumes in spring until the plants go to seed. Leeks are sliced and used fresh or cooked, and can be preserved by drying or freezing. The best part is the stalk, not the leaves.

Pests & Diseases Most gardeners will have none, but root maggots may be troublesome in some areas. See onions.

Lentils
(Leguminosae, *Lens culinaris*)

Description The lentil, attractive enough to take its place in any flower garden, is a bushy plant about 12 inches tall that produces dark green leaves and small white or pale blue flowers like sweet peas. Hardy, easy to grow and a source of soil nitrogen, it has recently become an important specialty crop in western Canada, but unfortunately it is less practical to grow on a small scale, as each pod produces only two or three lentils. Shelling is so time-consuming that most gardeners will choose to buy their lentils at the corner store.

Culture Plant any time in early spring, sowing seeds ½ inch deep and 4 inches apart. Water after planting if the soil is dry. Like peas, lentils do best in loose, cool, moist soil.

Harvest Leave the pods on the plants until they are dry, about two months after planting. Then harvest pods and shell them. Store lentils in a jar or paper bag in a cool, dry cupboard.

Pests & Diseases None of note.

Lettuce, Head
(Compositae, *Lactuca sativa*)

Description The lettuce with which North Americans are most familiar is head lettuce or, more specifically, crisphead lettuce. There are two other types of head lettuce as well: butterhead or bibb, which produces loose heads of tender, rounded leaves; and cos or romaine, with elongated, crisp leaves that are sometimes wrinkled. Some lettuces cross the class boundaries. All are more difficult to grow and more demanding of space than leaf lettuce. Lettuce is not as nutritious as other salad greens but its mild, sweet flavour is very popular. The young seedlings or transplants can withstand temperatures of 20 degrees F (-6 degrees C) if properly hardened off, while the mature heads will not bear frost, and must be covered if frost threatens before they are ready to harvest. Lettuce will germinate and continue to grow as long as the soil temperature is at least 40 degrees F (4 degrees C).

Culture Head lettuce is often started indoors in flats or containers six or seven weeks before the last frost date so that it will mature before the hottest summer weather causes it to bolt to seed prematurely. But it may also be seeded directly outdoors two or three weeks before the last frost or until early summer, as long as the plants are allowed about three months to mature before the first fall frost.

Germination is fastest around 75 degrees F (24 degrees C); growth is best from 60 to 65 degrees F (16 to 18 degrees C). Sow seeds thinly in very shallow furrows 1 foot apart, or broadcast seed over the soil surface, pressing it down and watering with a fine spray. When the plants have two or three true leaves, thin them to stand 1 foot apart. Keep plants watered until they are about 4 inches tall. Then they can be mulched with organic matter to retain moisture. Then water every two weeks with manure tea or fish fertilizer.

Harvest Thinnings may be eaten. The head is ready to harvest when it feels firm under light pressure, or when it has attained full size for the cultivar.

Pests & Diseases The worst pest is the slug, particularly in wet gardens. Press saucers or jar lids of beer into the soil around the plants, or dust plants and surrounding soil with diatomaceous earth after every rainfall. Fungal diseases are also most likely to strike lettuce in wet gardens, causing leaves to wilt or discolour. Choose fungus-resistant or quick-maturing leaf varieties, and rotate crops every year. Tipburn may result when temperatures vary widely from day to night. Counter with resistant varieties and a limited nitrogen supply.

Lettuce, Leaf

Description If head lettuce is a demanding crop, looseleaf lettuce is among the easiest, and the final product is just as tender and sweet as the foliage of the heading cultivars. Some types have broad leaves; some have curly, savoyed leaves; others have reddish leaves. The colour develops best in direct sunlight. Leaf lettuce is fully mature about two months after seeding, with some varieties more resistant to bolting to seed than others. Check the seed catalogue descriptions for long-standing types (often, unfortunately, not the sweetest). The plants will bear light frost both early and late in the season. Under row covers or in a cold frame, they may survive more than a month past the first fall frost.

Culture Sow indoors five or six weeks before the last spring frost, transplanting seedlings outdoors three or four weeks later. Successive sowings can be transplanted outdoors all season, with mid-summer transplants going into a spot overshadowed by a crop that will be harvested in late summer. Or sowing may be done directly in the garden as for head lettuce. When there are two or three true leaves, thin plants to stand 6 to 8 inches apart. Keep watered, and fertilize with manure tea or fish fertilizer every two weeks. An organic mulch will help retain soil moisture. Choose heat-tolerant (bolt-resistant) cultivars for late planting.

Harvest Thinnings can be eaten. Single outer leaves can be pulled from several plants, or the entire head can be pulled, trimmed and served. Store in plastic bags in the refrigerator.

Pests & Diseases As for head lettuce.

Luffa
(Cucurbitaceae, *Luffa cylindrica*)

Description A gourd of many uses from the far East, the luffa is a conversation piece for Northerners. Some years it may produce a crop; many times it will not. It takes the name "Chinese okra" from the shape of the fruits, which may be eaten young or used as bath sponges if allowed to mature – luffa sponges, made of the inner fibres of the gourds, are expensive items in bath shops. Luffa, extremely frost tender, needs a warm season of at least 115 days, a very sunny location and fertile soil.

Culture Plant seeds four weeks before the last spring frost, two or three seeds to a 4-inch container or peat pellet, pinching off all but the strongest seedling. Like other cucurbits, luffas will tolerate little root disturbance, so they must be sown in containers that can be planted (peat pellets or peat pots) or in ones that can be torn away from the root ball. If the plant outgrows a peat pellet, the entire pellet must be planted in a larger container. Plant outdoors about two weeks after the last frost date in a sunny, sheltered place, with plants 1 foot apart. The luffa likes to climb and may extend 10 to 15 feet – 30 feet in a very good year – so plant it by a fence or trellis, or by a south-facing wall from which netting has been hung. Plastic mulch and hot caps will help get the plants started, and the mulch should be left in place all season.

Harvest For culinary use, pick the gourds when they are less than 6 inches long. Pare off the ridges with a potato peeler and cook or serve raw like zucchini. The mature gourds, which may weigh 5 pounds, are harvested after the vine has been killed by frost, and then soaked in warm water to remove

The fruit of the luffa can be eaten when it is young or, when mature, it can also be dried and used as a bath sponge

the skin. The husk is dried and the seeds emptied out, leaving a luffa sponge.

Pests & Diseases See cucumber.

Malabar Spinach

(Chenopodiaceae, *Basella alba*)

Description An Asian biennial treated as an annual in the North, *Basella alba* produces glossy, spinach-like greens that are very frost tender but will not bolt to seed with summer's heat and long days; in fact, the higher the temperature, the better it grows. Leaves are mature about two months after sowing, but may be harvested sooner. The plant produces a long, creeping stem that can be supported on a fence or trellis. Cover plants if frost threatens.

Culture Start seeds indoors about two weeks before the last frost and transplant outdoors three weeks later, or sow directly outdoors in a sunny place around the last frost date. Sow seeds about ¼ inch deep at 2-inch intervals, later thinning or transplanting to stand 9 inches apart.

Harvest Use raw or cooked throughout the season, like spinach.

Pests & Diseases As for dandelions.

Mushrooms

(Fungi, *Agaricus bisporus*)

Description There are many edible mushrooms growing wild in the North and, armed with a suitable manual, even a beginner can safely identify a few of them. For those who prefer the standard supermarket variety, *Agaricus bisporus*, several seed companies stock the spawn or "seed." It requires a cool, damp, dark place indoors or outdoors. Conditions being somewhat easier to control indoors, mushrooms are usually raised on composted manure in boxes in a basement.

Culture For outdoor sowing, select a shady spot in spring, roll back the sod and spread the spawn evenly on the soil, water if necessary, then replace the sod. Mushrooms should appear in about seven weeks and continue for several "flushes" thereafter. Indoors, the spawn is sown in a box of thoroughly composted livestock manure — avoid manure that has been contaminated with disinfectants. Compost the manure outdoors by layering it with gypsum at the rate of 20 pounds per ½ ton of manure. Or, on a smaller scale, the Atlantic provinces recommend a compost made of 1 cubic yard of horse manure, ½ to 1 bale of hay, ½ bushel of poultry manure, 10 pounds of gypsum and 1 pound of ammonium nitrate. This should fill a bed 10 feet long, 3 feet wide and 8 inches deep. Some home gardeners have reported success with composted horse manure (including bedding) used alone.

When the pile is thoroughly composted (see directions on pages 42 to 44), pile it into boxes 8 to 10 inches deep and apply the spawn according to package directions. Throughout the growing process, the compost must be kept moist and within the temperature range of 52 to 70 degrees F (11 to 21 degrees C). It must also be kept in the dark. In two or three weeks, a cottony layer of mycelia, the working part of the mushrooms, will appear on the top of the compost. Cover it with 1½ inches of a wetted mixture of equal parts by weight of peat moss and calcitic limestone. Cover this with a layer of plastic or with newspaper that is sprinkled with water daily. In 10 days, remove the paper. Mushrooms should begin to appear within a week.

Harvest Once a mushroom begins to open, it will not become any larger. Snap it at the soil level when it reaches the preferred stage of maturity, usually about a week after emergence. New flushes should continue for two to five months, with each harvest less abundant than the previous one. Total yields of 3 pounds per square foot are possible. Mushrooms may be used raw or cooked, or they can be preserved by drying or freezing.

Pests & Diseases The growing bed is prey to many insects and diseases, including unwanted fungi; all are best controlled in a very clean growing area and a well-composted growing mixture that is never sodden.

Muskmelon

(Cucurbitaceae, *Cucumis melo*)
Cantaloupe

Description The cantaloupes grown in northern gardens are almost always muskmelons, fruits of Asian origin that are much more popular than their name. More than a century ago, Sir John A. Macdonald wrote to his daughter Mary, "The garden looks fine now. . . there are some fine melons. . . . You must pick them for dinner and feed the chickens with the rind." Although melons are extremely frost tender, such quick-maturing varieties have been bred that, grown under cover and hand pollinated, they will take advantage of the long days to produce a crop even north of the 60th parallel. In experiments at the University of New Hampshire, fruit maturity was as much as 13 days earlier for plants grown with black plastic mulch under a slitted row cover than with the black mulch alone. Daytime temperatures under the row covers averaged 39 to 41 degrees F (22 to 23 degrees C) above outside air temperatures. Further south they will do fine outdoors, though sometimes requiring the boost of an early hot cap or a season-long plastic mulch. Select the earliest varieties available of either the orange-fleshed muskmelon or green-fleshed honeydew. By starting them indoors and coddling them along, almost any gardener can produce one of the most delicious and exotic of the garden's offerings — vine-ripened, sunwarmed melon. Nothing in the grocery store can even come close.

Culture Start melon seeds indoors four or five weeks before the last spring frost. Sow two or three seeds per container, choosing fairly large ones such as milk shake cups or milk cartons that can be torn away in transplanting. Or use peat pots — peat pellets are too small. The roots will not stand any disturbance in transplanting. Germination takes place in four to 14 days at 68 to 86 degrees F (20 to 30 degrees C), and is best at 72 degrees F (22 degrees C). Seeds will not germinate below 60 degrees F (16 degrees C). Thin seedlings to one per container by pinching off the weaker ones. Transplant outdoors into warm, fertile soil about two weeks after the last spring frost date, allowing 3 feet all around each hill of two or three plants. Vining (not bush) varieties can be encouraged to climb. Plant them 1 foot apart along a fence or trellis, training the vines upward and supporting the fruit as it develops. The use of hot caps or plant shelters will help the plants during their first two or three weeks outdoors but, later, insects must be allowed to visit the flowers or else they must be hand pollinated (see page 111). Mulching young plants will help discourage weeds and will keep the fruit of sprawling plants clean. Adequate moisture is especially important directly after transplanting and again when the fruit begins to form. Do not move vines while cultivating.

Harvest The fruit is ready to pick 70 to 100 days after transplanting, when the skin colour changes from green to slightly orange. The fruit then becomes fragrant and will "slip" easily off the stem — do not force it. Fruit picked slightly prematurely, however, will ripen indoors if the skin is not cut. It can be eaten fresh, or cubed and frozen to preserve.

Pests & Diseases As for cucumbers. As well, wireworms may penetrate fruit resting on the ground or mulch; rest each fruit on a squat tin can which has had its top and bottom removed. Cold weather late in the season may cause the plant to wilt; in cool-season areas use plastic mulch or crop covers, and ensure that the soil is moist and fertile. The main problem confronted when raising muskmelon in the North is cool soil. See pages 61 to 63 for details on warmth-enhancing plant protectors.

Mustard cabbage, with its preference for cool, damp weather, is one of the bonuses that gardening in the North provides

Mustard Cabbage
(Cruciferae, *Brassica chinensis*)
Chinese mustard cabbage, Looseleaf Chinese cabbage, Bok choy
Description This staple of Oriental cuisine most closely resembles Swiss chard, with very pronounced white ribs and stems and dark green leaves. A cool-weather plant, it survives light frost but will bolt to seed quickly in warm weather. It matures from seed in about eight weeks but may be harvested much sooner. Wild mustards of the *Brassica* genus are also edible.
Culture Sow indoors eight weeks before the last spring frost, transplanting outdoors four weeks later, or sow directly in the garden from that time until about 10 weeks before the first fall frost. Sow seeds ½ inch deep and about 1 inch apart. Thin to stand 4 to 6 inches apart. Mustard cabbage requires a steady supply of moisture and appreciates fertile soil. Water every two weeks with manure tea or fish fertilizer.
Harvest Pull single leaves or entire plants. Leaves are used raw or cooked, like spinach, while the stems may be chopped and used like celery or as-

paragus. This vegetable is a popular addition to stir-fry dishes.
Pests & Diseases As for dandelions.

Mustard Greens
(Cruciferae, *Brassica juncea*)

Description This tall, hardy plant produces peppery leaves that do not, in fact, taste like mustard, though its seeds may be used for home preparation of the condiment. It is available in both broad and curly-leafed cultivars. The vegetable matures in about 45 days from seed, though thinnings may be eaten about two weeks earlier. It is frost resistant. However, it bolts to seed quickly in hot weather.
Culture As for mustard cabbage.
Harvest Harvest and use like spinach.
Pests & Diseases As for dandelions.

New Zealand Spinach
(Tetragoniaceae, *Tetragonia expansa*)

Description *Tetragonia expansa*, like Malabar spinach is a spinach-like green that will not bolt to seed in hot weather. It thrives in high temperatures and is sensitive to frost. It is thus most highly valued where summers are hot. It is planted in spring to take over when spinach bolts, providing salad greens until fall. A native of New Zealand, the plant produces 2- to 3-foot trailing branches with fairly small, fleshy leaves. New Zealand spinach is well suited to hanging baskets — one to three plants in a 10-inch-diameter container.
Culture To speed germination, soak the large seeds in lukewarm water for 24 hours before planting. Around the last frost date sow seeds ½ inch deep and 1 inch apart in a sunny place, thinning later to stand 8 inches apart.
Harvest Harvesting may be done every two to four weeks throughout the summer once the plants are 8 to 10 inches long. Snap 3 to 4 inches off the tips, which are used like spinach, raw or cooked.
Pests & Diseases As for dandelions.

Okra
(Malvaceae, *Abelmoschus esculentus*)
Gumbo

Description An unusual vegetable to find in northern gardens, okra is usually associated with the cuisine of the deep south, where it grows prolifically to heights of 7 feet. Yet fairly fast-maturing, small-fruited varieties have been developed, so that any gardener who can grow eggplant can also grow okra – both thrive in the same temperature range, and so appreciate plastic mulches and crop covers. The part eaten is the long, grooved pod, which must be picked while very young and tender.

Culture Sow indoors as for muskmelons, transplanting outdoors 1 to 2 feet apart two weeks after the last spring frost. One to four plants are sufficient for most families.

Harvest The seed packet will indicate the best harvest size for that variety, usually about 4 inches. The pods are sliced and cooked in soups, curries and stews, where they have a thickening effect. Harvesting every few days will ensure that plants continue to bear until the first frost, or until the soil becomes too cool. Freeze to preserve.

Pests & Diseases None of note.

Onions
(Liliaceae, *Allium cepa*)

Description Available in various shapes and sizes, some biennial, some perennial, onions of some sort should be included in every garden. The most popular onions include:

• Globe onions, of which there are red, yellow and white-skinned varieties, some of them especially hard and therefore long lasting in winter storage. Check the seed catalogue for this information. Sweet Spanish onions are just as easy to grow as regular globe onions but they usually take longer to mature. They do not store as long

• Egyptian, tree or top onions are very hardy plants that will overwinter in most of the North. On the top of each stalk they form bulblets that can be eaten or planted for propagation or for the production of spring onions

• Spring onions, also called scallions or bunching onions, can be grown from seeds or sets. While any onions can be harvested young for scallions, the true spring onions (*A. fistulosum*) produce clusters of greens but no bulbs. They were given a second-place rating among vegetables in terms of space efficiency by the National Garden Bureau

• Pickling or pearl onions are mature when still very small. Because the skins are white and the necks are smaller than those of immature globe onions, these varieties are best for pickling

• Shallots produce garlic-like bulbs that have a delicate, mild flavour. They are not as frost hardy as garlic (described on page 82), but are planted in early spring and harvested in fall. Otherwise, grow and tend them as garlic

All of the onions are quite frost hardy and pest and disease resistant. All may be interplanted among other crops as long as they are not overshadowed in the process. All do best in light, well-drained, fertile soil high in organic matter. Shallow-rooted, they should be mulched or watered regularly. Do not cultivate deeply around them, but keep weeds in check. Growth interruptions caused by weeds or drought can produce unpleasantly hot onions.

Culture Globe onions are usually started indoors in flats about 10 weeks before the last spring frost, and transplanted outdoors about a month later, or any time until the last spring frost date. They may be clipped to 4 inches tall if they become overgrown before the garden is ready for planting. Allow transplants 4 inches in all directions – slight crowding speeds maturation. Most onions grown from sets or cloves can be given the same spacing, and all are set out at the same time. Plant the sets so that the pointed tips are even with or just under the soil surface. Sow the seeds of bunching onions by broadcasting them thickly on the soil surface from early through late spring, covering them with about ¼ inch of soil. Be sure that all onion seed is covered, as germination is retarded or prevented if seeds are exposed to light. A packet of bunching onion seed should cover about 5 to 6 square feet and provides 20 to 25 bunches of onions. To grow sets, sow seed of a suitable, long-storage variety such as Ebenezer or Stuttgarter in early spring. Seeds are sown very thickly, 200 per square foot. Harvest when the tops are dry and brittle, cure, and store in a cool, dry place until the following spring. In some mild areas, onions can be seeded in fall and mulched to overwinter, providing early greens and bulbs the next year.

Harvest Any type of onion can be harvested young, before the bulbs swell, and used as scallions. Bulb onions are mature when the tops die down; afterwards, they may rot if allowed to stand in the garden. The best storage onions do not form flower stalks. Those that do, and all others that have a thick stem after harvesting, must be used first, as they will not store well. The formation of flower stalks, bolting, is often caused by the use of over-sized onion sets, which should be no larger than ½ inch in diameter when purchased. It can also be caused by prolonged cold weather early in the season. If the tops have not fallen two weeks before the first fall frost date, bend them to one side.

On a sunny day about a week later, pull the onions and place them on newspaper in a sunny place, turning them occasionally. Continue curing them in this way for several days, bringing them indoors at night or when rain or frost threatens. When the skin and tops are thoroughly dry, bring the onions indoors to store in a dry place at about 40 degrees F (5 degrees C). As they keep best when air circulates around them, store them loose in baskets, boxes, in string bags or old nylon stockings, or braid them together and hang them.

Pests & Diseases In most gardens, onions will suffer no damage at all, and may even have a pest-repellent effect that will help protect neighbouring plants. The most serious pest of onions is the onion maggot, the larva of a small fly that lays its eggs on the soil near onions. The maggots then crawl into the soil to attack the bulbs. If maggots are a problem, rotate the onion patch among plants of different families (see the chart on page 38), and cover the soil around the onions with diatomaceous earth.

Parsnips
(Umbelliferae, *Pastinaca sativa*)

Description The Latin *pastinaca*, "a thing dug up," describes the parsnip – a large, white root well suited to most northern gardens because its delicate flavour sweetens with fall frost. Parsnips are an easy crop to grow but do require patience; they germinate and grow slowly, taking about four months to mature from seed. Like all root crops, parsnips do best in deeply worked, light-textured soil. The parsnip is longer than most garden roots, so give the parsnip bed a thorough spading before planting. Parsnips will often self-sow if allowed to go to seed the spring after planting.

Culture As soon as the soil can be worked, sow seeds 1 inch apart and ½ inch deep, in rows about 6 inches apart. The minimum germination temperature is 36 degrees F (2 degrees C), though the seedlings may not emerge for three weeks. During this time, keep the seed bed weeded and watered. Thin seedlings to stand 4 inches apart in all directions.

Harvest Although thinnings can be eaten earlier, roots are mature in late fall and become sweeter with each frost. The best roots are dug in early spring after the soil thaws but before the parsnips go to seed. In most areas, they will overwinter even without a mulch, although a heavy organic mulch may keep the soil from freezing, so that roots can be harvested all winter. Parsnips can be stored like beets, sliced and frozen or dried.

Pests & Diseases Parsnips suffer from few ailments in home gardens, as long as they are grown in moist, deep soil. Hand pick parsleyworms.

Peanuts
(Leguminosae, *Arachis hypogaea*)

Description Spanish or Valencia peanuts, the types grown in the North, are very attractive plants but, like lentils, may produce little to harvest. The plant develops orange blossoms that bend and touch the soil after pollination, and the peanuts then develop in clusters on "pegs" under the soil surface. Thus, the plant needs a very light, preferably sandy soil in which the nuts can expand. It also needs a long, warm season of two or three months – the longer the season, the more nuts are produced. Peanuts are more frost hardy than snap beans, but less so than peas.

Culture Shell carefully, without damaging the membrane on the nuts, and, in a sunny location about a week before the last spring frost date, sow them in rows 1½ inches deep and 3 inches apart with rows 1½ feet apart, or in a bed, allowing 8 inches all around each plant.

Harvest Dig up the plants and nuts after the first fall frost. Break the pods off and spread them in a warm, dry place to cure for about two weeks, after which the pods should be brittle. Nuts can be stored in the pods in a cool, dry cupboard or roasted on cookie sheets in a 300-degree-F (150-degree-C) oven for an hour, stirring occasionally. Discard any mouldy peanuts.

Pests & Diseases None of note.

Peas

(Leguminosae, *Pisum sativum*)
Snow peas, Snap peas, Soup peas

Description Sweet and nutritious, the garden pea's love of cool weather has made it a northern standby. Peas do best at temperatures under 81 degrees F (27 degrees C). There are two main types: those with wrinkled seeds, which are the longest-maturing, sweetest peas, and those with smooth seeds, earlier and more cold tolerant but not as sweet. Peas can also be classified according to the shape and edibility of their pods. The standard shelling pea produces the smallest harvest per plant, while edible-podded snow or snap peas may double the weight of the harvest. Some seed companies sell green or yellow soup peas which are planted like other peas but harvested about three months later, like dry beans. Although all peas will climb if given the opportunity, their need for support varies with the length of the vines which ranges from 1 to 10 feet. Coating the seed with nitrogen-fixing inoculant, available from some seed outlets, will help ensure a vigorous crop that enriches the soil with nitrogen. The plants are quite frost hardy, but pea pods are not, so after the flowers have begun to bloom, the plants should be covered when frost threatens. Peas will grow as long as the soil temperature is above 41 degrees F (5 degrees C), with most ready for harvest about two months after sowing.

Culture Peas may be planted four weeks before the last spring frost date or at any time during the season as long as the soil temperature is not much above 60 degrees F (16 degrees C). Seeds will not germinate well later than mid-June in most areas, so a late crop should be pregerminated indoors in a towel dampened with cool water, then sown outdoors in a spot shaded by an early-maturing crop. In calculating the planting time for a fall crop, allow sufficient time for pods to mature before the first heavy frost, and prepare to cover the plants during light frosts. Fall crops are always less dependable than spring crops. Plant seeds 1 inch deep and 1 inch apart in a double row by a fence or trellis, or plant seeds of short-vining varieties in beds, allowing 2 inches around each seed. Strong twigs can be set upright throughout the bed to provide some support. Seeds take five to eight days to germinate at 39 to 75 degrees F (4 to 24 degrees C), and grow best between 50 and 60 degrees F (10 and 16 degrees C) in moist soil rich in organic matter. The application of an organic mulch when plants are about 4 inches tall, will help retain moisture and discourage weeds.

Harvest Shelling peas and snap peas are ready to harvest when the pods are well rounded but have not yet begun to look leathery. Snow peas are ready when the pods are full-sized and the peas inside have just begun to swell. Picking them every three or four days will prolong the harvest. Harvest and store soup peas as for dry beans, allowing them to dry on the vine or harvesting the mature pods for indoor drying. With all varieties, pull the pods off the plants gently so that the plants are not damaged. Snow peas and snap peas may have strings that should be removed before they are eaten; break off the top end and pull strings downward. Peas can be eaten raw or cooked; or they may be preserved by freezing or pressure canning. **Pests & Diseases** None in most gardens, but aphids can weaken plants and spread disease. Control with insecticidal soap diluted according to the manufacturer's directions. Aphids spread a disease that causes vines to yellow and die; remove and destroy affected plants. The spotted cucumber beetle can be controlled with rotenone or pyrethrum.

Peppers

(Solanaceae, *Capsicum annuum*)

Description Bell peppers and hot peppers, both cultivated by the Aztecs for thousands of years, assume a position halfway between the eggplant and the tomato in their need for warmth and their likelihood of producing a crop in the North. A gardener who can grow eggplant can grow peppers in much the same way, but a gardener who can grow tomatoes will not necessarily harvest peppers as well. The plant needs a sunny, sheltered position, prefers sandy soil and requires almost three months of warm weather – or the same length of time under cover – to produce a crop. If in doubt, choose the fastest-maturing varieties available. Early strains usually produce smaller fruit with thinner walls than do later ones. The "no pepper syndrome" may be caused by nights below 50 degrees F (10 degrees C) in early summer. Do not rush the season, and plant more than one variety for bet-hedging. Green-fruiting peppers may turn red later – red colour development is best between 64 and 75 degrees F (18 and 24 degrees C) but stops at 55 degrees F (13 degrees C) when the fruit begins to rot instead. In addition, cultivars are available that produce elongated or globe-shaped yellow fruit, which turns orange or red as it matures. For instructions about hot peppers, see chile peppers on page 138.
Culture As for eggplant.
Harvest Pick the peppers when they are glossy and large. If watery spots appear, pick them immediately and remove the damaged sections. Peppers can be kept fresh for eight to 10 days at 44 degrees F (7 degrees C), or else they can be preserved by freezing or by drying. Use the fruits raw or cooked.
Pests & Diseases As for eggplant. Aphids, usually a problem with plants under cover, can be controlled with insecticidal soap diluted according to the manufacturer's directions. The beet armyworm and corn ear worm can be controlled with *Bacillus thuringiensis*. Fruit infested with pepper maggots must be removed and destroyed. Chilling injury manifests itself in surface pitting of fruit, and can occur after two days at 32 degrees F (0 degrees C), 7 days at 34 degrees F (1 degree C) or 14 days at 45 degrees F (7 degrees C).

Potatoes

(Solanaceae, *Solanum tuberosum*)

Description After it arrived in North America from South America via Europe, the potato became this continent's most popular starchy vegetable. Canadian horticulturist W.T. Macoun wrote in 1918: "The potato succeeds well everywhere in this country where the season is long enough for the tubers to develop before the tops are killed by frost; hence potatoes are cultivated in practically every settlement in Canada, even up to and within the Arctic Circle." The part eaten, the tuber, is the food-storage swelling of an underground stem. Tubers of the most popular North American cultivars have either brown or red skin and white or golden flesh. Producing a crop in almost any soil, the potato does best, however, in light, well-drained, slightly acidic soil where a legume grew the previous season. Although it is cold tolerant, and prefers cool, moist growing conditions with night temperatures around 54 degrees F (12 degrees C), the greens will be killed by frost – but the tubers contain sufficient nutrients that the plants often revive when suitable conditions recur. Left in the soil over winter, tubers will often sprout in the spring. In short-season areas (80 days), plants should be surrounded with plastic mulch. Early, mid-season and main-crop strains of potato are available. Some of the most common North American potatoes include the following:

• Chieftan tubers have red skin and mature in mid-

season (about three and a half months after planting). The yield is high. The tubers do not store very well, but plants are resistant to scab and late blight
• Irish Cobbler is an early strain that has been on the market for more than a century. Its chief advantage is its good flavour; its chief disadvantage, susceptibility to scab. The tubers are lumpy in shape
• Kennebec is a high-yielding strain that matures in mid-season. The tubers are especially susceptible to greening when exposed to light, but plants are resistant to scab and fungus diseases
• Keswick is best suited to far Northerners. It is, like Kennebec, resistant to scab and fungus diseases
• Netted Gem is also known as the Russet Burbank or Idaho Baker. It produces large tubers that are superb when baked and that store very well if they are sound. This is the most demanding of popular potatoes, requiring optimal growing conditions and plenty of space – 18 inches between plants and 3 feet between rows – for top-quality tubers. Knobby, misshapen potatoes are likely to result if they are crowded or the weather is changeable. The tubers are scab resistant, but the plants are susceptible to late blight
• Norland produces medium-sized tubers with deep pink skins. The tubers are particularly well suited to early harvesting as new potatoes
• Red Pontiac produces heavy yields of red-skinned, round potatoes in mid-season. It is most popular in the United States
• Sebago is a late-maturing potato that produces large, smooth tubers in great quantity. The tubers store dependably well for only about three months
• Superior is an early, white-skinned strain that, like Norland, is especially prized for new potatoes. Superior does best in well-drained soils that are neither cold nor hot

Culture Traditionally, potatoes are grown from eyes, pieces of tuber used to clone the parent plant. Seeds do not normally reproduce true and so are not used for garden propagation, but "true seed" is now available, which must be started indoors like tomato seed. Certified potato eyes, disease free and suitable for planting, are available at garden outlets, country general stores and from some mail-order sources. Each potato can be planted whole, or cut the day before planting into two or three egg-sized pieces, each bearing at least one eye.

About three to five weeks before the last spring frost, when the soil has warmed to about 42 degrees F (6 degrees C) or as long as a month thereafter, take a spade and dig holes about 8 inches deep and 18 inches apart in rows the length of the potato patch. The day after cutting them into sections, lay one piece of potato, eye upward, on the bottom of each hole, covering it with about 2 inches of soil. Water if necessary. As the plant grows, fill in the hole but do not bury all of the foliage. This hilling is done because tubers develop above the eye, and must be protected from exposure to light, which causes greening. Once the holes are filled level with the soil surface, mulch with plastic (in short-season areas) or with organic matter that will keep the soil cool and retain moisture. As they develop, cover any exposed tubers with soil or mulch.

Gardeners who have a plentiful supply of mulching materials can simply lay the potato eyes on the ground in rows, then cover the potato patch with at least a foot of organic mulch. Although animal predation is a possibility with this system, planting and harvesting are greatly simplified.

Harvest Early new potatoes can be dug as early as a month after hilling is complete. These tender, sweet tubers can be found by digging directly under a plant and removing one or two, or by digging up entire plants. Potatoes are fully mature when the tops die; after this the tubers will keep in cool soil but should be dug fairly soon because they are susceptible to damage by grubs and worms. The fall potato harvest should begin on a sunny, dry morning after the plant tops have died. Using a spade, pitchfork or potato fork, dig straight down about 1 foot from each plant stem, and pry up the soil toward the plant. Dig carefully so that few tubers are damaged – any that are undersized or damaged should be set aside for immediate use; they will not keep well. Lay the others on a bare patch of soil or mulch and turn several times during the day to cure. Brush off any clumps of soil while doing this. At the end of the day, put all the sound, large tubers in boxes, feed sacks or paper bags – they must be exposed to air but not light – and store them in a cool, airy, dark place (45 to 50 degrees F, 7 to 10 degrees C). Remove any green parts before serving, as they contain solanine which can cause indigestion or sickness. Potatoes that are not diseased can be used as next year's eyes.

Pests & Diseases Potatoes attract pests and diseases in almost every garden, though the entire crop will seldom be lost. The worst pest is the larva of the Colorado potato beetle, which has a voracious appetite for potato foliage. Search for and destroy its egg clusters in late spring – the bright orange eggs are found on the undersides of leaves. Later, the orange larvae may be hand picked or dusted with rotenone. The adults, black and orange striped beetles, will appear throughout the season; usually they can be knocked off and squashed. Other pests include wireworms and the fat, white larvae of June beetles which tunnel into tubers and are best controlled by crop rotation. The most damaging diseases, such as early and late blight, are caused by fungi, and are worst in warm, wet weather. Do not set the plants too closely, do not mulch in very damp areas and do not tend wet plants. Hollow-heart of potatoes is caused by irregular weather conditions, while scab is the result of overly alkaline soil. Neither disorder affects the edibility of the tubers.

Purslane

(Portulacaceae, *Portulaca oleracea*)
Wild portulaca

Description Like the dandelion, purslane with its smooth, reddish stems and small, fleshy leaves has taken well to northern gardens. Besides the weedy strains that produce leafy mats between garden vegetables in summer, cultivated strains with larger leaves, some upright in habit, are carried by a few seed outlets. All are quick to grow, nutritious and tasty, and thrive in hot, dry gardens where many other greens wilt. If they are allowed to go to seed, however, they will spread like weeds in later years.

Culture Broadcast seeds thinly on well-worked soil in a sunny location any time after the last spring frost. Press seeds down and water with a fine spray. Thin plants to stand 4 inches apart.

Harvest Cut when plants are 4 to 6 inches tall and use fresh or cooked like spinach. The weed may be used in the same way.

Pests & Diseases None of note.

Radish

(Cruciferae, *Raphanus sativus*)
Daikon

Description The garden's fastest-maturing root vegetable is the common globe radish, ready about three weeks after sowing, while winter storage varieties may attain weights over a pound and take about two months to mature. All radishes prefer cool, moist soil and do best with a fairly short day length – in the far North, choose small-rooted and fast-maturing cultivars to discourage premature bolting to seed. Mild radishes result from steady, quick growth in cool weather; any checks in development may produce unpleasantly peppery, tough roots.

Culture Sow from early spring through early summer and again in late summer in rich, moist, cool soil. Plant the seeds ½ inch deep and ½ inch apart. In hot weather, choose a spot shaded by another crop. Radishes require only 1 inch around them, and so can be interplanted with other crops. As they are very quick to sprout, germinating in four to six days at 45 to 70 degrees F (7 to 21 degrees C), they are often sown with slow-emerging seeds such as parsnip, asparagus, carrot and beet. Their emergence breaks up the soil crust and marks the row. Storage radishes, such as the Oriental types, are planted in early spring or late summer, if sufficient time for maturity before the first frost date is allowed. Mulching or regular watering helps ensure good root quality – in too-wet soil roots may crack, while in too-dry soil they become woody, as they do when overmature.

Harvest Pull small-rooted types any time after the root begins to swell until it is about 1 inch across, after which it becomes hot and woody. Harvest larger cultivars according to the maturation rate mentioned by the seed company. Washed radishes will keep several weeks in perforated polyethylene bags in the refrigerator or cold room. Keep storage varieties as you would beets.

Pests & Diseases Flea beetles and cabbage root maggots. See broccoli.

Rhubarb

(Polygonaceae, *Rheum rhaponticum*)

Description Although technically a vegetable, sweetened rhubarb has a flavour sufficiently fruity that it is treasured for use in northern desserts and preserves. A native of Asia that has become a welcome member of almost every Canadian garden, this hardy perennial is quite pest and disease free. Of the two types, red-stalked and green-stalked, the former is sweeter and more flavourful, but less productive than the latter. Red-stalked cultivars include Valentine, Crimson Red and Canada Red; green-stalked include Victoria and Sutton's. As green-stalked cultivars are better for winter forcing than red-stalked ones, rhubarb aficionados should plant a bed of each: red rhubarb for spring and fall use, green for winter forcing, when its stalks will be light pink and very tender.

Culture Plants can be grown from seed, although this is a slow procedure with unpredictable results. Usually, roots are planted in early spring as soon as the soil can be worked or, if necessary, in late fall just before freeze-up. Set plants 2 to 4 feet apart, the tips of the buds just even with the soil surface in a sunny location in soil that has been thoroughly weeded and mixed with compost or well-rotted manure. As the bed will be in place for many years, the initial preparations have long-lasting consequences. Rhubarb will grow on any well-drained soil but does best on sandy loam. Every year, add manure or compost and a layer of organic mulch to the rhubarb bed. After about 10 years, or when stalks have become spindly, divide plants early in spring as soon as the buds break through the soil. Dig up the plant and cut it vertically into several pieces, each one with two or three good buds and part of the root attached. Set these 2 to 4 feet apart

as usual. Rhubarb that is at least two years old can also be divided in spring for propagation, or in fall for indoor forcing. For forcing, dig the roots before the soil freezes, divide them and spread them on the garden, lightly mulched, where they will remain through several light frosts. Then replant the roots in boxes or pots of wet sand, soil or peat moss, allowing each one about 2 square feet of soil surface, and place them in a dark room at 50 to 60 degrees F (10 to 15 degrees C). Keep the soil moist but not sodden. The most productive forced roots will be those from which stalks were not harvested the previous year.

Harvest Do not harvest stalks for the first year from roots planted outdoors. The second year, harvest the largest stalks for only two weeks in spring. Thereafter, stalks may be pulled in spring and fall, but allow the plants about two months in summer to build up strength. Removing seed stalks in spring will prolong the early harvest. Harvest stalks by tugging or twisting them from the crown, not by cutting. Forced stalks are ready to pick about a month after they are brought indoors and for three to eight weeks after that. Discard the roots after forcing. Rhubarb leaves, which contain toxic levels of oxalic acid, must never be eaten or fed to livestock; put them on the compost pile. Rhubarb freezes well.

Pests & Diseases Rare in the home garden.

Rocket

(Brassica, *Eruca sativa*)
Arugula, Roquette, Ruchetta

Description Among Europeans this is a highly prized vegetable, but it has only begun to develop a following in North America, where its radish-like leaves with their horseradish flavour are quite different from the usual salad and sandwich fare. Rocket is similar to spinach in its affinity for cool weather. It goes to seed rapidly in summer. The plant grows about a foot wide and a foot tall.

Culture Sow the seeds at ¼-inch intervals outdoors about two weeks before the last spring frost date, thinning the plants gradually until they stand a foot apart. A steady supply of water will ensure that tender, fairly mild-tasting leaves develop. As soon as the plants bolt to seed in summer, they should be removed from the garden and replaced with heat-tolerant seedlings of another vegetable. Or seeds may be allowed to mature for collection and sowing next season.

Harvest Use thinnings in salads and sandwiches. Six weeks to two months after seeding, the entire plant may be cut and eaten.

Pests & Diseases None of note.

Rutabagas

(Cruciferae, *Brassica napus*)
Swede, Turnip

Description This large, gold-fleshed root is often called a turnip, a word that more properly refers to one of its ancestors, the white-fleshed turnip, *Brassica rapa*. The rutabaga, which probably takes its name from the Scandinavian *rotabagge*, "round root," takes longer to mature and is more frost hardy. Like other root crops, it requires well-worked soil, even though much of the root develops above the soil surface. It is frost hardy throughout the season.

Culture The rutabaga's main attraction is its provision of winter vitamins – it is nutritious and easy to store. Its maturation time of about three months is subtracted from the first fall frost date to indicate the best time for sowing – usually a few weeks after the last spring frost, following an early planting of lettuce or spinach. In shorter-season areas, the rutabaga can be sown in the same manner as Brussels sprouts or early cabbage, either indoors or outdoors. Roots should have a final garden spacing of 1 foot all around, and a soil pH above 6. Water regularly or mulch, because checks in growth will produce tough roots.

Harvest Leaves of the young plant are tender and nutritious and can be used in place of turnip greens, collards or kale. Harvest roots when they are about 6 to 10 inches across, or according to the maturation date suggested by the seed company.

Roots can remain in the garden until just before the soil freezes. Cut off the tops and store the same way as for beets, for as long as six months. Waxing is not recommended. Roots can also be sliced and dried or frozen.

Pests & Diseases A soft brown interior is usually symptomatic of a soil boron deficiency; apply agricultural borax according to the recommendation of a soil test report. Black leg, black rot and turnip mosaic virus can all be combated with crop rotation and disposal of infected plants. Control flea beetles, which attack seedlings, with rotenone or pyrethrum. Clubroot may be a problem in acidic soil and areas of high rainfall; purchase seed of resistant cultivars, such as Fortune and York, and try to lower soil acidity.

Salsify

(Compositae, *Tragopogon porrifolius*)
Oyster plant, Vegetable oyster

Description, Culture & Harvest This long, white root is thinner than a parsnip and has a distinctive flavour reminiscent of oyster. Plant, tend, harvest and serve as for parsnip. A biennial, it is frost hardy and matures in about four months.

Pests & Diseases None of note.

Scorzonera

(Compositae, *Scorzonera hispanica*)
Black salsify

Description, Culture & Harvest Scorzonera is much like salsify but its root has dull white flesh and black skin. It too is frost hardy and slow to mature, like parsnip. Plant, tend, harvest and serve as for parsnip.

Pests & Diseases None of note.

Sorrel

(Polygonaceae, *Rumex sp.*)
Sourgrass

Description Sorrel, which is related to buckwheat and the weed dock, has a flavour that some find reminiscent of citrus fruits, and that others describe as just plain sour. While the plant is not likely to be considered a staple vegetable — its seeds, in fact, are often listed among herbs in seed catalogues — sorrel lends a distinct *haute cuisine* flavour to some dishes, especially soups, salads, and casseroles. A leafy, bushy plant that grows about 10 inches tall and is a perennial in its native southern Europe, it is grown as a hardy annual throughout most of the North. French sorrel (*R. scutatas*) has broad leaves, while garden sorrel (*R. acetosa*) has narrow leaves. The plant may self-sow if allowed to go to seed in summer.

Culture Seeds are sown outdoors about four weeks before the last spring frost in a sunny or shady spot of fertile, moist soil. The plant tolerates light frost and does best in cool weather. When the seedlings are about an inch tall, thin them to stand 8 inches apart, using the thinnings in the kitchen.

Harvest The young leaves have the mildest flavour and are best for salads and sandwiches, while older, stronger-tasting leaves complement soups and casseroles best. The leaves may be harvested at any time, as long as the plant is not weakened by overpicking. Leaves may be dried for storage, but some of the distinctive flavour will be lost.

Pests & Diseases None of note.

Spinach

(Chenopodiaceae, *Spinacia oleracea*)

Description The Moorish *is-fanakh* has become today's spinach, with sweet, nutritious foliage of distinctive flavour. Its ability to produce a crop in cool weather, and even to resist light frosts, has made it a northern favourite. Spinach will, however, sprout to seed quickly in hot weather. Choose long-standing, bolt-resistant cultivars. The best spinach grows in spring and fall in moist, well-worked, very fertile soil with a pH of 6 to 6.8. Spinach contains appreciable amounts of calcium, iron, potassium and vitamin A. Lamb's quarters, *Chenopodium album*, a spinach relative, grows wild in many gardens and is a very nutritious substitute, tasting best if harvested very young.

Culture Sow spinach outdoors six weeks before the last spring frost and until the last frost date, or seed a fall crop in late summer. In mild areas, seeds can be sown in early fall and mulched to overwinter for early spring greens next season. Alternatively, seeds may be sown in flats indoors and transplanted outdoors four weeks later; in hot weather, transplant into a shady spot. Seeds will germinate and plants will grow at a soil temperature of just 36 degrees F (2 degrees C). Allow each plant 4 inches all around in fertile, well-drained soil. Water once a week with manure tea or fish fertilizer.

Harvest Single outer leaves can be pulled from plants as soon as they have six to eight true leaves; thereafter, harvest leaves as needed or pull entire plants. Leaves may be eaten raw or cooked, and can be frozen or dried to preserve. Heads will keep for about a week in a plastic bag in a refrigerator or cold room.

Pests & Diseases Few. Hand pick caterpillars and control aphids with insecticidal soap diluted according to the manufacturer's instructions.

Squash, Summer

(Cucurbitaceae, *Cucurbita moschata* or *pepo*)
Crookneck, Straightneck, Patti-pan, Scallop, Vegetable marrow, Zucchini

Description Summer squash cultivars are those that are harvested while immature, when both seeds and skins are still soft and edible. Such a variety of colours and shapes of summer squash fruits exists that any gardener who likes these frost-tender but quick-maturing (six to eight weeks) vegetables should plant more than one type. But don't overdo it — one or two plants will serve two people. Crookneck produces club-shaped, crooked fruit with yellow skin that may be bumpy or smooth. Straightneck squash is, as the name suggests, a straight version. Patti-pan or scallop produces flat, round, scallop-edged green or white fruits. Vegetable marrow also has green or white skin, but is fat and elongated, while zucchini is long and slender with green or yellow skin.

Culture Plant and tend as for cucumbers, but vining varieties should be 1 foot apart along a fence or trellis. There are, as yet, no seedless cultivars — all plants have both male and female flowers.

Harvest Like cucumber, frequent picking will encourage a greater fruit set. Most fruits are best soon after they begin to form, when 6 to 8 inches long and 1½ to 2 inches wide. Pick scallops when 3 inches across. Use all young fruit whole – skin, seeds and all – raw or cooked. The flowers are also edible. Fruits left to mature may be used in baking or as livestock feed. They will store for several weeks in a cool, dry room.

Pests & Diseases As for cucumbers. Blossom end rot may occur in soils deficient in calcium or after a long, rainy period. The disease should disappear as conditions improve. Apply calcium according to soil test recommendations.

Squash, Winter

(Cucurbitaceae, *Cucurbita maxima*,
C. moschata or *C. pepo*)
Acorn, Buttercup, Butternut, Delicata,
Delicious, Hubbard, Hungarian mammoth,
Tahitian, Turban, Pumpkin, Vegetable spaghetti

Description Unlike the summer squashes to which these are closely related, winter cultivars are left to mature fully, until the seeds are hard and the skins are tough and unpalatable. As such, they take much longer to mature, three to five months from seed, depending upon weather and cultivar. In general, the bigger-fruited cultivars take longer to mature than do the smaller ones like butternut and acorn. The latter, also called pepper squash and the most common supermarket squash, weighs 1 to 5 pounds and is heart-shaped with grooved green or orange skin, maturing in 80 or 90 days. It does not store especially well. Buttercup and turban squash are squarish, usually with a cup-shaped indentation at the stem end. They mature in 80 to 100 days to weights of 3 to 7 pounds and are among the best keepers. Butternut squash is pear-shaped and golden, weighing about 2 pounds at maturity, about 80 days after seeding. Butternut also keeps well, but is more likely to be damaged by frost or low temperatures than are buttercup or Hubbard squashes. Bearing oblong fruit with green- and white-striped skins, Delicata or sweet potato squash produces 1-pound fruits that mature in about 100 days and store very well. Hubbard squash, with green or yellow, often warted skin, is roughly lemon-shaped, may weigh 12 pounds and takes 120 days to mature. Hungarian mammoth squash also requires a very long season of about four months, bearing pumpkin-shaped fruits of such size – sometimes over 400 pounds – that it is the subject of "pumpkin"-growing contests. Pumpkins, on the other hand, tend to weigh less than 100 pounds and the best pie cultivars, those with the sweetest flesh, are closer to 5 pounds at maturity. There are, in addition, "naked-seeded" pumpkins whose shell-less seeds are easily roasted and eaten. Golden nugget squash produces small, 1-pound, pumpkin-type fruits. Tahitian or melon squash, with club-shaped fruits up to 5 feet long and weighing up to 40 pounds, needs a long start indoors if it is planted in the North at all – it requires four or five warm months, though it will ripen somewhat indoors after picking. All squash is frost tender and grows best in warm, fertile soil with a temperature of at least 55 degrees F (13 degrees C). Hot caps or cloches will urge all seeds or seedlings along to a good start.

Culture In most gardens, seeds can be sown directly outdoors, although in very short-season areas the seeds should be started indoors. See muskmelon. Seeds of naked-seeded pumpkins should be pregerminated indoors (see page 53) because their germination outdoors is undependable due to their lack of normal seed coats. When the roots are ½ inch long, plant them ½ inch deep in warm soil and water. Two or three transplants, or six to nine seeds, all the same variety or a mixture of different types of squash, may be planted in hills outdoors a week or two after the last frost date, with hills made according to the instructions on page 57. Thin seedlings to three per hill and allow 6 feet around each hill for vining varieties, which can be trained up a fence or trellis, but the developing fruit must be supported in slings of fabric or netting. This method is most successful with the small-fruited types, but is seldom practical with large-fruited squashes like pumpkins. Vines can also be trained onto a lawn, patio, or where they will not occupy garden space. Bush types will take less space; check the seed packet for recommendations. The area surrounding the stems should be mulched with plastic in cool areas, elsewhere with organic mulch that extends as far as the vines will spread in the garden. This will control weeds and keep the fruit off the ground. About three weeks before the first fall frost, begin pinching off growing tips, flowers and new fruits, as they will not mature before the first frost and will slow the development of older fruit. Cover the plants with plastic or fabric if frost threatens before fruits are mature.

Harvest Flowers and seeds of all types are edible. Some fruits change colour when mature; green-skinned fruits are ready when the bottom has turned orange. All can be harvested when the skin is tough enough that it cannot be easily dented with a thumbnail. In any case, do not leave harvesting past the first light frost unless plants can be easily covered during frosty weather. The first light frost is likely to damage only foliage and sweeten the flesh, but if the fruit is touched by frost its keeping quality will deteriorate. When picking, leave 4 inches of stem attached to each fruit, slicing through it with a knife or pruning shears. Cure fruits in a warm, dry place for about 10 days, then store them, not touching, at 50 to 55 degrees F (10 to 12 degrees C) for two to six months, depending upon variety. Most squash tastes best in late fall, and then the flavour and quality start to deteriorate. Spaghetti squash is prepared by boiling or baking the entire squash, after which the meat is scooped out and served as pasta.

Pests & Diseases See summer squash.

Sunflowers

(Compositae, *Helianthus annuus*)

Description The sunflower is hardly the most space-efficient member of the vegetable garden, but its colour and cheer make up for what it lacks in practicality. Still, the plant does produce edible, very nutritious seeds, as visiting squirrels and birds will prove if given the chance. Sunflowers vary in height from 3 to 10 feet, and the width of their seed-filled heads varies accordingly. The smaller types

are ready to harvest about two months after sowing, the larger ones about two weeks later. Because the sunflower shades nearby plants, it is a poor companion plant but it can be given its own patch or used to line a driveway attractively or to back a flower garden. It will tolerate light frost.

Sunflowers, which are as decorative as they are useful, provide beautiful blooms and seeds that are high in protein

Culture Around the last spring frost date sow seeds in a fertile, sunny spot, ½ inch deep and 4 inches apart, later thinning or transplanting them to stand 1 foot apart. The plants grow quickly and require little care. Plastic mulch and plant covers will give them a boost when young, and the mulch can be left in place in cool-season areas.

Harvest The seeds are mature when they turn brown or when the backs of the heads turn yellow. Cut the entire heads and dry them indoors or in the sun for a day; then thresh by rubbing the seeds off. To hull the dried seeds, crack them with a rolling pin or food chopper, drop them into cold water and stir vigorously. The kernels will sink and the shells will float. Dry the kernels, then roast or store. Whole seeds may be stored in a cool, dry place and used as bird feed or livestock feed throughout the winter. If heads become overmature in the garden, volunteer plants may appear the following spring.

Pests & Diseases The most notable are birds and rodents, though some gardeners consider these visitations pleasant rather than pesky. Heads must be picked as soon as they are mature, if animals and birds are not to make off with most of the seeds.

Sweet Potatoes

(Convolvulaceae, *Ipomoea batatas*)

Description Even though the names of the common potato and the sweet potato are both derived from the South American Indian word *batata*, the two plants are unrelated and quite different. The sweet potato is such a tender plant that it is virtually unknown as a northern garden vegetable. Still, there are a few early varieties that will mature in about 100 days, provided they are coddled along the way and never exposed to frost. They grow best in a soil not too high in organic matter, which encourages rough or cracked roots. At the time of writing, these early cultivars are not available in Canada and must be imported from the United States, according to the directions in Sources on page 185.

Culture If sweet potatoes are bought from a seed outlet or nursery, the gardener will receive small shoots or slips. One can also grow one's own shoots from a mature sweet potato. About two weeks before the last spring frost, place the root in a pan of warm water in a warm place. Meanwhile, heat a sunny, raised bed or ridge of soil with plastic mulch. A week or two after the last frost date, break the shoots off the root and set them into the soil through holes in the plastic, covering the plants with hot caps or crop shelters for the first week or until the weather is dependably warm. Plants should be 1½ feet apart in all directions. Throughout the season, plants must be covered if frost threatens, and crop shelters should be available for augmenting the sun's heat in cool weather.

Harvest Dig the plants before the soil temperature drops below 55 degrees F (12 degrees C) or before the first fall frost. Cure the roots indoors by covering them with perforated plastic for one week at 85 degrees F (30 degrees C) or two weeks at 75 degrees F (24 degrees C), at high humidity. Store sweet potatoes at 55 to 60 degrees F (12 to 15 degrees C) in moderate humidity.

Pests & Diseases Cold soil is the most immediate danger to sweet potatoes in the North; any other malady is insignificant in comparison.

Swiss Chard

(Chenopodiaceae, *Beta vulgaris cicla*)

Description Called by western Europeans "Swiss chardon" to distinguish it from the "French chardon" or cardoon (a relative of the globe artichoke), chard is one of the most practical, easy and productive plants for the northern garden. Spinach-like in flavour and nutrients, its leaves are edible throughout the season. Swiss chard is frost resistant and does not bolt to seed with hot weather as spinach does. Chard is a leafier version of the beet, and its culture is similar. It grows well in pots and satisfactorily in shade, and comes with white, red or golden leaf ribs.

Culture Seed may be sown in the garden as soon as the soil can be worked in spring, or any time while the soil is still relatively cool; the seed germinates in four to 10 days within its preferred soil temperature range of 45 to 70 degrees F (7 to 21 degrees C). Sow seeds about 1 inch apart and ½ inch deep, gradually thinning plants until they stand 6 inches apart. Thinnings may be eaten. Chard requires little care, although the best greens will grow in soil that is quite fertile and watered once a week with manure tea or fish fertilizer.

Harvest Single outer leaves may be pulled once the plants have developed four or five true leaves. It is best to pull the entire plants only during thinning or at the end of the season, when the leaves begin to deteriorate after the first light frost. Use leaves as you would spinach, raw or cooked. Preserve by drying or freezing. Ribs and stems can be prepared as for celery or asparagus.

Pests & Diseases See spinach.

Tampala

(Chenopodiaceae, *Amaranthus gangeticus*)
Vegetable amaranth, Chinese spinach

Description Tampala, very popular in the far East where several cultivars are grown, is a highly nutritious, green leafy vegetable, closely related to grain amaranth which contains quality protein in generous amounts. Tampala shares with Swiss chard, New Zealand spinach, Malabar spinach and beet greens the ability to produce spinach-like greens in hot, dry weather, after spinach has bolted to seed. The leaves of tampala are, however, most tender and tasty when they are young. The same can be said of its wild counterpart, redroot pigweed or green amaranth, *Amaranthus retroflexus*, and both can be harvested as nutritious spinach substitutes.

Culture Around the last spring frost, plant seeds about ½ inch deep and 1 inch apart in rows 1 foot apart. As they grow, thin plants to stand 1 foot apart. Thinnings can be eaten.

Harvest As for Swiss chard, but older plants become tough and less flavourful. With pigweed, pick only the young leaves for best flavour and texture.

Pests & Diseases None of note.

Tomatillos

(Solanaceae, *Physalis ixocarpa*)

Description A cousin of the ground cherry, the tomatillo is a larger version that grows fruit of golf-ball size, also in an attractive Chinese lantern husk. Tomatillos are used quite often in authentic Mexican cooking, but can be substituted to provide a different colour (green) and mild flavour in any dish demanding whole tomatoes. The bushes grow about 3 feet tall, and are quite bushy and spreading.

Culture Sow indoors as for tomatoes, four weeks before the last frost date. Set transplants outdoors leaving 2 feet around each one, on the last frost date. The plants require little care, and are more weather resistant than tomatoes. The fruit is ready to pick about 10 weeks after transplanting.

Harvest Harvest fruit when it is deep green and the husks are tan-coloured. Husked, it can be eaten raw or cooked, or preserved by freezing or canning. To store, leave fruits in the husks and spread them 1 layer deep in a cool well-ventilated area.

Pests & Diseases As for ground cherry. In addition, blister beetles may infest fruit. Use rotenone or pyrethrum for severe problems.

Tomatoes

(Solanaceae, *Lycopersicon esculentum*)

Description Tomatoes are the single most popular garden vegetable. In the North, they are certainly not the easiest of plants to grow, but even far Northerners will go to almost any lengths to include in the garden a tomato plant or two, or four, or eight. . . . Fortunately, plant breeders have responded to this desire for fresh tomatoes by producing some very fast-maturing cultivars. Others grow best under cover, extending the tomato's range to wherever there is light and heat, even if artificial. Tomatoes are available in various fruit colours and shapes and in small and large-fruiting cultivars, the former generally earlier than the latter. There are also determinate and indeterminate cultivars. The former, including most of the earliest tomatoes, are bushy in shape and produce a single crop of fruit, sometimes virtually simultaneously. Most seed catalogues refer to determinates as bush tomatoes. They need not be staked and should not be pruned. The indeterminates grow tall and produce tomatoes for as long as the weather permits; they are usually staked and pruned. And then there are semi-determinates, cultivars that include qualities of both types. Toward the end of the season, the tips of indeterminate and semi-determinate plants should be pinched off so that the plant's energy is concentrated on developing fruit. All plants are very frost tender and virtually all should be given an early start indoors. In choosing a spot to grow tomatoes, avoid low-lying areas, shady places or any place where water collects. The plants also do best where air circulates freely. The use of plastic mulch will promote fruit production in cool-season gardens. Elsewhere, organic mulch can be applied in early summer when the soil is warm and plants are about 1 foot tall.

Culture Start seeds indoors six to eight weeks before the last spring frost date, sowing seeds in flats or containers, ¼ inch deep and ½ inch apart in rows 1 inch apart. Seeds germinate in four to seven days in moist soil in their preferred temperature range of 70 to 85 degrees F (21 to 29 degrees C), but take 25 to 30 days at 50 degrees F (10 degrees C). The seeds do not need light for germination, but as soon as the seedlings emerge, containers must be placed in a sunny window or heated crop shelter. Once they have their first true leaves, thin them, or transplant them, so that each seedling has at least 1 inch of space all around. About three weeks later, transplant the seedlings into larger containers, burying them as deep as the seedling leaves. The plants are usually set outdoors around the last frost date – be prepared to cover them if frost threatens. In a system developed at Morden, Manitoba, seeds are sown April 15th; transplants are set outdoors May 15th and covered with hot caps ventilated with a 1½-inch slit in the peak. Enlarge the opening when the temperature rises above 75 degrees F (24 degrees C). When frost threatens, place a second protector over the first. Allow the plants to grow out of the protectors freely. In most gardens, crop protectors will not be necessary, but gardeners may elect to delay outdoor transplanting for a week after the last frost date.

Set staked tomatoes 18 inches apart in rows and unstaked plants 2 to 3 feet apart. For each plant, dig a hole wider and deeper than the root ball, and place the root ball in the hole so that the soil will be filled in to the level of the first true leaves. Fill the hole with compost or fertile soil, and surround each stem with a collar that extends above and below the soil level by 1½ inches to deter cutworms. Water. If plants are to be staked, 5-foot poles should be pounded 1 foot into the earth directly behind each plant now, when there is no danger of root damage. Fasten the plant loosely to the stake with a figure 8 of fabric encircling both stake and stem. Tomatoes may also be supported in wire cages, or indeterminates may be trained up strings that descend from a horizontal wire or pole supported 6 feet above a row of plants. Every few days, twist the plant stem around the string. All staked or twining indeterminate tomatoes must be pruned or they will become unmanageable. Regularly throughout the season, pinch out the suckers that form in branch axils. Incidentally, pruned suckers planted in the soil and kept moist will root and grow into full-sized plants, producing late fruit. See pages 22 and 23 for diagrams of tomato support systems.

After the first fruit has set, water the plants about every two weeks with manure tea or with a fish fertilizer solution.

Harvest Tomatoes are ready to pick when they are somewhat soft, fragrant and full-coloured. If pests are a nuisance, fruits may be ripened indoors as soon as they have become "mature green" (whitish), although the flavour will not be as good as if they were vine-ripened. Similarly, fruit may be brought indoors to ripen when frost threatens. Store ripe fruit at 40 degrees F (5 degrees C).

Pests & Diseases Tomato plants and fruit are susceptible to a number of disorders, pests and diseases. Blossom end rot of fruit is caused by drought or by a soil calcium deficiency; have a soil test done, and apply calcium according to the report's recommendations. Oddly shaped fruit may be caused by a cold snap during pollination. It cannot be helped, but the fruit is edible. Tomatoes are very susceptible to injury from some herbicides such as 2,4-D and 2,4,5-T, a problem in gardens near lawns or farm roadsides where weeds are sprayed.

Nematodes are tiny worms that can attack roots, weakening plants. Some control comes from the planting of French marigolds, *Tagetes patula* (all marigolds are good companions for tomatoes), around plants. Resistant tomato varieties are available. Some cultivars are also resistant to the fungus diseases verticillium and fusarium wilt. The latter is seldom a problem in the North, but the former may cause discoloration of leaves and wilting. Early blight, usually seen on early, determinate tomatoes, causes spotting of foliage and wilting of plants. All fungus diseases are best combated with resistant varieties, good air circulation, and proper plant spacing. Among pests, the tomato hornworm and tobacco hornworm are the largest, but they are easily hand picked. Slugs, crickets and other insects and worms that devour fruit can be controlled somewhat by staking plants. It may be necessary to remove an organic mulch if pests are really troublesome. Tomatoes must not be planted within 40 to 50 feet of a walnut tree because an exudate, juglone, causes "walnut wilt" and death of tomato plants.

Turnips
(Cruciferae, *Brassica rapa*)
Summer turnip, White turnip

Description The turnip can be considered, in its growing preferences, as a large radish without the hot flavour. Like a radish, the turnip does best in cool weather when allowed to grow quickly and steadily, thanks to fertile soil and an adequate water supply. It is frost hardy and ready to harvest about two months after seeding.

Culture As soon as the soil can be worked in spring until the last spring frost date, sow seeds outdoors ½ inch deep and apart, gradually thinning or transplanting seedlings until the plants stand 4 inches apart. Thinnings may be eaten. Checks in growth produce tough, fibrous roots. Late sowings should be left in the soil until it almost freezes because the sugar content of turnips, like parsnips, increases with frost.

Harvest Greens may be eaten raw or cooked. The roots may be pulled any time after they have reached a diameter of about 4 inches. Use as rutabagas. Unlike rutabagas, however, turnips do not store well, so they should be harvested gradually and kept in a polyethylene bag in a refrigerator or cold room until needed.

Pests & Diseases See rutabagas.

Watercress
(Cruciferae, *Nasturtium officinale*)

Description Watercress has adapted well to its North American habitat, and is now found growing wild along streams and in boggy meadows throughout much of the country. It can also be cultivated, but does demand cool weather and plenty of water for the best growth of its peppery, nutritious greens. Thus, it is the best choice for wet garden spots where no other vegetable grows well. Grown in suitable wet locations, it will self-sow annually. Watercress is ready for harvesting about 50 days after sowing.

Culture Six weeks before the last frost, preger-minate seeds in a cool, moist paper towel, then sow in growing medium, two seeds per peat pellet or small pot set in a pan of cool water. Transplant outdoors two weeks later in a shady, moist spot. Alternatively, seeds can be sown directly into the wet soil of a stream bed or in a wet garden.

Harvest The leaves are best in spring and fall. Pick out the side shoots and use raw or cooked.

Pests & Diseases None of note.

Watermelon
(Cucurbitaceae, *Citrullus lanatus*)

Description The watermelon seems an unlikely resident of a northern garden, and yet can be expected to mature anywhere muskmelon ripens, provided the gardener chooses early cultivars, which will mature as early as 70 days after transplanting. These cultivars produce smaller fruit than that sold in supermarkets, but they are unexcelled for sweetness and flavour, whether the flesh is red or yellow. Watermelon is extremely frost sensitive and will not grow in cold weather. Plant them under cover in short-season areas.

Culture As for muskmelon, but leave 4 feet between hills of vining cultivars. If they are trained up a fence or trellis, the fruit must be supported. Bush varieties cannot be trained to grow vertically.

Harvest One of the most puzzling garden quandaries is the identification of a ripe watermelon. Some produce a white or yellow belly when they are ripe, but others are not ripe when the underside is light. There are gardeners who claim to know the difference between the "plunk" of an unripe melon and the "plink" of a ripe one when tapped. First check the maturation time noted by the seed company. Then make sure the tendril on the vine nearest the melon has dried. Finally, as the British Columbia Ministry of Agriculture recommends, "If unsure about the ripeness, wait a little longer." If melons are harvested unripe, they can nevertheless be used for pickling or candying in the same way as citron, a melon grown exclusively for that purpose.

Pests & Diseases As for cucumbers, squash and muskmelon.

The Blooming of Summer

"I have contemplated a well-hoed ridge of potatoes on that bush farm with as much delight as in years long past I had experienced in examining a fine painting"

– Susanna Moodie
Roughing It in the Bush, 1852

Throughout the North there occurs, sometime between the end of one winter and the beginning of the next, a rapid and momentous transformation. One day vegetation struggles along, an invisible insect manages an early bite of a winter-whitened forearm and birds arrive sporadically, like latecomers to a play. And then the next day the drama begins: The lawn has to be mowed, sunrise brings heat, and the garden begins to burst with life, with insects, worms, birds, squirrels, weeds growing like, well, weeds – and, praise be, the first vegetables ready for harvest.

Coping with summer is generally the least of the northern gardener's concerns. Better to concentrate your energy on those tricky borderline times, spring and fall. If the gardener is spared untimely frosts, the summer may be spent in the garden doing little more than weeding and harvesting. But in most areas, summer means less rain and higher temperatures than most vegetables can tolerate. It also brings vegetable-eating insects that must be kept within bounds. Watering, mulching and pest control become vital to the leafy summer routine.

Watering

Most gardens need a thorough soaking with about an inch of water once a week. A particular garden's need for water varies, however, with many things: with the weather – hot, windy weather speeds evaporation from plants and soil – with the layout of the garden, and with its soil. Soil high in organic matter is able to retain what water there is far better than soil that is chiefly silt, clay or sand. A very important part of a gardener's drought-proofing program comes from soil improvements, as described in Chapter II.

Whatever the soil type, it is the plant roots within it that make the best use of water. Watering foliage wastes water and encourages fungus diseases, especially in calm, hot, damp weather. So a watering system that applies the water directly to the soil surface around the plants will conserve water while helping to maintain a healthy garden. Sprinkling, on the other hand, requires high water pressure and can waste about half the sprayed water to evaporation, even more to pathways. If you must use a sprinkler, try to do so on calm evenings when evaporation is minimal, and do not enter the garden until the foliage has dried, as you may otherwise spread diseases among the plants.

Better systems include perforated hoses or tubing

which can be laid on the soil next to plants. A special trickler irrigation hose has been manufactured for this purpose, and can be purchased at garden shops and from some mail-order suppliers. Such a system can be connected directly to the home water supply but, as it requires little pressure, may

Plastic mulches help warm the soil, while organic mulches contribute soil nutrients and discourage weed growth

even be gravity-fed from a plastic garbage can, cistern or metal drum raised above the level of the garden. This holding tank can also be used for filtered manure tea, which is then distributed through the trickle system. Household "grey" water, from washing and bathing, can be used for about half the irrigation if it has been filtered and does not contain borax, fabric softeners, bleaches or detergents (although some soap is fine). The same cistern arrangements can catch the runoff from a roof and can be connected with a faucet to a regular garden hose for hand watering. Although labour-intensive, hand watering has the advantage of placing water exactly where it is most needed.

A traditional irrigation system, in which the water follows channels throughout the garden, involves a great deal of preparatory work and may waste a considerable amount of water unless the excess is recycled. Other labour-intensive systems involving watering cans or buckets filled from the home or a cistern are best in very small gardens or for container plantings.

A gardener can most easily determine when plants need water by watching for wilting. Wilting

in the afternoon or evening on a hot, windy day happens quite frequently, even when soil moisture levels are adequate, but if plants are still wilted in the morning or begin to wilt before noon they must be watered immediately.

Mulching

Augmenting or even replacing watering systems are synthetic or organic mulches, both of which help retain moisture in the soil, especially if applied after a heavy rain. Plastic mulches also help warm the soil, as described on page 63. Organic mulches do not warm the soil, although their insulating properties will help retain its warmth on summer nights and in fall, but they do control or curb weeds and help maintain soil moisture. With a deep organic mulch on the garden, it is actually possible that no watering at all will have to be done, even during long, dry spells. In her constantly mulched garden in Connecticut, Ruth Stout, the "mother of mulch," never watered or weeded and seldom fertilized. Connecticut is, however, a relatively warm area, and such a year-round mulch system can seriously slow soil warming and therefore retard spring growth in short-season gardens. There are, in fact, a couple of cases in which organic mulches should be used sparingly or not at all. Where the season is very short or cool, do not use them except in pathways. In very wet gardens, mulches will worsen slug and disease problems; here, confine the mulches to pathways and drier areas of the garden or forgo their use entirely.

The most suitable organic mulching materials for a particular garden depend upon availability and cost; the best ones, of course, are free. Rural gardeners often find that straw and spoiled hay are the easiest mulching materials to obtain, while city gardeners may be able to find good supplies of fallen leaves and grass clippings, especially if they can count on the contributions of neighbours and city parks. Do not use grass clippings from a lawn recently sprayed with herbicides. Fallen leaves are best piled in fall and applied to the garden next spring or, even better, the following spring. Researchers from the Connecticut Agricultural Experiment Station have noted: "During initial decomposition of leaves, substances are released that apparently inhibit growth of vegetable plants and reduce their subsequent yield." The inhibitory effect is not long lasting, however. Composted leaves or leaf mould had a positive effect on the experimental gardens. In any case, never use the leaves of walnut trees as they contain juglone, a potent fungicide that is harmful to some vegetables.

For those who can obtain it, seaweed is an excellent mulching material. It need not be rinsed to remove salt before use. Freshwater weeds are a substitute for the landlocked. Compost is another very good mulch, but it is usually in too-short supply to be used as anything other than a soil conditioner and mild fertilizer.

Organic mulches have a further advantage in their contribution of organic matter and nutrients to the soil. Straw, for instance, contains about .5 per cent nitrogen, .2 per cent phosphorus and 1 per cent potassium as well as many other nutrients. Sawdust contains a little less nitrogen and potassium but slightly more phosphorus. Seaweed contains even less nitrogen and phosphorus, but may rate an astonishing 4.6-per-cent-potassium content.

The mulch material's contribution of nutrients and fibre to the soil depends not only on its fertility, but also upon its carbon to nitrogen (C:N) ratio. In general, drier, older materials contain a higher proportion of carbon than do fresher, moister substances, the preferred mulches. Manure and grass clippings have a lower C:N ratio than straw or paper. While the C:N ratio of paper is about 173:1, that of grass clippings is about 20:1, of sewage sludge, 6:1. Materials high in carbon will eventually add fibre and fertility to the soil but they do so initially at the expense of soil nitrogen. For that reason, wood chips, sawdust and paper should be used sparingly or confined to pathways. After they have decomposed, the resultant organic matter can be hoed into growing beds. Despite its high carbon content, newpaper is so helpful in weed control that single or double layers of it are often used around plants.

While plastic mulches may be laid very early in spring so that soil warming precedes sowing or transplanting, the application of organic mulch should be delayed because it has the opposite effect. Mulch applied too early slows the warming of the soil and can seriously retard plant growth. Mid-June is about the right time for mulching in most northern gardens, with the soil warm and plants growing rapidly. First weed the garden and then, after a rain, lay down newspaper between rows,

A rotary tiller may be expensive, but it can prepare the soil and provide pathway weed control throughout the season

weighing down its edges with soil. Then cover it with a further 4 to 6 inches of another mulch, which may reach right up under the plants and around their stems. In the small spaces between plants, newspaper is impractical; here, straw, grass clippings, compost or leaf mould can be piled. If mulching materials are in short supply, concentrate those that are available on the cool-loving crops such as potatoes and leafy vegetables. Next, apply mulches around those plants whose fruit would otherwise rest on the ground: sprawling tomatoes, cucumbers or melons.

Weeding

Because mulches not only conserve water but also control weeds, they are very popular with gardeners, few of whom really enjoy the otherwise endless task of weeding. Weeds grow faster than virtually all vegetables and, left on their own, these sturdy native or naturalized plants will take the lion's share of the light, moisture and soil nutrients, leaving the vegetables waning in their shadows.

Weeds not only take care of their immediate needs with gusto, they also ensure that their progeny will inhabit future gardens. One hedge mustard plant can produce half a million seeds; redroot pigweed and purslane produce about 200,000, and the seeds of some weeds such as lamb's quarters, purslane, pigweed, and wild mustard can spring to life 40 years after being buried in the soil. No wonder successive tillings bring new flushes of weeds.

Perennial grasses are among the garden's most tenacious weeds, spreading both by seeds and by underground rhizomes

Some of the hardy biennial or perennial weeds such as dandelions and burdock have long taproots that must be dug almost entirely if the plant is not to rebound. Quack grass, which infests fields and gardens across the country, has a system of underground stem-like rhizomes with a number of buds or growing points, any of which can develop new shoots when the plant is broken up. It also spreads by seed, and so is an exceedingly persistent plant that requires diligent digging of roots. It is the newly cleared garden plot that produces the greatest crop of perennial weeds.

No one ever really wins the battle with the weeds, but then weeds are not enemies as much as competitors. They do have their good points, bringing up nutrients from deep in the soil and contributing organic matter to the garden when they are hoed or to the compost pile when they are pulled. And many are as edible as the vegetables they grow with. Lamb's quarters, purslane, wild mustard, redroot pigweed and dandelion are highly nutritious and tasty, especially when very young.

Despite the use of mulches, some weeding will have to be done in any garden. Weeds are most eas-

ily removed when young, when a scrape over the soil with a hoe or the edge of a trowel will decapitate them, and the tops can be left where they are. If this is repeated every few days, weeding need never be a back-breaking chore. When weeds do become more mature, they must be pulled. This is most easily done after a rain when the soil is soft. As they may reroot if tossed on the soil, remove them to the compost pile or leave them, roots up, on the mulch. Quack grass should be confined to its own pile at the edge of the garden.

Insects Friendly and Unfriendly

Following weed control in importance is pest control. Most pests seem to arrive in droves — a sudden rise in plant damage can be clearly related to a sudden rise in the population of pests. In fact, many pests overwinter in the garden and many more are there as mating adults or eggs long before any damage appears. Removing plant debris from the garden in fall is one of the best ways of keeping the pest population under control. Rotating crops and keeping related plants apart also helps, as does anything else that encourages the steady growth of sturdy, healthy plants. Insects and diseases are far more likely to attack plants weakened by weather, overfertilization or poor soil.

Physical barriers are also effective means of pest control in some cases. These include cardboard collars to discourage cutworms, collars of window screening to keep slugs from climbing plant stems, and cheesecloth or screening on a wooden frame that covers plants vulnerable to moths or flies. Hot caps and cloches will also help prevent some pests from making their way to their favourite plants.

If the pests do infest the plants, the best way to control them — "best" in terms of controls that are in no way harmful to the gardener or the garden allies — involves hand picking the pests or their eggs. If this seems distasteful, you can use a stick to knock the offenders into a jar, which can then be carried out of the garden and the insects squashed or drowned. As well, insect pest egg masses can be removed still attached to the part of the leaf on which they were laid. The use of baits, such as beer for slugs or molasses for grasshoppers, helps the hand-picking process, and some birds will quite happily

Companion planting, the positioning of plants according to their effects upon one another, produces an attractive garden

do the work for the gardener. If they find suitable nesting sites around the garden, swallows and purple martins will spend virtually all their time in pursuit of flying insects. While the range of the purple martin does not extend very far north, swallows can be found throughout most of the continent.

Companion Planting

Another very benign method of pest and disease control is companion planting, which involves arranging garden plants according to their beneficial effects upon one another. In a small garden it is unavoidable, of course, that plants from different families will find themselves growing next to one another, and usually this is just as well. Pole beans and corn, for instance, are traditional companions; beans contribute nitrogen to the soil while corn is a heavy feeder. If the corn is given a head start of a couple of weeks, the beans can use the corn stalks for support. Explorer Samuel de Champlain noted just this system in use by native Indians when he travelled the St. Lawrence in 1604. The Indians planted the corn in hills of three or four kernels, each hill 3 feet from the next. Then, wrote Champlain, "with this corn they put in each hill three or

four Brazilian beans [kidney beans] which are of different colours. When they grow up, they interlace with the corn, which reaches to the height of from 5 to 6 feet, and they keep the ground very free from weeds."

But companion planting is more than the sensible use of interplantings or crop rotations to make the best use of light, space and soil nutrients. The theory is that some garden plants have an immediate, positive effect on others, often on pest control, and that, furthermore, the wrong companions may have a detrimental effect. The evidence for this has been in small part scientifically documented, in large part a matter of subjective observation and, as such, is liable to change with the climate, the cultivar grown, and with weather and pest populations during any particular season. For instance, some gardeners have found that nasturtiums help produce healthy, pest-free brassicas, while in his experiments at Cornell University, Richard Root found that nasturtiums increased the population of flea beetles on collards. Tests at Prince Edward Island's Ark project produced similar results and research in 1981 in Alberta showed that neither flea beetle nor cabbage worm damage to cabbage was lessened by the use of any of nine species of recommended companion plants. Several of the companions, moreover, competed with the vegetables for water and nutrients, stunting cabbage growth. And, in addition to feeding on the cabbage, flea beetles also ate tansy flowers and nibbled the nasturtiums.

Nasturtiums are not only reputedly valuable as companion plants, they are also edible. See Chapter VII for information

Still, one thing is clear. Nasturtiums are colourful, edible and, whether companionable or not, certainly provide the gardener with a more pleasant place to work. Thoroughly companion-planted gardens, those designed according to a book such as Louise Riotte's *Carrots Love Tomatoes* (Garden Way Publishing), are among the most attractive one can find anywhere, a pleasing mix of herbs, flowers and vegetables.

Some companions have been proved beneficial. The French marigold *Tagetes patula*, available from most seed houses, has a repellent effect that can save tomatoes and potatoes from nematode infestation if the flowers encircle the vegetables. The tall Mexican marigold *Tagetes minuta*, available from some specialty houses such as J.L. Hudson, has a repellent effect on wireworms. Horticulturist Root found that interplanting collards with potatoes, tomatoes or tobacco lessened flea beetle damage to the collards. Garlic oil has been found to be a potent larvicide. Garlic, then, becomes a suitable companion with everything except other onions, provided the garlic is not so badly overshadowed that its own maturity is endangered. All onions

seem to have some repellent effect and so may be grown throughout the garden.

Pesticides

Although sprays or powders made from some insect-repelling plants have become part of the organic gardener's arsenal, they are decidedly less prefer-

All onions, including the Egyptian, top or tree onion, are valuable as companion plants and in organic pesticide sprays

able than the pest control means already described. Remember that pests, intelligently controlled, will very seldom mean the loss of a crop. The "pruning" they do early in the season can actually help produce healthy plants. Often, too, the damage they do produce is only cosmetic and of little concern to the enlightened gardener who sees such damage as proof that the food is indeed edible. Many insects such as yellow jackets, ants and dragonflies do not have a direct influence on plants.

The following pesticides are *not* synthetics, which are usually powerful substances that do not biodegrade easily and may present a danger to beneficial insects, birds, pets, squirrels and even the gardener. Nonetheless, some of the following substances are powerful in their own right, capable of killing toads, lady beetles or honey bees and sometimes toxic to humans within a certain period of time. Use them if you must, but use them carefully.

Bacillus thuringiensis (Bt) Sold in concentrated form, bacterial spores are diluted with water before the spray is applied to plants. Bt is sold under such trade names as Dipel, Biotrol, Bactur, Thuricide and Sok-BT. It is an expensive but effective and very selective control of the larvae of butterflies and moths (Lepidoptera) such as cabbage loopers, tomato hornworms and parsleyworms, all of which die about three days after spraying. A new strain is effective against the larvae of Colorado potato bee-

tles. Apparently neither strain has a harmful effect on humans, animals, birds, fish or earthworms.

Conveniently, the gardener may extend his supply of Bt indefinitely. Dale Pollett of Louisiana State University advises the gardener to gather a

The Bedside Companion: Vegetable Pollination

In the 1930s, a book was published entitled, *Just Like the Flowers, Dear: A Botany for Parents.* A couple of generations later, both gardeners and parents still consider "the birds and the bees" with more than passing interest, although the gardener's manual might well be called *Not Very Much Like People, Dear: A Sex Manual for Gardeners.*

Plants lead a very passive love life, depending upon various active agents – the wind, insects, water, passing animals – to be their matchmakers. The way in which various vegetables make use of these go-betweens is of concern to the gardener for several reasons: It influences plant spacing, the segregation of varieties, seed saving, and has a bearing on whether or not plants will produce fruit. As far as the harvest is concerned, plant pollination is most critical with the fruit-bearing crops (defined on page 65); others produce the vegetable first and go to seed later.

Fruiting crops that are insect pollinated, for instance, will produce no crop if there are no suitable insects in the garden. There may be few or no honey bees if the garden is downtown, if it is near an area recently sprayed with insecticides, or if the plant is growing in a greenhouse. In such cases, pollination must be done by the

gardener if he is to pick any fruit, especially from any of the cucurbits: the cucumbers, squashes, melons and pumpkins.

All of these plants are termed monoecious; although the plant bears both male and female reproductive organs, each is segregated in its own flower. Female flowers, which often appear a little later than the males, are easily distinguished by a small, immature fruit – cucumber, squash or melon – at the base. If there are bees in the area, pollination will likely take place as soon as the flower opens; otherwise, the gardener must transfer pollen from a male flower to the stigma – the centre of the female flower – using a small paintbrush or a swab. With small flowers such as cucumbers, the entire stamen – the pollen-headed filament – in the male flower can be removed with tweezers and touched against the stigma. After pollination occurs, the petals drop and the fruit begins to swell and mature.

Most other fruit-producing crops – beans, peppers, tomatoes, peas, eggplant and such – are primarily self-pollinated. These plants are termed hermaphroditic: Each flower contains both male and female organs, and pollination is achieved when the plant is moved in the wind, bumped by a passing gardener or perhaps visited by an in-

sect. Hand pollination of these plants is needed only when they are grown under cover – they or their blossoms can be simply bumped or touched – or when their crossbreeding is controlled for seed production, as described in the next chapter.

Like the melon family, corn is monoecious but, in this case, pollination is assisted by the wind which transfers pollen from the spoke-like tassels, high on the plant, to the silks atop each ear. Every strand of silk must be pollinated in order for the kernels to fill the entire cob. Because this is very much a hit-and-miss affair, each corn cultivar must be grown in a block rather than just in a single row. Details are on page 77.

Of course, lack of fruit formation need not always be caused by the lack of a suitable pollinating agent. Fruit will form irregularly, if at all, when the plant is under stress. Usually, in northern gardens, this happens because temperatures are too low; but it also occurs when temperatures are too high, when plants are diseased or malnourished, when drought conditions persist, or when the soil is so rich in nitrogen that the plant develops leaves, but not fruit. All in all, successful production of fruit is the sign of a good working relationship between the gardener, the garden and the weather.

handful of Bt-sprayed larvae that are almost dead, mash or blend them in a pint (50 millilitres) of milk, let the mixture stand at room temperature for three days, and then strain it and add enough water to make one gallon (4 litres).

Rotenone A botanical pesticide produced in the roots of several tropical legumes, rotenone is so expensive and powerful that it is usually sold in concentrations of only about one per cent. It is an effective control against many beetles, aphids, caterpillars, larvae and bugs, but is also highly toxic to cold-blooded creatures such as fish, frogs and toads. It is harmful to humans when fresh, although its toxicity disappears soon after the powder is applied or when it becomes old. Buy rotenone fresh every year. Apply it with care and do not use it during the week before harvesting vegetables.

Pyrethrum Another botanical pesticide, pyrethrum or pyrethrin comes from the blossoms of pyrethrum daisies, some of which are grown in the North — seeds are available from Richter's and several other mail-order houses. A contact poison, it provides fast "knockdown" of pests, killing a range of caterpillars, aphids, beetles and thrips (minute insects) almost upon contact, then biodegrading quickly in the garden. Pyrethrum is toxic to cold-blooded animals such as fish, toads and snakes, and is also harmful to humans when fresh. Do not apply pyrethrum during the week before harvesting vegetables. Pyrethroid, synthetic pyrethrum, is stronger and longer-lasting.

Mineral Oil One-quarter of a teaspoon of light mineral oil placed at the tips of corn silks just after they have wilted helps control corn ear worms. Heavier dormant oil sprays are applied to fruit trees before the buds begin to open in spring. Both are very localized in their effectiveness and are toxic only to eggs or pests coated with oil.

Insecticidal Soap Sold under two main brand names, Safer's and Fossil Flower, insecticidal soap is an effective control of aphids, whiteflies, mealy bugs and spider mites. It is not otherwise toxic and readily biodegrades.

Diatomaceous Earth This is the pulverized remains of tiny hard-shelled sea creatures called diatoms. Its particles are so sharp edged that they can be effective in piercing the skin of soft-bodied pests such as slugs and snails or the very hard shells of beetles. As diatomaceous earth is usually sold in combination with rotenone or pyrethrum, its effectiveness by itself is difficult to measure, but it is most effective on plants and soil that are dry. This

Aphids, tiny, soft-bodied insects that live in colonies, weaken and very occasionally kill garden plants by sucking their sap

means that reapplication is necessary after a rain.

Other Remedies Using the cedar tree's own pest-repelling properties, a tea of cedar bark and water may be used to control squash bugs and Mexican bean beetles. A tea made from fresh tomato leaves is said to help repel diamondback moths from brassicas. Garlic oils and hot pepper sprays, sometimes in combination, also have repellent properties. To any such spray, add a few drops of mild soap or dishwashing liquid to facilitate mixing and adherence to plants and to increase its effectiveness. A hard jet of water applied to foliage may be enough to remove some pests.

Beneficial Imports Beneficial insects such as ladybugs and praying mantids can be bought for release into the garden. This is not recommended because, of course, the imports cannot be conveniently contained within the garden but are likely to depart almost as quickly as they arrived. Every garden will quite naturally attract its own population of native beneficial insects in numbers the garden can support. Take care of these rather than buying new ones. The exception is greenhouse gardening, where purchased or collected beneficial insects are automatically confined.

Know These Bugs

Aphids This tiny, soft-bodied sap-sucking insect thrives in colonies on all sorts of plants, especially cucumbers, melons, brassicas, peas and peppers, and most often when they are grown in dry, hot in-

The Colorado potato beetle lays its orange eggs in clusters on the undersides of leaves of Solanaceae, especially potatoes

The northern garden's largest larval pest, the tomato horn-worm can be controlled by hand picking or spraying with Bt

door conditions. Aphids exist in many colours including white, green, purple and black. They weaken plants and sometimes spread disease. They may kill young plants. Eggs may overwinter in the garden or greenhouse. Insecticidal soaps provide the best garden control, while a tea of walnut leaves may be used on plants other than Solanaceae.

Cabbage Loopers or Cabbage Worms Several similar larvae infest brassicas, chewing holes in foliage and inflorescences: the imported cabbage worm, the diamondback moth larva, and the cabbage looper. All of them are green. Their round or oval whitish eggs can be scraped off leaves in spring, soon after cabbage butterflies are seen in the garden. Later the green caterpillars can be hand picked, sprayed with *Bacillus thuringiensis* or, in severe cases, with rotenone or pyrethrum.

Colorado Potato Beetles Because adults can overwinter in the garden, rotating the potato patch from place to place will help foil these orange and black beetles. In early spring, masses of orange eggs found on the undersides of potato leaves can be destroyed. The orange or brown larvae that hatch from these eggs chew the foliage of potato plants,

and also occasionally infest other Solanaceae. Hand pick or, in severe infestations, apply rotenone.

Cucumber Beetles Whether striped or spotted, cucumber beetles are found mostly in the northeast, where they are likely to infest Cucurbitaceae – cucumbers, melons and squashes – eating the foliage and sometimes spreading disease. The spotted cucumber beetle is yellow-green with 12 black spots, while the striped cucumber beetle has three lengthwise black stripes on a yellow background. They occasionally spread to corn, beans, peas and blossoms. For severe infestations, use rotenone.

Cutworms Existing in hundreds of different species throughout the continent, these plump, hairless caterpillars vary in colour from grey to brown to black. They live underground, chewing plant stems at the soil line at night, with some crawling up the stems to strip foliage. All are most easily disposed of in spring when tilling or spading exposes them. Later, they are most likely to attack tender plants like the transplants of tomatoes, peppers and eggplant, and the seedlings of beans and corn. Most damage occurs in May and June. Protect transplants with cardboard collars that extend

The yellow jacket presents a greater danger to the gardener than the garden, but it will not sting if left undisturbed

Cucumber beetles infect many garden plants, but prefer the blossoms and leaves of cucumbers, melons and squashes

1½ inches above and below the soil line. If few or no seedlings emerge from warm soil, cutworms might be at work. Dig in the soil to check. If a seedling is lopped off, dig around it the next morning to find and destroy the cutworm.

Flea Beetles Tiny beetles that jump when disturbed, flea beetles perforate foliage and can destroy seedlings, especially those of the cabbage family, eggplant, peppers, tomatoes, potatoes and radishes, and usually early in the season. The crucifer flea beetle is blue-black, while the striped flea beetle bears two yellow stripes on a black background. Because flea beetles do not usually destroy entire plantings, succession planting and heavy sowing of seeds can make up for losses. In severe cases, use rotenone or pyrethrum.

Grasshoppers In most gardens, the grasshopper is an occasional visitor whose damage is not severe. When infestations are really serious, very little can be done to protect plants other than covering them with screening or cheesecloth. Tomatoes and corn are usually consumed first. For light outbreaks, push cans containing 1 inch of a mixture of water and molasses into the soil throughout the garden.

June Beetle Larvae Sometimes, and appropriately, called white grubs, these large, pale, C-shaped larvae are most likely to infest newly cleared ground following their three-year cycle of growth. Damage, then, is most severe once every three years, with root crops, especially potatoes, the worst hit. Check for larvae and adults — large, rust-brown beetles — while spading or tilling in spring. Rotate potato plantings. Buried chunks of potato may be used as bait among other crops. Dig them up and replace them throughout the season.

Lady Beetles One of the gardener's best friends, the lady beetle is carnivorous. It does not live on plants, but on plant-eating insects such as aphids. The eggs are orange and laid in clusters on the undersides of leaves; they are smaller and more cylindrical than those of the Colorado potato beetle. The larva is flat and greyish. Lady beetles can have red, orange or white wing casings that may or may not be spotted.

Onion maggots The larva of a small fly, *Hylemya antiqua*, the onion maggot, which lays its eggs on the soil near onions, tunnels into onion bulbs. Control of the ⅓-inch-long larva is by crop rota-

The larva of the black swallowtail butterfly, the parsleyworm is most often found on plants in the Umbelliferae family

Wet weather, like that common on the west coast, encourages the growth of slugs, which will eat almost all vegetables

tion and applications of diatomaceous earth to the soil around onions in affected gardens.

Parsleyworms The larva of the black swallowtail butterfly eats the foliage of Umbelliferae – parsley, parsnips, carrots, dill and other herbs. Hand pick.

Praying mantids Various species of this long, 2½-inch insect (also known as a praying mantis) prey upon insects, flies and bugs in most North American gardens. Although they do not discern friend from foe, their predation is welcomed by most gardeners. The eggs are laid in a hard, foamy mass on stems or twigs.

Slugs Molluscs that can vary in length from ⅓ inch to 10 inches, slugs and their relatives, snails, prefer cabbage, lettuce, cauliflower, tomatoes, potato tubers and bean pods, but will eat almost anything, particularly in the damp, shady conditions they prefer. Depressing saucers or jar lids of beer into the soil around affected plants will attract and drown slugs. Or, lay boards or cabbage leaves on the ground near the plants; slugs, which are nocturnal in habit, will congregate under them at night and can be removed in the morning. Collars made of window screening and put on the plants

will prevent molluscs from climbing the stems.

Squash bugs Grey, dark brown or black in colour, these flat bugs congregate near the base of cucurbits, especially squash and pumpkins, sucking juice from leaves, stems and vines. The eggs, which are laid on the undersides of squash leaves in early summer, are first yellow but soon turn brown. Control the bugs with cedar bark tea or by placing boards or shingles around the bases of plants. Like slugs, they gather under the boards at night and can be removed in the morning.

Tomato Hornworms Three or 4 inches long, these larvae are so large that their damage is easy to spot and they themselves are easy to hand pick. Control may also be maintained with *Bacillus thuringiensis*. The yellow-green eggs are laid on host plants, which include Solanaceae.

Wireworms These fast-moving, tough-skinned, cylindrical worms, usually reddish-brown, are the larvae of click beetles. They consume seeds, roots and tubers. Remove wireworms that are exposed through tilling or spading. As well, pieces of potato can be buried as bait. Dig the pieces up, destroy and replace them throughout the season.

Plant Diseases and Disorders

Plants, like people, are subject not only to predation by insects but also to a host of diseases and disorders. And, like people, the best-fed, best-tended plant specimens tend to suffer least. In the usual well-managed garden, diseases are generally scarcely noticeable. Drops in productivity may occur, but seldom will the entire crop of a vegetable be lost.

Diseases and deficiencies are often difficult to diagnose because many have similar symptoms, because a plant may suffer from more than one, and because those symptoms may signify something other than a disease or nutrient problem. A long cold spell can cause heat-loving plants to fade and die even if frost does not occur. Air pollution, too much water, or too little water, can all produce unhealthy plants. Many plants, too, will die as soon as their propagation requirements have been fulfilled; early peas turn yellow and die in mid-summer, while potato and onion foliage dies in mid to late summer.

When death occurs from natural causes, the harvest will be as large as your soil, garden and climatic conditions permit. Diseases and disorders, however, almost always cause a drop in productivity — something you may not be able to measure

A corn disorder resembling smut, but actually caused by drought, typifies the difficulty of diagnosing plant diseases

until you have gardened for several seasons. In any case, good soil maintenance, proper crop rotations and the use of suitable varieties and growing methods will help to alleviate all serious problems, whether they are caused by soil nutrient disorders, pests or diseases.

Diseases most frequently appear in mid or late season when the weather is hot, foliage is dense, and disease-spreading insects are moving from plant to plant. Diseases may be caused by bacteria, fungi or viruses. Some of the most common in the North include:

Bacterial Diseases These are most prevalent during hot, humid weather when bacteria in the soil multiply freely, attacking nonresistant varieties. Rotate crops and, if you have problems, buy fresh seed of a new variety next year. Destroy affected plants.

• Bacterial blight causes pea stems to turn purplish or black at ground level, and small, water-soaked spots to appear on leaves and pods

• Bacterial ring rot affects potatoes, causing leaf margins to turn inward and become leathery and tubers to have a dark ring just inside the skin

• Bacterial soft rot affects lettuce, cabbage and tap-roots such as carrots, turning them into soft, pulpy masses. Outer leaves of cabbage and lettuce rot first

Viral Diseases Highly infectious, these diseases are often spread by aphids or beetles. Covering plants with cheesecloth, which prevents contact with disease-carrying insects, may help.

• Mosaic is a common disease that can infect almost all garden plants, especially tomatoes, potatoes, cucumbers and summer squash, producing mottled, mosaic-like designs on fruit and leaves. Mosaics can be spread to plants in the Solanaceae family from tobacco; smokers should wash their hands before gardening

Fungal Diseases Responsible for most disease problems in the northern garden, fungi may produce moulds, galls, watery or rotten spots on leaves or fruit. All except smut and scab are most severe in hot, humid weather. Thin plants to encourage air circulation, choose resistant varieties, and rotate crops. Do not tend wet plants.

• Anthracnose affects many garden plants. Mature tomato or pepper fruits have small black bumps or wrinkled, uneven areas of decay. Bean seed coats bear dark brown indented spots and lower leaves may have dark red or purplish veins. Also affected are rhubarb and all cucurbits

• Black leg affects most Solanaceae and Cruciferae (see page 38 for a list of plant families). They exhibit a black lesion at the base of the stem that causes the plant to wilt, topple over and die

• Botrytis produces a greyish mould on globe artichokes, cucurbits, lettuce, berries and fruit. Resistant cultivars are available. Botrytis rot of onions is often not evident until after they are harvested. Because it usually appears at the top of the bulb, it is also known as neck rot

• Clubroot affects all Cruciferae, especially in wet, acidic soil. Leaves become yellow and plants may wilt even when watered. When pulled up, the roots appear large and misshapen, eventually becoming mushy or mouldy. Some resistant varieties are available. Raising the pH of the soil helps

• Damping off attacks young seedlings before or after emergence (see page 54)

• Downy mildew produces cottony white patches on the pods or leaves of onions, lettuce, lima beans and peas. Stake the peas and beans, thin the onions and lettuce and, in wet areas, grow them in well-drained soil, perhaps in raised beds

• Early blight, or alternaria, is "early" because it attacks plants while they are still blossoming. This disease affects all plants in the Solanaceae family. On tomato, eggplant and pepper fruit, the rot begins in cracks or areas where there has been pest damage, gradually spreading into flattened, black spots. Leaves bear concentric circular spots, which led to another name for the disease, target spot. Early tomatoes, particularly, are likely to contract this disease late in the season

• Late blight, which caused Ireland's potato famine, attacks solanaceous plants after they blossom, and is most serious in areas where the weather is cool and damp late in the season. Dark watery spots suddenly appear on branches, fruit and leaves, spreading rapidly. A whitish mould may grow under the leaves. When severe, the disease produces a foul smell. Plants usually die. Sebago is one of the most resistant potato cultivars

• Powdery mildew produces a white, powdery coating on the surface of cucurbit and pea leaves, fruit and stems. There are resistant cultivars

• Scab produces corky, brown marks on potatoes, turnips, beets and radishes. Although unsightly, it does not affect the edibility of the vegetables. It is most severe in warm, dry alkaline soils. Lowering the pH should eradicate it. Do not save scabby potatoes for use as seed

• Smut is among the most destructive of corn diseases, producing galls (swellings) that may be tiny or several inches across. Destroy all affected plants before the galls burst, releasing black spores. Dry weather, late planting, poor soil or an overabundance of nitrogen all encourage smut

• Verticillium wilt affects plants in the Solanaceae family around blossoming time. Leaves wilt and die progressively from the base of the plant upward. Yields may be lowered or plants may die. Do not rotate solanaceous plants with others in the same family, or with strawberries, raspberries or Brussels sprouts. Resistant tomato cultivars bear an initial "V" after the name

As You Reap So Shall You Sow

"A few large carrots should be laid by to plant out early in spring for seed. Onions the same, also beets, parsnips, and some of your best cabbages"

– Catharine Parr Traill
The Canadian Settler's Guide, 1855

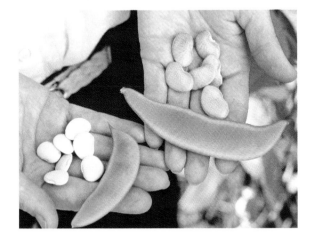

At the time when Catharine Parr Traill was advising Upper Canadian settlers to save their own garden seeds, high-quality seeds of desirable vegetable varieties were difficult to come by. Purchased seed might be dirty and contaminated with weeds, and might produce plants quite inferior to those advertised by the salesman. Seeds for a favourite Old World vegetable might not be available at all – unless the settler had the foresight to include a few in his trunk.

Today the situation has changed utterly, with seed selection problems more likely the result of too many choices rather than too few. And all of those choices are likely to be top-quality, clean seeds. In Canada, freshness and therefore good germination is virtually assured by seed regulations that demand that the year of packaging or the designation "Canada no. 1" or "Canada no. 2" be marked on each packet.

And yet there are still very good reasons for gardeners to save seed from their own plants. One reason is subtle, and was as true in Traill's day as in our own. There is a certain satisfaction that comes from seeing the gardening process through from beginning to end to beginning again. Your knowledge of botany and of the peculiarities of your own garden cannot help but grow. Along the way, a gardener who carefully saves seed from his best plants is likely to end up after several years with custom-designed cultivars that suit his own garden better than anything on the market. Another reason is more immediately apparent. Saving seed saves money. The cost of seeds is increasing dramatically, the dollar packet now little more than a fond memory at a few seed houses. Ironically, it is often the most expensive seeds – bulky ones like beans and peas – that are the easiest to save at home. Just one plant may provide next year's seed.

Although saving your own seeds has personal significance, it has broader consequences as well. A seed retailer can carry only a limited selection of cultivars, so every year as new selections are introduced older ones must be dropped, sometimes never to reappear. The home gardener who has been saving a personal seed supply can still grow the discontinued cultivar and perhaps produce enough seed to share with other gardeners. Seed exchanges have been established in both Canada and the United States for the barter and sale of hard-to-find or heirloom vegetables.

Hybrid vs. Standard

Hybrids, the first generation offspring of two inbred parents, have qualities of vigour and uniformity that have made them popular with many gardeners and farmers. Corn is one plant that has changed dramatically through hybridization, with

At the National Seed Storage Laboratory in Colorado, seeds are counted by being dropped through a counting board

bigger cobs and bigger, sweeter kernels available on hybrid plants. As well, greenhouse "seedless" cucumbers are markedly different from their open-pollinated counterparts, and some hybrid melons are remarkably early.

If hybrids are popular with some growers, they are even more so with many seed companies. This is not necessarily because hybrid seed is usually quite expensive — it is more costly to produce — but because the seed produced by hybrid plants is not worth saving in most home and farm situations. Gardeners or farmers who grow hybrid crops must return to the seed company every year for a new supply of seed. Understandably, such guaranteed yearly sales are extremely attractive to seedsmen, who often promote hybrids heavily. The offspring of a hybrid vegetable may look like its parent, but more likely it will hark back to a tough-skinned or small-fruited forebear. The seed of hybrid plants may even be sterile.

Standard or open-pollinated vegetables, on the other hand, will produce seed that grows into vegetables very much like the parents, provided cross-pollination among different cultivars is avoided.

Any gardener who wishes to save garden seed is strongly advised to buy nonhybrid seeds, some of which grow into vegetables whose own seed is very easy to collect. There is a mystique surrounding seed production that is not justified in many situations, although there are a few crops that present

Seeds are then germinated in a special chamber kept at the ideal conditions of high humidity and 20 to 30 degrees C

seed collection problems, often because the northern season is too short or too wet for success, and because the isolation of cross-pollinated crops is difficult to ensure in crowded urban or suburban areas. A great deal of commercial seed is produced in areas such as Idaho and California, where the seasons are long and dry, and where variety isolation is carefully controlled.

Plant Selection

Some experimentation will be required before you know which seeds you can most easily collect. Because properly stored seeds last longer than one year, it is not necessary to save the seed of every crop every year. In fact, with a little cooperation among several gardeners, seed saving could be reduced to just one vegetable a year for each gardener.

In general, the seeds of annual plants, those that go to seed the same year they are sown, are easiest to save — check the chart "Pollination of Vegetable Crops" on pages 122 and 123. Biennials, the plants that go to seed in their second year, often present more complications. Also, self-pollinating crops are easier to handle than those that cross-pollinate. With cross-pollinators, it's always best to grow just one cultivar for seed. With seeds that usually self-pollinate but occasionally cross, the gardener can grow different cultivars at opposite ends of the garden or plant them at different times. For instance, if both green and yellow snap beans are to be saved, the two crops could be grown as far apart in the garden as possible, or one might be planted in early June, the other in early July. Any late-forming blossoms will have to be removed from the early crop once the late one begins to bloom.

In an urban or suburban situation where there are many gardens close to one another, seed purity of most cross-pollinated crops is difficult to ensure. Here, it is best to work with only the crops that primarily self-pollinate: tomatoes, lettuce, peas, beans. In addition, seed saving of cucurbits and corn, whose cross-pollination can be controlled fairly easily, will usually be worthwhile for city gardeners who welcome a challenge.

Isolation of varieties and consequent seed purity is very important to commercial seedsmen with reputations to maintain and government regulations to meet. It is far less important in most home situations, where an accidental crossing, if it occurs at all, may have a happy conclusion. When crossing is frequent, however, a decline in vegetable quality is almost inevitable. The gardener who saves beet seed from a garden next to one where Swiss chard has bolted may end up with seeds that grow into plants that are more leaf than root. The gardener whose bolting carrots cross with a neighbour's hybrid carrots may end up a year later with little more than weedy Queen Anne's lace. In most gardens, however, few or no biennial plants are left long enough to go to seed, presenting little problem to the gardener saving seed. Have a look around the neighbourhood vegetable gardens before you begin to save cross-pollinating seeds. You may find that your seedy cabbages are actually growing in what, for practical purposes, amounts to isolation. Most rural gardeners are usually in an enviable position when it comes to seed saving, with the next garden perhaps more than a mile away.

Always choose the healthiest, most productive, earliest-bearing plant for seed. This requires a considerable amount of will power: The bush bearing the earliest beans must be marked and those beans allowed to mature and dry on the branches while you are anxiously awaiting your first harvest. Remember to take the whole plant into consideration. A 4-pound tomato may look tempting, but if it is the only fruit the plant has produced, it would

While hybrids like these Burpee's Early Pick produce unreliable seed, the seed of standard varieties is worth saving

be much better to save the seed from a plant bearing many smaller tomatoes. Plants at the ends of rows or in a patch of fertile soil will look better than less favoured ones, but such productivity will not be carried with the seed.

Seed Storage

Whether seed is grown commercially or domestically, it must be mature in order to keep over the winter and, later, to germinate successfully. Fruits, then — tomatoes, peppers, squash and such — must be fully mature but not yet rotting when they are cut open for seed collection. If they cannot be left to ripen on the vine they can spend the final week or two indoors. Pods such as those of beans, peas, radishes and cabbage should be papery dry and the seeds inside hard. Again, maturation is most successful if it occurs on the plant, but almost-dry pods can, if necessary, be brought indoors for final drying. Seeds borne on umbels — those of carrots, dill, parsley and parsnips — are ready for harvest when they are brown and papery. Onion seeds will begin to fall from the seed heads when they are shiny, black and mature.

All seeds must be thoroughly dry to keep well.

After they first appear dry, allow seeds a further week in a warm place where air circulation is good. They must not be exposed to very high temperatures (no more than 100 degrees F, 37 degrees C), nor should they be allowed to become wet during drying. If they are dried outdoors, bring them indoors every night and during damp weather.

Home-stored seeds often contain bits of dried stem, leaf or pod. Some of this can be removed by hand or by winnowing (allowing the seed to drop from one container to another while an electric fan or stiff breeze carries the chaff away). Don't be too concerned about clean seed, however. Bits of dry plant material will not affect seed germination or usefulness for planting.

Even those gardeners who do not wish to save their own garden seeds should save commercial seeds left over from spring planting. Most will keep for several years if storage conditions are suitable — dry and cool. Write the date of purchase or collection on seed packets that do not already bear the date of packaging. Home-collected seeds can go in envelopes, paper bags, jars or cans. Place envelopes or bags, marked with the cultivar name, in airtight jars or cookie tins with some moisture-absorbing material such as silica gel, cotton wool, or a couple

Pollination of Vegetable Crops

Family	Vegetable	Pollination			Seed-bearing habit
		Self	Cross	Method*	
Liliaceae	Asparagus	–	100%	insects	perennial
	Chives	–	100%	insects	perennial
	Garlic	–	100%	insects, bees	biennial
	Leeks	–	100%	insects, bees	biennial
	Onions	–	100%	insects, bees	biennial
	Shallots	–	100%	insects, bees	biennial
Chenopodiaceae	Beets	–	100%	wind	biennial
	Spinach	–	100%	wind	annual
	Swiss chard	–	100%	wind	biennial
Umbelliferae	Carrots	–	100%	insects	biennial
	Celeriac, Celery	–	100%	insects	biennial
	Parsley	–	100%	insects	biennial
	Parsnips	–	100%	insects	biennial
Compositae	Artichokes, globe	95%	5%	wind, insects	annual
	Artichokes, Jerusalem	–	100%	insects	perennial
	Endive	95%	5%	wind, insects	annual
	Lettuce	95%	5%	wind, insects	annual
	Salsify	–	100%	insects	biennial
Cruciferae	Broccoli	–	100%	bees, insects	annual
	Brussels sprouts	–	100%	insects	biennial

of spoonfuls of skim milk powder wrapped in a few layers of facial tissues. Peas and beans need to breathe, and so should go in paper bags or in jars with perforated lids. Place the containers in a cool, dark cupboard. Incidentally, mice will overwinter happily on the gardener's stored seeds. If there are mice in the house, keep all seeds in metal or glass containers, not paper, cardboard or plastic.

Dampness is the worst enemy of seed storage, causing germination or rotting. The general rule is that the best storage conditions occur when the sum of the percentage of relative humidity and the temperature in degrees Fahrenheit totals less than 100. Avoid temperatures over 70 degrees F (21 degrees C) in storage if possible.

The approximate longevity of properly stored seeds is:

1-2 years corn, okra, onions, parsley, parsnips, potatoes

2-3 years leeks, peppers, salsify

3-4 years asparagus, beans, carrots, celery, lettuce, peas, spinach, sunflowers, tomatoes

4-5 years cabbage and its relatives, beets, Swiss chard, squash, pumpkins, radishes

5-6 years cucumbers, endive, ground cherries, muskmelon, watermelon

Family	Vegetable	Pollination			Seed-bearing habit
		Self	Cross	Method*	
	Cabbage	–	100%	insects, bees	biennial
	Cauliflower	–	100%	insects, bees	biennial
	Cress	–	100%	insects, bees	annual
	Horseradish	–	100%	insects, bees	perennial
	Kale, Kohlrabi	–	100%	insects, bees	biennial
	Radishes	–	100%	insects, bees	annual or biennial
	Rutabagas, Turnips	–	100%	bees, insects	biennial
	Watercress	–	100%	insects, bees	perennial
Solanaceae	Eggplant	55%	45%	wind, insects	annual
	Peppers	70%	30%	wind, insects	perennial
	Potatoes	100%	–	wind	annual
	Tomatoes	95%	5%	wind, insects	annual
Cucurbitaceae	Cucumbers	25%	75%	bees, insects	annual
	Melons	25%	75%	bees, insects	annual
	Squash, Pumpkins	25%	75%	bees, insects	annual
Leguminosae	Beans	90%	10%	tripped by bees	annual
	Peas	97%	3%	tripped by bees	annual
	Peanuts	–	100%	insects	annual
Graminae	Sweet corn	5%	95%	wind	annual

* the most common is mentioned first

To check the viability of old seeds, place 10 of them in warm, moist paper towelling about a month before the seeding date in spring. If after three weeks five seeds have not germinated, consider discarding the seed and buying a fresh supply. If a few have germinated, the seed can be sown thickly to compensate for germination failure.

Seed Saving of Annuals

Beans & Peas Beans and peas are among the easiest seeds to save. Most flowers self-pollinate, though enough crossing occurs that the gardener should keep different varieties as far apart as possible. Leave the pods on the plants until they have become dry and papery or, if this is not possible, harvest almost-dry pods to finish drying indoors. Harvesting can be left until after the first light fall frost, which will not harm pods that are almost dry. Shell them, then continue to dry indoors until they cannot be easily dented with the teeth.

Broccoli Broccoli is one of the more difficult annual candidates for seed saving. Occasionally it will go to seed before producing an edible head, especially if the transplants were overly mature before they were set outdoors, but usually it takes a very long time to go to seed — the head, the part eaten, is a mass of unopened flowers which must bloom and then produce seed stalks whose seed must ripen. Also, broccoli cross-pollinates readily with all other members of the same species, *Brassica oleracea* — cabbage, Brussels sprouts, cauliflower, kale, collards, turnips, rutabagas and kohlrabi — pollination occurring easily among plants separated by less than 100 feet. This is of no concern, however, to gardeners who have not allowed any of the other crops, all biennial, to overwinter and go to seed. Broccoli raised for seed should be started early indoors (see Chapter III), or it can be sown outside in fall in very mild areas. Because broccoli may be self-sterile, two plants of the same cultivar should be allowed to go to seed. Do not harvest the heads that form on the healthiest, most productive plants, but allow them to produce flowers and, later, seed pods. After the first fall frost, or when the first pods have become brittle, remove the seed stalks and place them in a large bag, cut ends protruding. Place the bag in a warm, dry place indoors until all

seed pods are dry. Then bang the bag against a wall to dislodge the seeds and pods, remove the stalks from the bag, and discard them. Remove bits of pod from the seeds by hand.

Corn Open-pollinated corn seed is fairly easy to save but is seldom grown. When it is the cultivar of choice remember that, both for seed saving and for eating, it should be kept isolated from other cultivars that mature at the same time. As corn will cross-pollinate over about 1,000 feet, the home gar-

Tassels are the male, pollen-bearing organs of the corn plant. Their pollen must reach the silks before pollination can occur

The broccoli head is a cluster of immature flowers that will bloom and eventually produce seed if the head is not picked

dener should plant one cultivar only or several that mature at different times, or stagger plantings at two-week intervals. Plants are not normally self-fertile (the tassels should not pollinate the silks of the same plant), and so cobs must be saved from more than one plant to retain vigour in future generations. To ensure that cross-pollination does not occur among different cultivars – if, for instance, a neighbour nearby is growing a different cultivar – cover the earliest developing ears with paper bags as soon as the silks have formed. When pollen is produced on the tassels of more plants of the same cultivar, remove the bag, break off part of a tassel from another plant and sprinkle pollen on the silks. Repeat for three or four days in succession. Between pollinations, replace the bag and leave it on the cob until the silks turn brown.

Leave the cobs on the plants until the kernels are dry, even if this means leaving them past the first few light frosts. Then pick the cobs, husk them and hang them indoors to dry until the kernels are brittle. The kernels can be left on the cobs all winter, or rubbed off and stored in jars or cans.

Cress When the plants begin to go to seed, pull them up and hang them under cover with a paper bag tied over the head to catch seeds as they fall. When it has completely dried, shake any seeds remaining on the plant into the bag.

Cucumbers Gardeners who wish to save cucumber seed should grow only one cultivar and, of course, it must not be hybrid. For further insurance that cross-pollination will not occur – if, for instance, a neighbour 100 feet away is growing cucumbers of a different cultivar – you should hand pollinate at least one female blossom as described on page 111. In this case, you will have to race the bees to the blossoms, a race the bees are almost sure to win unless your garden doesn't have any. Check female blossoms every afternoon. When one is fully formed but not yet open, enclose it in a small bag attached to the stem with a paperclip. The following morning, pollinate the blossom and then replace the bag, scratching the immature fruit with an X to designate that it is to be saved for seed – the mark will remain on the growing fruit. When the petals have fallen off, the bag can be removed. If the fruit drops off, pollination has not been successful and must be repeated on another blossom.

Fruits should be allowed to mature fully – until the skin is golden or white. They can be left on the vine until after the first frost, but should then be harvested and, if necessary, left to ripen further indoors. Then cut the fruit lengthwise, scoop the seeds into a jar and ferment as tomato seed, following the same procedure through drying.

Eggplant In the North, maturing eggplant fruit is usually sufficient triumph without the gardener also trying to save seed. Nevertheless, gardeners who intend to save eggplant seed should grow only one cultivar. When the fruit is ripe enough to eat, the seeds are almost ripe. Allow the fruit an extra week on the vine or indoors. Then mash the fruit into a bowl and gradually wash away the pulp from the seeds. Spread the seeds on a lightly greased screen or cookie sheet to dry, stirring occasionally and removing remaining bits of pulp.

Lettuce The tendency of lettuce to go to seed in hot weather is somewhat frustrating to gardeners lusting after summer salads. For the longest-standing lettuce in future years, collect the seeds of the last plant or plants to bolt – as long as those plants have other desirable characteristics as well. Very slow-bolting cultivars may have to be started early indoors so that they will bolt early enough for seed collection. Seed from looseleaf types is easier to collect than that of heading lettuce. Because lettuce usually self-pollinates, different cultivars can be placed quite close together, although seed purity will be more certain if different cultivars are set apart in the garden – or if all cultivars but one are harvested before bolting. When, about a month after bolting, the flowers begin to feather the way dandelions do when going to seed, shake the seed heads into a bag. Because the seeds mature over several days this procedure can be repeated from time to time. In mild areas, seeds may be sown in fall for seed collection the following summer.

Muskmelon Follow the same procedure as for cucumbers, again growing only one open-pollinated cultivar, and hand pollinating if other muskmelons are being grown within 100 feet. In this case, however, the seed is ripe when the fruit is normally harvested. Follow the same fermentation and drying procedure outlined for tomatoes.

Peanuts The crop is dug and pods dried in the same way whether for eating or for use as seed, although peanut seed must not be roasted (see peanuts, Chapter IV). If the seeds are to be saved for planting, do not shell them until spring.

Peppers Peppers must be fully ripe for the seed to be mature. Some peppers are not ripe until they have turned red. In other cases, leave fruit to ripen about a month past its first indication of ripeness. Mark the fruit so that it is not picked early. It can, if necessary, be ripened further at room temperature indoors. Peppers usually self-pollinate but, just to ensure purity, gardeners wishing to save seed should keep different cultivars about 25 feet apart. When the fruit is fully ripe, scrape out the seeds and dry by spreading them on a lightly greased screen or cookie sheet in a warm, dry place, stirring occasionally.

Potatoes As long as the potato crop is not diseased, sound tubers may be saved indoors for planting the following spring. Potatoes store best at 45 to 50 degrees F (7 to 10 degrees C) and must be kept in the dark. Cut into eyes and plant as usual in spring. The fruit borne by some potato plants contains seeds that may be dried and saved but, for genetic reasons, the quality of tubers that result from planting such seed will be unpredictable.

Radishes Grow only one cultivar if seed is to be saved, as radishes cross-pollinate over a quarter of a mile. Impure seed may result if other gardeners have allowed radishes to go to seed. Small domestic radishes allowed to mature completely will produce seed pods, which can be allowed to dry on the plant or picked to dry indoors. When the pods are papery, shell them; label and store the seeds. Treat biennial radishes (the winter storage or Oriental types) as carrots.

Spinach Spinach pollen may be carried more than a mile on the wind, making variety isolation, and hence seed purity, difficult to achieve in most garden situations. The gardener himself must allow only one cultivar to go to seed. Select the last plants to bolt, picking the entire plants when they are fully grown and bringing them indoors to dry further for one or two weeks. Hand pick seeds,

which are actually dried fruits (clusters of several seeds). Spread on screens or cookie sheets to dry.

Squash & Pumpkins Summer squash, winter squash and pumpkins cross-pollinate readily with any members of the same species growing within 100 feet, but crosses can even take place over a quarter of a mile. Therefore, gardeners who wish to save seed should ensure that hand pollination occurs with the fruits that are to be saved for seed (see cucumbers, page 125), or should grow no more than one selection from any of the following species of *Cucurbita*:
- *maxima* buttercup, hubbard, delicious, banana
- *moschata* butternut, sweet potato squash
- *pepo* all common summer squashes, acorn, pumpkin, Delicata, Lady Godiva, spaghetti squash

As the seeds of all squashes are ready to harvest when the fruits are mature, summer squashes, like cucumbers, must be left on the vine past their normal harvesting date. The skin will become as hard as that of winter squash and may change colour. All squash for seed may be left on the vine past the first fall frost. Then scoop out seeds, wash them and spread them on cookie sheets or screens to dry for about a week in a warm, dry place indoors.

Sunflowers Sunflower seeds that are fully mature and well dried will store for several years, provided they are left unshelled. Discard seeds that are undersized or damaged. Harvest and store in the same manner as seeds used for eating (see page 99).

Tomatoes Nonhybrid tomato seed is easily collected and stored. Tomatoes generally self-pollinate, but separation of different cultivars is still wise if seed is to be collected. On the best-producing plant, allow one fruit to become overripe but not rotten — mark the tomato with a ribbon so that it is not harvested early by mistake. Then pick the tomato, crush it in a quart jar and let the mixture ferment in a warm place (about 70 degrees F, 21 degrees C) for one to three days. After this the pulp will be soft and will readily separate from the seed and skin. Fill the jar with water, stir vigorously and then let the seeds settle for a minute. Pour off some of the mixture, refill the jar, stir and pour off again, repeating the refilling and emptying several times. Pour the seeds into a sieve, remove any remaining bits of tomato by hand and shake off excess water. Spread the wet seeds on a lightly greased screen or cookie sheet to dry in a warm, dry place.

Watermelon Follow the same procedure as for cucumbers, again growing only one open-pollinated cultivar and hand pollinating one fruit if necessary. The seed is ripe when the melon is ready for harvesting. Wash and spread on cookie sheets to dry.

Seed Saving of Biennials

Biennials are those plants that must survive one

Most bell peppers turn red when mature, at which stage those from nonhybrid plants can be harvested for seed collection

While potatoes are almost always cloned from eyes, small pieces of potato, the Explorer variety is grown from seed

winter before they will go to seed. Of all of them, parsnips are the easiest garden candidates for seed saving, overwintering in most northern gardens even without mulching. Others usually require mulching or even hilling (being covered with about 6 inches of soil) in order to survive the winter. The mulching should be done with at least 1 foot of straw, hay or leaf mould. Both mulch and most of the hilled soil are removed from the plants in spring after the ground thaws. Some crops must be dug in fall, stored indoors over the winter and replanted in the garden in spring, when they will go to seed. Because plants going to seed become tall and bushy, taking up more space than they did the previous year, they should be thinned or transplanted to twice the usual spacing.

Note Remember that all varieties of *Brassica oleracea* will cross-pollinate readily, so the seed of only one of them must be saved in any season; that is, only one of broccoli, Brussels sprouts, cabbage, kale, kohlrabi, collards, turnips, rutabagas or cauliflower. Plants growing within 300 feet of one another are quite likely to cross-pollinate if they flower at the same time.

Beets As beet pollen can travel for several miles, seed purity may be difficult to attain in some gardens. The gardener himself must allow only one cultivar to go to seed, and must not allow beets and chard to go to seed in the same year. Beets can be stored over winter in many gardens if they are hilled and mulched, or they can be stored indoors in a cold, humid root cellar. In spring, replant them in the garden, the tops even with the soil surface. When the seed stalks are dry, strip seed clusters from the stalks by hand.

Brussels Sprouts Mulch the plants heavily in late fall before freeze-up or, in the far North, store roots indoors as cabbage roots, setting them outdoors in spring. Collect seed as described for broccoli. See note above about *Brassica oleracea*.

Cabbage In fall before the ground freezes, dig cabbage roots, cut off the heads for table use if they have not already been harvested, and store roots in polyethylene bags or in damp peat or sand in a cool root cellar. Save at least two plants of the same cultivar, as the flowers are self-sterile. In spring, replant the roots outdoors. Collect seed stalks in the manner described for broccoli. See note on page 127 about *Brassica oleracea*.

Carrots Save only one cultivar of carrot for seed, as crossing can occur over more than 200 feet. Carrots are more cold hardy than beets, and will often overwinter successfully in the garden under a heavy mulch, especially if hilled first. Alternatively, roots stored in a cool root cellar can be planted in the garden in early spring, the shoulders just under the soil surface. As carrots will cross readily with the weed Queen Anne's lace, do not grow them for seed in areas where the weed grows profusely, or else keep the weed under control until after the carrot seed has been collected. Remove seed heads as the seeds ripen and turn brown. Hang the heads indoors to dry further and then rub the seeds from the seed heads into bags.

Cauliflower Cauliflower seed is one of the most difficult to save. Not only will cauliflower, even under mulch, not survive the winter in most northern gardens, but the roots will not tolerate winter in a root cellar. As is the case with broccoli, the part of the cauliflower that is eaten, the head, is a tight mass of immature flowers. In this case, however, the plant must experience cold before it will go to seed, which makes it a biennial and not, like broccoli, an annual. In his book *Growing Garden Seeds* (available from Johnny's Selected Seeds; see Sources for address) Rob Johnston suggests that in the North, seeds be sown under cover in early fall and the young plants kept from freezing over the winter. In late spring, set the plants two feet apart in the garden. Do not harvest the curds that develop but allow them to form yellow flowers and later, seed pods. Cover plants whenever frost threatens. Harvest seed as for broccoli. See note about *Brassica oleracea* on page 127.

Celery & Celeriac Plants may be hilled and deeply mulched in fall or, in areas where winter is more severe, the entire plants can be dug in fall and roots replanted in moist sand in a root cellar. Pick celery spears and trim decaying foliage throughout the winter, keeping the sand moist at all times. In late spring, set the roots in the garden. Allow only one cultivar of either celery or celeriac to go to seed, as

celery cross-pollinates over at least 200 feet with other celery cultivars or with celeriac. When the flower heads turn brown in late summer, treat them like those of carrots. Celery seed may be used as a seasoning, in which case it does not matter whether cross-pollination has occurred.

In its second year of growth, the globe onion produces a round seed head whose seeds become black as they ripen

Kale Kale can be heavily mulched in fall to overwinter in most gardens. Otherwise the roots must be dug as cabbage. Proceed as described for broccoli (page 124) and cabbage (page 127).

Kohlrabi See broccoli (page 124) and cabbage (page 127).

Onions Onions will cross-pollinate over about a quarter of a mile, so not only must just one cultivar be saved for seed in the garden, but seed purity may be lost where other gardens nearby contain bolting onions. Unharvested onions will often survive the winter, their globed seed heads appearing the following summer. Some types of onions, too, are perennial, producing seed heads every year. Bulbs that have been overwintered indoors in a cool, dry place can be planted in spring, the neck just above the soil surface. As soon as some of the black seed is exposed in the seed head, pick the entire head and shake it into a bag, or bend the head carefully over a bag and shake the seed loose. Seeds will continue to mature gradually, so the shaking of heads can be repeated over several days.

Parsley Parsley will overwinter in most areas without mulching and go to seed the following

Garlic is not propagated from seed but from cloves, the sections into which the mature bulb can be easily divided

summer. Allow only one cultivar to go to seed. As crossing can occur over 200 feet, seed purity may be difficult to maintain where gardens are near one another. When the seed heads are mature and the seeds have turned brown, rub the seed off the head into a paper bag. Seed may be used as a seasoning, in which case it does not matter if cross-pollination has occurred.

Parsnips With the easiest seed to save of all biennials, the parsnip usually overwinters in the garden without mulching, later presenting the gardener with large, papery seeds that are easy to strip from the seedstalks. The only problem with parsnips is that, like carrots and parsley, varietal crossing can take place over long distances. As few varieties exist, however, this is seldom a problem, even in city gardens. Where winters are severe, dig roots in fall to store in a cool root cellar and replant in spring.

Rutabagas In many areas, roots can be hilled and mulched in fall to overwinter in the garden and go to seed next spring. See note on page 127 about *Brassica oleracea*. Otherwise roots are brought indoors for storage in a cool, humid root cellar over the winter. Two weeks before the last spring frost,

remove them from the dark and place them in a well-lighted indoor place. In a week, discard any that have not begun to produce leaves. Plant the others outdoors, the top third above the soil surface. As soon as the seed pods have started to become papery, cut the seedstalks just above the root. Follow the directions given for broccoli.

Swiss Chard Like the beet, Swiss chard has fine pollen that can be carried more than a mile by the wind, so seed purity may be almost impossible to ensure in some situations. The gardener himself should allow only one cultivar to go to seed, and not in the same year that beet seeds are harvested. In most gardens, Swiss chard roots will overwinter under a heavy mulch applied after the first light frost. Remove the mulch in spring after the soil thaws. Harvest seed as described for beets.

Seed Sharing

As an historical addendum to the subject of seed saving, keep in mind a little advice from Catharine Parr Traill: "If you have more than a sufficiency for yourself do not begrudge a friend a share of your superfluous garden seeds. In a new country like Canada a kind and liberal spirit should be encouraged; in out-of-the-way country places people are dependent upon each other for many acts of friendship."

A Northern Bouquet Garni

"There were others that are known to the Natives and make a part of their food, especially fern roots, a root of licorice taste, and some others unknown to me..."

– the Journals of Captain James Cook, 1778

In describing the Nootka Indians of what is now coastal British Columbia, Captain Cook noted their use of plants that may have been consumed for either culinary or medicinal purposes, perhaps both. Certainly, all plants have an effect, good or ill, on the body. But most of the especially strong-tasting edible plants we call herbs are divided, principally by flavour, into those usually consumed as seasonings and those usually reserved for headaches, colds and even bad tempers.

The division is a vague one. Some plants once considered mostly curative are now considered essential only in the kitchen. Rhubarb is a good example. Sage's botanical name, *Salvia*, suggests that it has life-saving qualities, and indeed was once reputed to mend broken bones and cure nervous disorders. Now it is far more often found in turkey stuffings than in curative teas.

The essential oils that give these plants their characteristic flavour and fragrance – and their medicinal properties – are part of the plant's own insect- and herbivore-repelling strategies. Obviously, the ploy has done little to repel man, but it does mean that herbs have very few pest problems. Still in possession of the defensive faculties of their wild ancestors, herbs are also virtually disease free, and many of them thrive in infertile soils where vegetables would languish.

All of the herbs in this chapter have some reputed effect upon human health, but that is not why they have been included. They are here because they are the easiest, most dependable culinary herbs for Northerners to grow. Whether or not they are therapeutic, they will certainly enliven casseroles and minister to bland salads.

Herb Gardens

Because herbs are generally quite resilient and because a family usually wants only a few plants of any particular variety, herbs can be accommodated in almost any garden situation: in containers, flower gardens or the border along a driveway. All, however, must be sheltered from harsh winds and all do best in well-drained soil; indeed, without it some perennials will not be winter hardy in areas where they would normally survive. The best plan for a herb garden, then, will include sandy soil, perhaps in raised beds to help drainage. Only parsley, chervil, mint, lovage and bergamot will thrive in moist soil. Gardeners in the driest areas of the country will be able to get away with heavy soil that may even require a summer mulch, but in most areas a mixture of 1 part sand with 2 parts topsoil and 1 part compost will produce an adequate herb garden soil, piled into beds raised with stones, cement blocks, railway ties or boards. Raised beds produce an attractive display of herbs.

sometimes included in traditional gardens. All plants must be placed close together, just 3 to 4 inches apart, to achieve a continuous effect. They must also be kept trimmed, suckers and volunteer plants must be removed, and any dead plants replaced. In short, knot gardens are really not suita-

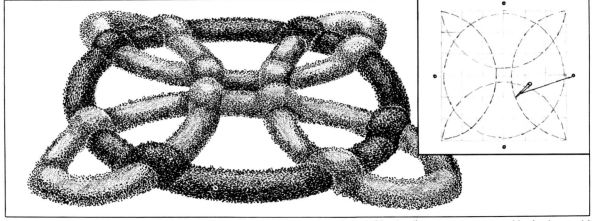

The knot garden, which gained popularity in the 16th and 17th centuries, featured bushy, low-growing perennial herbs that could be clipped to maintain an intricate pattern. The gardens were said to refresh the viewer's vision when they were seen from above

At one time, far more intricate herb gardens were popular. The knot gardens of Tudor and Stewart England featured complex, carefully groomed designs planted with low-growing herbs whose prunings made their way into soups and stews and medicines. The gardens were meant to be viewed from above, from a high window where, as William Coles wrote in 1656, there would be no better way to refresh one's vision "than to view the pleasant greennesse of Herbes. . . . "

In England, where many perennial herbs are winter hardy, such a garden is more practical than it is in the North, where there are fewer suitable selections — that is, fewer herbs that are perennial and lend themselves to pruning and shaping. Chives, sage, thyme, winter savory and hyssop, however, would be fine for a knot garden in many northern areas. Some perennial medicinal herbs such as horehound and wormwood could be used as well. Where lavender is hardy, its grey-green, fragrant foliage is a beautiful addition. Annual flowers, too, low-growing choices such as dwarf marigolds and alyssum, can be planted every spring to fill in areas of the design. Alpine strawberries were

ble for any but the most devoted of gardeners.

To make the knot garden illustrated above, first clear a square patch of soil of a suitable size, about 10 feet by 10 feet. Then find the centre of the square by tying string across both diagonals and marking the spot where they intersect. At this point, drive a stake into the ground and tie a string to it. The string should be long enough to reach almost to the mid-points of the sides of the square. Tie a peg to the outward end of the string and walk around the central stake, marking a circle in the soil. Go around the circle again, marking it deeply and clearly. The knot design is completed by describing arcs with the peg and string tied to a stake driven into the mid-point of each side of the square (see diagram above). The empty space between the lines of herbs can be covered with gravel or bark chips, or seeded to a creeping ground cover such as wild thyme. However, if grass is seeded within the knot, it will have to be clipped by hand.

Annual herbs can, of course, be raised in the vegetable garden, and this is usually done with basil, borage, summer savory, chervil, anise, nasturtiums, chile peppers and dill. A biennial such as parsley is also well suited to the vegetable garden, but remember not to till or spade the roots in fall or in spring before they resprout. If the perennial herbs are to be grown in the vegetable garden, give them a corner of their own and plan their positions carefully; some of them, like mint and horseradish,

Suited only to dedicated gardeners, knot gardens must be diligently maintained to retain their distinctive outlines

tend to spread; some, like lovage, grow very tall; others are small and easily crowded out.

Herb Propagation

Except for parsley and the annual herbs, culinary herbs are generally purchased as transplants or, in the case of horseradish, as root cuttings. Neither horseradish nor French tarragon nor peppermint set reliably fertile seed, so there is no choice in the method of propagation. Many other herbs produce seeds that are exceedingly tiny, slow and difficult to germinate, and are very slow to develop into mature plants. The shortcut of planting herbs that are already well developed is definitely recommended for Northerners, provided plants can be purchased from nurseries or cuttings can be obtained from another gardener. But growing herbs from seed does have its practical aspects: It is less expensive than buying transplants and, if the gardener has success with the seed, he will have a quantity of plants to barter, share or sell.

Very fine herb seeds are sprinkled on the surface of a flat of finely textured, damp potting soil. The container is then set in a warm place and covered with plastic, or is set in a shallow pan of warm wa-

ter. Seeds usually sprout in two or three weeks, after which they are thinned or transplanted into larger containers. When they are about 2 inches tall, begin hardening them off (see page 55) in preparation for outdoor planting. Sowing very tiny seeds outdoors is hazardous and wasteful.

Later on, most perennial herbs can be propagated by dividing roots or root crowns, or by layering plant stems. (Lay a stem on the ground and cover it with soil about 2 inches from the tip. When the stem roots, cut it from the main plant.) Thyme and mint propagate in this manner naturally.

Overwintering

The fact that some herbs are perennials, producing a harvest year after year, is very attractive to gardeners, most of whom like a garden that requires as little care as possible. But whether or not a given herb will survive the winter depends on many things: the herb's own capacity to withstand cold, its need for dormancy, the climate in the garden during any particular winter, the temperature, the snow cover, and the moisture level in the ground. Very hardy herbs will perish in waterlogged frozen soil, while half-hardy ones might survive a winter with a deep snow cover, yet succumb in a winter that may be warmer but that has less snow.

Check with other gardeners, with nurseries and with local horticultural societies to discover which herbs are likely to be hardy in your area. If there is any doubt, mulch heavily with leaves or straw before heavy frost. Or, better yet, bring a cutting of the plant indoors to overwinter.

This process is not without its own hazards, of course, because indoor growing is not optimal for herbs, most of which require cool air and plenty of sunlight. Retain as much of a root ball as possible and set the cutting into a light soil or potting mixture. Water it whenever it is dry and, if you are harvesting leaves throughout the winter, fertilize it with fish emulsion every month. The hardy herbs must have some winter cold in order to continue to grow well; do not bring them indoors until just before the soil freezes. Protect tender herbs from frost, and bring them indoors before the days are cold.

The Harvest

Herb leaves and stems can be pinched off at any

time, provided you don't pinch off so much that the plant is seriously set back in its growth — always leave at least two sets of leaves at the base of the plant. The youngest (top) leaves are usually the most desirable. Harvest them in the morning as soon as the dew has dried and wash only if necessary. In fall or just before the plant goes to seed, whichever is appropriate for each herb, pick a single, large harvest for winter storage.

Unquestionably, the best herbs are fresh herbs. But if preservation is necessary, drying is usually most convenient — the processing is very inexpensive and the finished product takes up little space. In recipes, substitute 1 part dried herbs for 6 parts fresh — that is, ½ teaspoon crushed, dried herbs instead of 1 tablespoon fresh.

Herb drying is most successful if it takes place fairly quickly in relative darkness and in temperatures of 70 to 95 degrees F (21 to 35 degrees C). Excessive heat and light cause additional flavour losses. Such conditions are not always easy to meet,

but the plants may be spread on screens or cookie sheets in a dry room, or in the open-doored oven of a warm woodstove. If you are drying herbs outdoors, leave them in a shady place in a box made of screening and be sure to bring them in overnight and whenever the weather is wet — any dampness during the drying process will cause darkening of leaves, loss of flavour and perhaps rotting.

Store paper-dry herbs in labelled glass jars, never in paper or cardboard, which will absorb essential oils. Place the containers in a cool, dark cupboard. If, after the first week or two, moisture can be seen condensing on the inside of the container, or if the herbs do not crush easily, they must be removed for further drying. Leafy herbs can also be hung upside down in bunches to dry, where they may be left until dry in four to six weeks, or throughout the winter. Bunches of thyme, sage, savory or oregano tied with ribbon can be quite decorative, although

Herbs, such as pineapple sage, that are not winter hardy in the North are often confined to indoor pots for convenience

they do become dusty. Do not crush dried herbs until just before use.

Herbs can also be stored by freezing – very successfully with chervil, tarragon, parsley and basil. The herbs are simply washed, packed in small plastic bags, labelled and put into the freezer. To make herb vinegar, add 4 parts vinegar to 1 part fresh herbs in a glass jar. In two weeks, strain off the liquid, add 1 part fresh leaves to it again and let stand for another two weeks. Strain and store, with one herb sprig added to the bottle for decoration and identification. Especially good herb vinegars are made with mint, basil, dill and tarragon. Herb vinegars, while not primarily a means of herb storage, do accomplish that end as do herb jellies or herbs stored in vegetable oils. Pesto, a mixture of basil, garlic, pine nuts, cheese and olive oil, is the most common herb-and-oil mixture. Salad dressing containing herbs is a popular version as well.

Most herbs are very well suited to preservation by drying, which is an easy process and requires only a warm, dry room

Because they are so easy to grow and store, at least one or two herbs should be part of the garden plan for any Northerner. Herbs could not possibly be called an essential part of the diet, but they are the *bouquet garni* of the garden, providing pleasure for the eyes, the nose and the taste buds.

Herbal Nutrition

While herbs are too strong in flavour to be edible in great quantity, and thus to influence one's nutrient intake significantly, they do contain nutrients just as other plants do. According to the U.S. Depart-

ment of Agriculture, a teaspoon (2.1 g) of:
• dill seed contains 32 mg calcium
• ground thyme contains 1.73 mg iron
• ground basil or tarragon contains 6 mg magnesium
• anise seed contains 9 mg phosphorus
• chile powder contains 50 mg potassium, 26 mg sodium, 1.67 mg ascorbic acid (vitamin C), .2 mg niacin and 908 International Units of vitamin A

Each of the above herbs contains other nutrients as well, and all the herbs not listed above are nutritious, too. But of the herbs that the U.S. government analyzed, these listings denote the highest rating available for each nutrient.

Anise

(Umbelliferae, *Pimpinella anisum*)

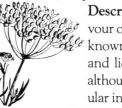

Description The licorice flavour of anise is now almost unknown beyond the candy store and liqueurs such as anisette, although aniseed cakes are popular in German cuisine. At one time, however, the herb was highly esteemed, and the early Romans considered it a cure for many ailments. Pliny the Elder claimed that, stuffed in a pillow, anise would help a sleeper avoid nightmares. The 16th-century herbalist, John Gerard, noted that the plant was "good against belchings and upbraidings of the stomacke. . . . Bechewed it maketh the breath sweet. . . . " Mrs. M. Grieve added in *A Modern Herbal* in 1931, "The taste is sweet and spicey, and the odour aromatic and agreeable."

The plant grows 1 to 2 feet tall, and somewhat resembles celery, producing its small greyish seed, the most favoured part of the plant, in late summer.

Culture An annual, anise is easy to grow but it does require about four months of warm, frost-free weather to produce seed. While the leaves of non-seed-producing plants can be used for teas and garnishes, Northerners who want seed have the best chance if they start their plants indoors in March or April, about four weeks before the last spring frost. Since the seedling forms a taproot and thus is difficult to transplant, seeds should be sown on peat pellets or in peat pots filled with potting mix. They will germinate in about a week at 68 degrees F

(20 degrees C). Set them outdoors 4 inches apart after the last spring frost date, choosing a sunny spot where the soil is well drained and free of weeds.

Harvest A few leaves may be picked from each plant from time to time and sprinkled on cooked vegetables or fruit salads or used as a soothing tea for colds. In August, each plant should produce up to half a dozen seed stalks, each bearing a small umbel of white flowers. As soon as a few seeds have ripened, cut the seed stalks and place them in a paper bag. In this way, the seeds will not be lost as they fall. The seeds are usually crushed before they are used in confectionary or baked goods. Some seeds may be saved for planting next spring.

Pests & Diseases None of note.

Balm

(Labiatae, *Melissa officinalis*)
Lemon balm, Melissa

Description A perennial in more southerly gardens, lemon balm, with its grey-green leaves, provides a delicious citrus-flavoured tea and can be used in many dishes, especially those including chicken and mushrooms. "The bees do delight in ye herb," wrote Dioscorides and, perhaps for the same reason, balm is well suited to use in potpourris. John Gerard noted in 1597 that balm "maketh the hart merrie and joiful and strengtheneth the vitall spirits." It grows 3 to 4 feet tall.

Culture It is often possible and, indeed, the best plan to buy plants from a nursery. Otherwise, in early spring, soak the seeds in warm water for 24 hours before sprinkling them on the surface of a container of finely textured potting mix. Keep it damp by covering the container with plastic or placing it in a shallow pan of warm water. The seed germinates in about a month. When the seedlings are 2 inches tall, transplant them into a sunny or partly shaded patch of well-drained soil at 1-foot intervals. In later years, the plants can be propagated by dividing the clumps. The plant may self-sow in the garden. Cut it back in late fall and mulch, or bring plants indoors wherever winters are severe. At the Devonian Botanic Garden in Edmonton,

the balm plants are overwintered in the greenhouse.

Harvest Do not harvest the first year after seeding. Thereafter, pinch off leaves and plant tips as they are needed. Cut off stems in fall and dry.

Pests & Diseases None of note.

Basil

(Labiatae, *Ocimum* sp.)

Description *Basileus* means "king" in Greek, an indication of this herb's standing in the culinary arts. A favourite accompaniment of tomatoes, this native of India and Asia has a pleasant, slightly sweet flavour that makes it suitable for use in all kinds of meat and vegetable dishes. Because it can be harvested as soon as six weeks after sowing in early summer (though it takes about three months to mature), basil can be grown in all northern gardens provided it is covered in case of untimely frost, to which it is very sensitive. There are several versions of the common sweet basil, O. *basilicum*; the one carried by most seed houses has large green leaves and grows about 18 inches tall. Opal basil has decorative purple foliage, while lettuce-leaf basil has larger foliage than normal. Bush basil is a low-growing, small-leafed version ideal for containers. In addition, other unusual types of basil can be purchased from seed houses specializing in herbs:

camphor basil, O. *kilimandscharicum*, is strong in flavour and odour, and is grown commercially for camphor. It grows about 5 feet tall

East Indian basil, O. *gratissimum*, has a stronger, more clove-like flavour and scent than common basil, and also grows about 5 feet tall

sacred basil, O. *sanctum*, also more clove-like than common basil, grows to about 20 inches

lemon basil, O. *americanum*, has a strong lemon fragrance that makes this form useful in teas, potpourris and fish dishes

Culture Although basil is perennial in southern Asia where it is native, it is grown as an annual in the North. Seeds may be sown indoors six weeks before the last spring frost date, or in the garden from the last frost date until mid-summer. Choose a sunny, sheltered spot where the soil is well drained. Seeds germinate in seven days at the preferred soil temperature of about 65 degrees F (18 degrees C). Thin plants gradually to stand 6 inches apart. Thinnings may be used sparingly in salads or as seasoning, or they may be transplanted into other garden areas. Mulching or regular watering will help produce tender leaves.

Harvest Leaves may be pinched off individually as needed until the plant flowers. To extend the harvest, pinch off flowers as they form. The harvest must be completed before the first frost and the entire plants cut and dried or the leaves frozen or preserved in pesto or vinegar.

Pests & Diseases None of note.

Bergamot

(Labiatae, *Monarda* sp.)

Beebalm, Oswego tea, Wild bergamot

Description Bergamot is one of the lesser-known herbs, mainly because it is a North American native and therefore was excluded from the old European herbals. But it is hardy and prolific, its showy bright red or pink flowers and green, mint-like leaves attractive at the back of the herb garden, where its 20- to 36-inch height will not shade other plants. Oswego tea, made from bergamot, became famous in Boston after the Tea Party and was used by the Indians for colds and stomach cramps. (Orange mint, also called bergamot, is used to flavour Earl Grey tea.) Chopped leaves may be used sparingly in salads, while flowers are an edible garnish. The scent of the perennial plant attracts bees and hummingbirds, and makes the leaves useful in potpourris.

Culture Although bergamot is usually propagated from root cuttings, the plants can be started from seed. Sow seeds in early spring in a sunny or lightly shaded spot with fairly moist soil. Thin or transplant seedlings to stand 18 inches apart. Plants should be divided about every three years.

Harvest Both leaves and flowers are used. Cut the leaves for drying when the flowers begin to form.

Pests & Diseases None of note.

Borage

(Boraginaceae, *Borago officinalis*)

Bee bread

Description "Borage for courage" advises an old saying, referring to a belief that the plant can induce euphoria – perhaps enough to induce a folly that would pass for bravery. Whether or not it encourages happiness, the foliage of borage has a cucumber flavour that suits salads, eggs and pickles. The young leaves can even be cooked as spinach, or used fresh to decorate summer drinks such as lemonade or punch. The older leaves are unpleasantly fuzzy. The dried flowers, which are bright blue, add colour to potpourris. An annual, borage grows 2 to 3 feet tall and has grey-green, velvety leaves. The plant attracts bees to such an extent it is nicknamed bee bread.

Culture Because borage is difficult to transplant, the seeds must be sown outdoors. About two weeks before the last frost date, sow seeds in a dry, sunny location or light shade. Thin seedlings to stand one foot apart. They mature in about 80 days, but can be sown every three weeks until mid-summer to prolong the harvest of young, tender leaves. If allowed to bloom, borage will often self-sow.

Harvest Pinch off young leaves as needed, and extend the harvest by pinching off flowers. Borage is only good fresh.

Pests & Diseases None of note.

Chervil

(Umbelliferae, *Anthriscus cerefolium*)

French parsley

Description Chervil is an annual with delicate, fern-like leaves that have a licorice flavour and are used in Béarnaise sauce, in salads, with chicken, veal and omelettes or as a garnish. The plant, which grows about 6 inches tall, will tolerate light frost.

Culture Because chervil is difficult to transplant, the seeds are best sown outdoors. Sow them in early spring on a shady patch of moist soil. Sprinkle the seeds on the soil and then press them down lightly, keeping the patch watered with a fine spray until the seeds sprout in about two weeks. When they are about 2 inches tall, thin seedlings to stand 6 inches apart. If allowed to flower, chervil may self-sow in the garden.

Harvest At first, cut only the outside leaves so that the centre will continue growing. Later the entire plant can be cut once or twice. Chervil leaves are far better fresh than dried, when they lose most of their flavour. They can, however, be frozen with quite good results. Seeds may be sown in a window-sill pot for a winter supply of fresh leaves.

Pests & Diseases None of note.

Chile Peppers

(Solanaceae, *Capsicum* sp.)

 **Description** All peppers, including the sweet peppers described on page 92, are sometimes called chiles to distinguish them from white or black pepper, the common seasoning. All are South American perennials that are usually grown as annuals in the North. But the northern palate is generally so unaccustomed to hot peppers that we have separated them, calling them chiles, into the herb section, since they are grown primarily for use as seasoning. These peppers vary greatly in the size of plant, the size and appearance of the fruit and its degree of hotness. Some of the more common chiles include:

cayenne – very thin, about 6 inches long, fiery hot, turning from dark green to red with maturity

tabasco – thin and about an inch long, hot, turning from light green to red with maturity

jalapeño – about 2 inches wide and 4 inches long, medium hot, turning from dark green to red with maturity

ancho – similar in size and shape to a bell pepper, mild to hot, turning from dark green to red to brown with maturity

Hungarian wax – a little longer than a jalapeño, medium to hot, and turn from yellow to red as they become mature

Ornamental peppers, whose seed is listed in the flower section of seed catalogues, produce very hot, tiny peppers on small plants that are ideally suited to window ledges or flower gardens. Allow a 6-inch pot of rich soil for each plant.

Culture See peppers; Chapter IV.

Harvest These peppers can be left on the plant until they are fully mature or, if the weather is inclement, they can be harvested at an immature stage. Their fruits must be protected from frost or picked before a frost, even if they are not ripe. Be careful in handling them. Some are so hot that the juice will cause painful, though not visible, burns. Fruits may be pickled, frozen, or dried whole or sliced. See the directions for drying food in Chapter IX. When thoroughly dry, store peppers whole or grind them for use as cayenne or chile pepper. Because few of these peppers are hybrid, their seeds can usually be saved for planting next year. See the instructions for saving pepper seed on page 126.

Pests & Diseases See peppers, Chapter IV.

Chives

(Liliaceae, *Allium* sp.)

 **Description** Hardy, spreading and very versatile in the kitchen, chives are an attractive addition to most northern herb gardens, where they will do well as long as they are adequately watered. A mild substitute for onions, chives are used fresh in salads, cooked in stir-fry dishes and with various meats and vegetables. Common garden chives, *Allium schoenoprasum*, grow into rounded clumps about 1 foot tall and bear rosy-lavender flowers. Garlic chives, *Allium tuberosum*, produce white flowers and flatter, paler green leaves with a mild garlic flavour. Garlic chives are somewhat taller and a little less winter hardy than common chives, but will overwinter in most marginal gardens if mulched.

Culture Chives are sufficiently popular and prolific that most gardeners should be able to obtain a few bulbs from a friend or a nursery. The plant can also be grown fairly easily from seed sown indoors or outdoors in the same way as onions. In early spring, but after heavy frosts are over, set

plants in groups of two or three at 1-foot intervals in a sunny or partially shaded location and fairly well-drained soil. Chives also do well in pots: A clump can be dug in fall and planted in potting mix to provide fresh chives indoors all winter, as long as the plant has adequate light and water.

Both the seed head and the foliage of dill, which is an annual herb, are esteemed for their unique flavour and fragrance

Harvest Because they can be picked all year and do not dry or freeze very successfully, chives are usually used fresh. Snip them off just above the base from the outside of the plant as needed. The flowers are also edible.

Pests & Diseases None of note.

Dill

(Umbelliferae, *Anethum graveolens*)

Description The umbrella-like heads of this blue-green herb are better known than are those of its relatives, carrot, parsley and parsnip. Dill is an annual that is usually planted in the vegetable garden where it is allowed to go to seed so that the seed heads can be used in pickling, potato salads, in eastern European dishes and in breads and dressings. The seed stalks grow 2 or 3 feet tall, but are not bushy enough to present a serious shading problem for neighbouring vegetables. Dill was said by John Parkinson in 1629 to have a therapeutic effect on the gastrointestinal system, "it being stronger than Fenel is of the more force to expel wind in the body. Some use to eat the seed to stay Hicock." Culpeper agreed a few years later that dill "stayeth the hic-

cough, being boiled in wine and but smelled unto."

Culture Dill does not transplant well, so seeds should be sown directly in the garden. If transplants are used, try not to disturb the roots. Around the last frost date, or early enough to allow the plants about 70 days to mature before frost, sow seeds in a sunny or partially shaded spot. Thin plants to stand 4 inches apart. Thinnings may be used fresh in salads or as seasoning. Dill often self-sows if the plant is allowed to drop some seed in the garden. Sown indoors in pots, dill is used for leaves but is not generally allowed to go to seed.

Harvest Dill leaves can be used as soon as they appear, or the heads can be cut as soon as they open but before the seeds fall. Leaves and seed heads may be dried, frozen or used in herb vinegar. After the seeds mature (turn brown), they can be stripped from the heads for use as seasoning.

Pests & Diseases None of note.

Horseradish

(Cruciferae, *Armoracia rusticana*)

Description One of the most persistent of perennials, horseradish has a tendency to take over the garden and is difficult to clear out of a spot once established. It is usually best relegated to a northern corner of the vegetable garden, where its 2-foot-tall, broad-leafed foliage will not shade or crowd other plants. Do not till the horseradish bed in spring because cut pieces of roots will grow into new plants. The root is usually grated and used as a seasoning or condiment, although horseradish was at one time considered a remedy for hoarseness, dropsy, rheumatism and palsy.

Culture Either buy roots from a nursery or obtain them from a neighbour. Horseradish cannot be grown from seed. Pieces of root about 3 inches long are placed 2 inches below the soil surface and 18 inches apart. They can be planted in early spring or in fall before the soil freezes. As with other root crops, the straightest, most fleshy horseradish roots grow in soil that has been deeply worked and is rich in organic matter, but horseradish is a hardy plant that will survive under almost any soil condition except standing water or a prolonged drought.

Harvest Roots are usually dug in fall after the first frost when they are at their largest, but they can be dug at any time as needed. Roots can be stored over the winter in a cool root cellar in the same way as beets or carrots. Peeled and grated, horseradish can be preserved in vinegar or lemon juice.

Pests & Diseases None of note.

Hyssop

(Labiatae, *Hyssopus officinalis*)

Description A hardy perennial native of southern Europe, hyssop is a very attractive plant that will overwinter in most northern gardens, especially under a mulch, but it is not likely to find a great deal of use in most kitchens. It is, in fact, as much a medicinal as a culinary herb. Nicholas Culpeper, who noted in the 17th century that "the plant is of a pretty strong aromatic smell," recommended that hyssop be applied externally for cuts and bruises. Mrs. M. Grieve listed hyssop tea sweetened with honey as a cure for rheumatism in *A Modern Herbal*. Bitter in flavour, hyssop is likely to be used only sparingly in salads and soups. But whether or not it is greatly used, the plant – which forms a bush about 18 inches high with small, evergreen leaves and blue, rose or white flowers – is a beautiful, easily grown addition to any herb garden, including a knot garden (see pages 132 and 133). It is a favourite with bees.

Culture Hyssop is easily grown from seed, which may be sown outdoors four weeks before the last spring frost date. Or they may be sown indoors a month before that. The seeds germinate in about 10 days, during which time they should be kept in darkness. Transplant or thin seedlings to stand 12 to 18 inches apart in any weed-free, well-drained spot. Hyssop tolerates sun or shade. The plant may later be propagated by dividing clumps. Also, the plant self-sows in most gardens, and new seedlings that appear in spring can be transplanted readily.

Harvest Before the plant flowers, pick leaves and branch tips to use in cooking.

Pests & Diseases None of note.

Lovage

(Umbelliferae, *Levisticum officinale*)

Description Lovage is not well known in North America, and yet it has a pleasant flavour reminiscent of two of its relatives, parsley and celery. In his *Complete Herbal*, Nicholas Culpeper wrote in the

Lovage has a flavour reminiscent of both parsley and celery, members of the same family, Umbelliferae, which it resembles

17th century that lovage tea "takes away the redness and dimness of the eyes if dropped into them; it removes spots and freckles from the face." Easy to grow in most areas, it is a hardy perennial that thrives in damp soil and partial shade, looks like overgrown, leafy celery, and grows very tall, up to 6 feet. The fresh leaves are used sparingly in salads or sandwiches; fresh or dried, they are used in soups, stews, breads and stuffings.

Culture As one plant will supply an ordinary family with all the lovage it needs, a single transplant is sufficient. Plants can also be started from seeds sown outdoors in moist soil in spring. Thin them gradually to stand 3 feet apart. Regular watering will ensure a constant supply of large, tender leaves. The plant may be propagated by dividing the clump as soon as shoots appear in spring.

Harvest Harvest branches and leaves as needed for fresh use. Seeds can be stripped from mature seed heads for use as seasoning. Leaves can be dried or frozen and young stems blanched and used as a cooked celery substitute. The root is also edible in soups and stews.

Pests & Diseases None of note.

Marjoram
(Labiatae, *Origanum* sp.)

Description Sweet marjoram (*Majorana hortensis* or *O. majorana*) is grown as an annual in the North. Bushy, with small, grey-green, rounded, velvety leaves, the plant grows about 10 inches tall, tolerates light frost and occasionally overwinters in milder areas. According to William Turner in 1551, marjoram leaves should be "layd unto the styngyng of a scorpyone with salt and vinegre." In 1629 John Parkinson added that the plant could be used in "sweete powders, sweete bags and sweete washing water." Now marjoram is used in soups and stews, and with lamb, carrots, mushrooms, veal and poultry. It is more highly esteemed for culinary use than is the closely related, more frost-hardy plant, oregano (see page 142).

Culture Buy transplants and set sweet marjoram outdoors a week after the last frost date. Or sow the fine seeds as described for balm. Germination may be poor and can take more than three weeks. Seeds should be kept in the shade until they sprout, after which they must be moved into sunlight. Transplant outdoors in a sunny spot with well-drained, sandy soil at 12-inch intervals. Sweet marjoram may be potted in fall and brought indoors to a sunny window sill for winter use, then replanted in the garden after the last spring frost.

Harvest Pinch off stems or leaves as needed and cut stalks as they begin to flower. The best flavour is in the green, knot-like buds that have given sweet marjoram the name "knotted marjoram." Leaves can be dried or frozen.

Pests & Diseases None of note.

Mint
(Labiatae, *Mentha* sp.)

Description Most mints are hardy perennials that spread by runners and tend to take over the garden if they are not pruned back every year. Native field mint (*M. arvensis*) grows 8 to 30 inches tall and looks much like its relative the stinging nettle, with hairy, toothed, pointed leaves and flowers growing in the leaf axils. It has less flavour and is less sweet than the cultivated mints, but was consumed as a tea and used as a condiment and medicine by many North American native tribes. Now, as well as a tea, it and the other mints are a fragrant addition to herbal baths, go well with fruit salads and summer drinks, and, of course, partner lamb dishes as mint jelly or sauce. Mint is the source of menthol, still used in cold remedies and as a flavouring agent.

Unlike most herbs, mint will tolerate shade, crowding and a great deal of moisture. There are many varieties. Some, such as peppermint, spearmint, watermint, woolly mint and curly mint, are upright and about 18 inches tall; some, such as orange mint, golden mint and silver apple mint, are bushy and about 6 inches tall; and one, Corsican mint, which is not hardy in the North, is creeping. The most common mints are:

peppermint or candymint, *Mentha piperita*, has purplish leaves and purple flowers that develop on a spike. It cannot be grown from seed

spearmint or garden mint, *Mentha spicata* or *viridis*, has a distinctive sweet flavour that makes it the most valued of mints in cooking. One variety, curly mint, has broad, crumpled leaves

apple mint, *Mentha suaveolens*, produces soft grey-green leaves with an apple fragrance. Pineapple mint, one variation, is a sprawling plant with variegated green and white leaves and a pineapple fragrance

orange or bergamot mint, *Mentha citrata*, has leaves with purplish margins and a slight orange fragrance and flavour

Culture Plants are best grown from purchased transplants, as seed is sometimes untrustworthy in its purity and variety, and tends to germinate poorly. Those gardeners who do purchase seed should follow the directions for balm. When seedlings are 2 inches tall, set them outdoors at 6-inch spacing. Because the plants spread quickly, only two to five plants are needed in most cases. Control the plants by digging up runners every spring – these can be used for propagation if desired – or by growing plants in large pots or drainage tiles submerged in the soil, the rim extending just above the soil surface.

Harvest Take leaves, branches and plant tips as needed. Mint can be dried or frozen, or preserved in vinegar or jelly.

Pests & Diseases Rust may appear on plants growing in overly rich soil. If it develops, dig up infected plants, burn or discard them and replant mint in a new location the following year.

Nasturtium

(Tropaeolaceae, *Tropaeolum* sp.)

Description This attractive Peruvian native with its showy blooms and saucer leaves needs little introduction to Northerners, but it is seldom appreciated as an edible plant. Indeed, its name is the same as the genus of watercress, *Nasturtium officinale*, whose leaves have a similar peppery flavour. There are both climbing and bush varieties of nasturtium. Climbers grow 10 to 12 feet tall on a trellis, while others grow about a foot tall.

Culture The large seeds are planted ½ inch deep about a week before the last spring frost date. They germinate and grow best at a soil temperature of 65 to 70 degrees F (18 to 21 degrees C). Gradually thin seedlings to stand 8 inches apart. The plants will bloom about two months after seeding, unless they have been sown in shade, where they will produce few blooms.

Harvest The young flower buds and the young green seeds can be pickled to use as a substitute for capers. They are simply washed, placed in sterilized jars, and covered with boiling cider vinegar and a sealer lid. Both the flowers and leaves are edible in sandwiches and salads and, of course, as garnishes.

Pests & Diseases None of note.

Oregano

(Labiatae, *Origanum* sp.)

Description This staple of Italian cuisine is closely related to marjoram and has a similar but stronger flavour. Oregano is good with pasta and pizza as well as lamb, guacamole and green beans. It was once esteemed as a gargle for sore throats, and John Gerard claimed in 1597 that it "healeth scabs, itchings and scurviness, being used in bathes." During the next century, Culpeper wrote that "it strengthens the stomach and head much; there is scarcely a better herb growing for relieving a sour stomach, loss of appetite, cough, congestion of the lungs." Greek or true oregano is a half-hardy perennial that must overwinter indoors in most of the North. Pot it before heavy frost in fall and set it beside a sunny window for winter use, replanting it outdoors after the last heavy frost in spring. Wild oregano, or common or pot marjoram (*Origanum vulgare*) is a hardy perennial, but its flavour is not as fine as that of true oregano. It produces a clump 2 feet tall and has broad oval leaves with blunted tips. The flowers range from pale pink to purple and attract bees.

Culture Oregano is best grown from transplants, although seed can be sown as for marjoram. Set plants at 1-foot intervals in light, well-drained soil in a sunny location. Growth is slow, and so the plants must be kept well weeded to prevent crowding. Replace plants every three or four years, starting new ones by layering stems (see page 133).

Harvest Pinch off fresh leaves as needed, and complete the harvest when plants start to flower. Pinching off the flowers as they develop will prolong the harvest.

Pests & Diseases None of note.

Parsley

(Umbelliferae, *Petroselinum* sp.)

Description A very hardy biennial, parsley will overwinter in most northern gardens and go to seed the following summer, often self-sowing year after year. Or it may be dug in its first winter and replanted, two plants to a deep, 12-inch pot for fresh greens all winter. Curled or moss curled parsley, the most usual type, is well known as a garnish. The plain-leafed varieties, French, Italian or Greek, with their small, celery-like leaves, have a more subtle flavour and are more winter hardy than moss curled. Hamburg or turnip-rooted parsley (*Carum petroselinum*) produces a slender, parsnip-like root that can be used in soups and stews and stored in a root cellar like beets or carrots. Parsley leaves can be used in almost every meal, in soup, stews, sandwich fillings, sauces, stuffings and, of course, as a garnish. Thomas Hyll wrote in 1568 that "chawinge of the fresh and grene Parceleye doth cause a swete smelling breath." The Greeks used the plant as a garden border.

Culture Sow seeds indoors eight weeks before the last frost, or outdoors as soon as the soil can be worked in spring. Soaking seed in warm water for 24 hours before sowing will speed germination, which usually takes about three weeks. During this time the bed must be kept moist and weeded. Plants also grow slowly, so must be kept well tended or they will be overshadowed. Thin plants gradually to stand 6 inches apart, using the thinnings as salad greens or seasoning. Plants will grow in full sun or, more slowly, in partial shade, and do best with a regular water supply. Mulching encourages good growth.

Harvest Pinch off leaves as needed. In late fall, pick most foliage for drying or freezing, or replant in pots as described above and bring plants indoors to a sunny window.

Pests & Diseases None of note.

Rosemary

(Labiatae, *Rosmarinus officinalis*)

Description This very attractive plant with its fine or broad evergreen leaves and woody stem has traditionally been associated with fidelity – "rosemary for remembrance." Peter Treveris' *Grete Herball* of 1526 recommended that those suffering from "weyknesse of ye brayne" inhale the smoke of rosemary that had been soaked in wine. Perhaps, his "brayne" strengthened, the patient would regain lost memories, thus fortifying the plant's reputation. Rosemary is perennial in its native southern Europe, where it may grow 6 feet or more in height, but in the North it is virtually always wintered indoors. In her book *Profitable Herb Growing at Home*, British Columbia gardener Betty

Jacobs noted that she found it hardy on southern Vancouver Island in "normal" winters but, when the temperature dipped to 0 degrees F (-18 degrees C) one "harsh" winter, her rosemary perished. Many Northerners keep the plants in pots, so that they can be easily moved indoors and outdoors.

Culture Rosemary germinates slowly and poorly, and then grows so slowly that none can be harvested for years. Instead, buy potted plants or take a cutting from the plant of a friend and root it in water before planting. Rosemary can also be easily tip-layered (see page 133). If the plant is potted, root the tip in another pot placed next to it. Once the tip has rooted, it can be cut from the parent plant. The plant can be set outdoors after the last spring frost in sandy, well-drained soil. It will tolerate full sun or partial shade, but must not be allowed to dry out for any length of time, a particular hazard for potted plants outdoors. Before bringing plants indoors, prune them lightly. Indoors, the plant does best in a bright, cool (45 degrees F, 7 degrees C) spot where the air is moist. Mist the plant occasionally, and do not let it dry out thoroughly. Harden the plant off (see page 55) before setting it outdoors again in spring.

Harvest Pinch off leaves sparingly as needed, for use with lamb and chicken, and in fruit salads, breads and medicinal teas. Leaves may also be dried for later use.

Pests & Diseases None of note.

Sage

(Labiatae, *Salvia officinalis*)

Description A Latin proverb of the Middle Ages posed the question, "Why should a man die while sage is in his garden?" The plant was reputed to cure everything from toothaches and coughs to wounds, failing memory and grey hair (which the juice was said to darken). "If it were possible," wrote one herbalist of Tudor times, "it would make man immortal."

Sage is also such an attractive plant, with its grey-green foliage and blue flowers, that it could easily fit into a flower garden. It grows about 18 inches tall and is a hardy perennial that will die back to the soil every winter in most gardens, resuming growth quite late the following spring. At the Devonian Botanic Garden in Edmonton it is not hardy and is grown as an annual.

Sage has a strong, distinctive flavour that complements poultry, sausages, peas, rabbit and fish, and is good in herb breads or mixed with cream cheese. Purple sage and tricolour sage, with its white, pink and deep red foliage, are termed half-hardy perennials, less hardy than the common variety but capable of overwintering in the garden in the mildest areas, especially if mulched. Golden sage and pineapple sage, with pineapple-scented leaves, are the most frost tender, and must be brought indoors for the winter and set back outdoors after the last spring frost.

Culture Since growth from seed is very slow and irregular, the use of transplants is recommended. Set plants about 1 foot apart in sandy soil in a sunny location.

Harvest Pinch off leaves and plant tips as needed, completing the harvest as the plant begins to flower. Dry the thick leaves slowly and thoroughly.

Pests & Diseases None of note.

Salad Burnet

(Rosaceae, *Sanguisorba minor*)

Description A perennial in most northern gardens, salad burnet has fern-like foliage that was at one time, according to herbalist John Gerard, "thought to make the hart merry and glad." In his herbal of 1551, John Turner described the evergreen plant as having "two little leaves like onto the wings of birds, standing out as the bird setteth her wings out as she intendeth to flye." Those "little leaves" have a slight cucumber flavour and fragrance. The plant grows 1 to 2 feet tall, producing crimson flowers in summer.

Culture The seed may be sown ½ inch deep outdoors in fall or early spring. Salad burnet will grow in any well-drained soil and does best in full sun, although it will also grow in shade. Transplants may be set outdoors at 12-inch intervals in early

spring. Later, the plant can be propagated by dividing the entire clump, although it is just as easily left to self-sow in the garden.

Harvest Pinch off the top leaves throughout the season, using only young leaves in salads and casseroles. Removal of the flower stalks will prolong the harvest, which should be discontinued once the flowers have bloomed. Allow the plant to go to seed if you intend it to self-sow. Leaves may be dried for later use, although some flavour will be lost.

Pests & Diseases None of note.

Savory

(Labiatae, *Satureia* sp.)

Description Winter savory (*S. montana*) is a low-growing, 8-inch hardy perennial with small, stiff, almost evergreen leaves. Its flavour is stronger and not as highly esteemed as that of summer savory, but it is used in much the same way. Summer savory (*S. hortensis*) is an erect, branching annual that grows about 1 to 1½ feet tall and, with its pink flowers and grey-green leaves, is attractive enough for use in borders and flower gardens. The mild-flavoured leaves are used in soups, sauces and egg and poultry dishes, as well as in bean dishes. Savory is sometimes called the bean herb – its German name is just that, *Bohnenkraut* – because it is such a good complement for cooked beans and bean salads, peas and lentils.

Culture Winter savory may be grown from seed, although transplants shortcut the growing process. To grow it from seed, follow the instructions for balm. Set plants outdoors after the last spring frost date, 1 foot apart, in well-drained soil and full sun. Summer savory does not transplant well and is much easier to grow from seed, which can be sown outdoors around the last frost date. Sow seeds 1 inch apart and do not thin. A clump of winter savory can be dug up and potted for indoor use during the winter.

Harvest Strip off leaves as needed, until flowers start to open in mid-summer, and then cut stalks for drying or freezing.

Pests & Diseases None of note.

Tarragon
(Compositae, *Artemisia dracunculus*)
Estragon

Description Said to soothe a toothache, tarragon was also once thought to be so repellent to snakes that, according to Pliny, someone who carried a sprig of it was safe from snake bites. No doubt it earned this reputation from the appearance of its snake-like roots. Its Latin species name, which means "little dragon," also reflects this supposed association with snakes. True or French tarragon is a hardy perennial with a strong anise flavour that is entirely lacking in Russian tarragon, *Artemisia dracunculoides*, which is scarcely worth growing as a culinary herb. French tarragon grows about 2 feet tall and has long, thin leaves that are much esteemed in *cordon bleu* cuisine, especially with fish, shellfish and spinach. It is also a very attractive plant, with dark green leaves and tiny white flowers.

Culture French tarragon can be grown only from transplants or root divisions. The seed sold is for the less satisfactory Russian tarragon. French tarragon will tolerate either sun or partial shade but requires well-drained soil – dampness will cause winterkilling. Cut back before the soil freezes and mulch plants heavily, removing the mulch in spring. Divide plants every third spring.

Harvest Leaves may be stripped from stems as needed, but are best before the plant blooms in mid-summer. Afterward, leave the plant to gain strength for winter. Leaves may be dried or frozen, although they are much better fresh. Tarragon makes a very good herb vinegar.

Pests & Diseases None of note.

Thyme
(Labiatae, *Thymus* sp.)

Description Semi-prostrate, bushy or creeping in habit, thyme in many varieties forms a fragrant, usually perennial mat in many northern border plantings, herb and rock gardens. A highly respected medicinal herb, it was believed to cure snake bites, skin disorders and toothaches, although it is better known today as a seasoning for soups, stews, vegetables and meats. Legend has it that Hercules became strong through his liberal use of thyme. There are almost 100 varieties of the plant, some of which, like wild thyme, *Thymus serpyllum*, are decorative, fragrant ground covers not commonly used in cooking. Unusual varieties can be purchased from seed companies specializing in herbs. The most popular types include:

common or garden thyme, *Thymus vulgaris*, comes in two types: English, German or winter thyme, which is up to 12 inches tall; and French or summer thyme, which is up to 18 inches tall and less hardy than English thyme

caraway thyme, *Thymus herba-barona*, has a distinctive caraway flavour and aroma. It is low-growing, forming a mat of small, dark green leaves and deep pink flowers. The name comes from the use of this herb as a seasoning for baron of beef in the Middle Ages

lemon thyme, *Thymus vulgaris citriodorus* or *T. lemoneum*, has a lemony flavour and grows about 12 inches tall. A yellow variegated leaf form is available, as is silver thyme, with grey-green leaves. These are less hardy than English or caraway thyme

Culture Thyme is most easily grown from transplants or from established plants propagated by the tip-layering method (see page 133). Gardeners who wish to grow thyme from seed should follow the directions given for balm. Around the last spring frost date, set plants outdoors 6 inches apart in a sunny spot with well-drained soil and little competition from other plants. In cold areas, mulch plants and, if there is a possibility of winterkill, overwinter some of the plants indoors.

Harvest Pinch off branches and strip leaves as needed. Flowers may also be harvested for use. All may be dried or frozen. As thyme can often be picked all winter, remaining evergreen under the snow, a fresh supply may be available where the snow cover is adequate or winters are mild. Always leave enough foliage on the plant in fall and winter to ensure that it is not weakened.

Pests & Diseases None of note.

Of Balconies, Bins & Boxes

"Young, middle-aged and elderly people were. . . so enthusiastic, in fact, that extra courses had to be given and a waiting list made for those wanting garden boxes"
— Susan Alward, Ron Alward & Witold Rybczynski
Rooftop Wastelands, 1976

I t has been said that city gardeners save no money at all by growing their own vegetables in containers. It has, in fact, been said by an authority on the matter, Witold Rybczynski, one of the leaders of McGill University's landmark roof gardening project in which a downtown Montreal roof became the site of compost bins, a solar greenhouse, and scores of wooden boxes filled with dirt and growing food plants.

While optimists among us nevertheless maintain that economic gains can be made by canny container gardeners, it is true that money is seldom their foremost preoccupation. Living on the newest horticultural frontier, today's high-rise gardener is an adventurer, an explorer seldom matched in dedication by his ground-floor counterparts who, whatever their location or soil conditions, have a much easier lot than that of the balcony gardener. He is so busy carrying bags of soil up the elevator, watering his charges and trying to fulfill their every need that he really hasn't the time to think about saving money.

Although container gardeners grow many of the same vegetables as anybody else, they do so with certain handicaps. One is the necessarily limited

amount of soil they can provide for each plant. The most frequent fault of container gardeners is their provision of too little root space for their plants, which can scarcely be given too much. Naturally, a compromise must be reached – space is limited, and very large containers are remarkably unwieldy – but it must not entail too great a sacrifice of soil or the plant will quickly become root bound; it will wilt, starve and generally produce little harvest.

Container gardeners must pay a great deal of attention not only to the quantity of soil, but also to its fertility and moisture content. While conventional gardeners sometimes rely entirely upon rainfall, watering is often a daily preoccupation for the owner of outdoor container plants whose soil should be moist just about all the time. Baked by the sun that reflects off building walls and desiccated by wind, boxed soil – what there is of it – dries out with discouraging speed.

Container gardening, then, should not be undertaken if you expect the plants to take care of themselves while you fly off to Florida for a week. If that's your style, a few small pots of herbs in a sunny window will probably suit you best. Double potting or mulching can, however, afford some short-term watering relief. In the first system, the container holding the plant is placed inside a larger, watertight one with a layer of several inches of charcoal or vermiculite at the bottom. Water is poured in to the depth of this layer, and the pot containing the plant is placed inside. Similarly, several smaller pots can be placed inside a large tray. A mulch of grass clippings — get them from the building superintendent, but refuse all that have been treated with weedkiller — will slow evaporation from the soil surface.

Soil-drying balcony winds also present problems to the plants themselves: Tender leaves wilt even before the soil has dried out and small containers sometimes topple over. It may be necessary to erect a cloth or wooden barrier on the windward side of some balconies.

Of course, all container-bound vegetables do not grow on balconies, rooftops, or indeed, even in cities. Containers can be useful and decorative on suburban patios or country porches or indoors, as long as adequate light is provided (see pages 50 and 51). In any situation, containers do have one major advantage: portability. In short-season areas, boxed peppers, tomatoes, or eggplants can be kept indoors under lights during cold weather and moved outdoors on sunny, warm days. Potted herbs may spend summers outdoors and winters on a sunny window sill.

Choosing Containers

Whatever the situation, suitable plant containers must meet three conditions: They must be big enough for the plant in question, they must allow water to drain from the bottom and they must hold soil securely for at least one season. Within these criteria, the range of possibilities is almost endless — packing crates, ice-cream pails, garbage bags or pails, wastepaper baskets. Big flower pots, cedar tubs or half-barrels have decorative advantages that may or may not be deemed worth their price. Perforate the bottom of any container that would otherwise be watertight.

In their Montreal rooftop experiment, the researchers at McGill used wooden packing crates that measured about 2 feet by 3 feet by 2 feet deep. One box, they found, would comfortably accommodate either one summer squash or broccoli plant, or two tomatoes or eggplants, or three miniature cabbages, or three rows of peas or two rows of beans. Or they could broadcast lettuce or carrot seed on the soil surface of a single box, later thinning plants to leave 2 to 6 inches between each.

The chart beginning on page 150, "The Best Vegetables and Herbs for Container Growing," lists minimum container size for each of the most space-efficient plants. Inefficient and impractical plants such as corn, potatoes and winter squash have been excluded. Although heading members of the cabbage family — cabbage, broccoli, cauliflower and Brussels sprouts — can be grown in containers, the return per square foot is so low that precious space is better spent on cut-and-come-again leafy greens, herbs or fruiting plants such as beans, peas, tomatoes, peppers and summer squash.

Soil Mixes and Fertility

A lightweight, well-drained growing mix is required for all container growing, indoor or outdoor, house plants or vegetables — a mixture that will not become overly compact as garden soil will when it is used on its own in such situations. In addition, the soil mix must be lightweight to avoid overloading a balcony or rooftop. Balconies are usually built to support about 50 pounds per square foot. A cubic foot of soil weighs about 25 pounds. On rooftops, situate all large containers near the edge or directly over structural supports. On balconies, keep the largest containers next to the building wall.

Any of the soil mixtures noted on page 53 should be adequate. The McGill researchers reported success with a heavier mix of seven-eighths good topsoil and one-eighth vermiculite, perlite and peat moss. Topsoil sterilization is not required. The McGill gardeners placed a 1-inch layer of half-and-

The same soil can be used for several seasons, although before spring planting about one-quarter of the old soil should be removed from the container and replaced with the same quantity of compost or with half-and-half topsoil and composted manure. After it has dried over the winter, the potted soil

Almost anything new or recycled can be a suitable vegetable or herb container, provided that it drains water from the bot-

tom, is reasonably sturdy, holds enough soil to support the plant or plants in question, and fits in the space available

half peat moss and vermiculite on the bottom of their large containers, to aid drainage and prevent soil leakage.

Because their roots are necessarily more restricted than they would be in a garden, and because earthworms and decaying plant matter seldom augment container soil fertility, potted plants must be fertilized more frequently than garden plants. Leaf crops — spinach, chard, lettuce, kale and such — should be watered every two weeks with manure tea or commercial fish emulsion diluted according to the manufacturer's directions. This fertilizer, available under several brand names, is sold in most garden shops. Fruiting crops should receive such waterings every three weeks from the time the first fruit is set. Except for basil and parsley, which are treated as leafy greens, fertilize herbs once a month.

On their rooftop, the Montreal researchers installed a compost bin into which leaves, plant material and household garbage were piled. They noted that the compost was "the ideal fertilizer" and used it whenever possible. But few container gardeners will have sufficient space for such a feature, no matter how desirable.

may need to have water worked into it before it is ready for use again.

Seasonal Routines

Very often, the plants for containers, any of those marked "T" on the table on the following pages, will be purchased as transplants from a nursery. While this will limit the gardener's variety options, it is often the most practical choice. Container gardeners usually want only a few plants, perhaps just one, and they seldom have the time or facilities to produce the best home-grown transplants.

As soon as the transplants are brought home, the hardening-off process can begin (see page 55). While they are still in their temporary flats or pots, begin leaving the plants in their outdoor growing spot for increasing lengths of time each day (provided the weather is amenable), starting with just an hour the first day. In about a week the plants can be left out all day and all night — but, of course, do not leave frost-tender plants outdoors on frosty nights.

As soon as the weather is suitable for the plants to take up permanent positions outdoors, fill the larger containers with soil mix and, in the position each transplant will occupy, dig a depression as

The Best Vegetables and Herbs for Container Growing

Plant	Balcony requirements	Seeds or transplants	Survives light frost	Minimum container size	Days from planting to maturity	Recommended varieties
Basil	some shade	S or T	No	6" dia., 6" deep for 1 plant	30-85	Any
Bay	some shade	T	Yes	6" dia., 6" deep for 1 plant	30-60	N/A
Beans, snap	some sun	S	No	8" dia., 8" deep for 3 plants	40-90	Choose early-maturing varieties, either yellow or green
Beets	some shade	S	Yes	Thin to 3" apart in soil 6"-12" deep, depending on variety	45-65	Choose variety to suit size of container, regular beets in 6" of soil
Carrots	some shade	S	Yes	Thin to 2" apart in soil 8"-12" deep, depending on variety	65-75	Choose variety to suit size of container
Cress	some shade	S	Yes	Any	10-20	Any
Cucumbers	some sun	S	No	8" dia., 12" deep for 1 plant	55-70	Choose early-maturing varieties
Dill	some sun	S	Yes	6" dia., 12" deep for 2 plants	30-70	N/A
Eggplant	full sun	T	No	12" dia., 12" deep for 1 plant	65-80	Choose the earliest available variety
Garlic	some shade	Cloves	Yes	6" dia., 6" deep for 1 plant	100-120	Any
Kale	some shade	S or T	Yes	8" dia., 8" deep for 1 plant	60-70	Any
Lettuce	some shade	S or T	Yes	8" dia., 8" deep for 2 looseleaf or 1 head	40-80	Looseleaf easier and more space-efficient than heads. Choose slow-bolting varieties
Marjoram & Oregano	some sun	T	See pages 141, 142	6" dia., 6" deep for 1 plant	30-75	Any

Comments

Can be seeded sparingly in pots with other plants

Bay forms an attractive bush. It will tolerate light frost and can be grown outdoors in zone 9, but otherwise must be overwintered indoors

Bush beans are compact. Pole beans mature later but are more prolific and must be staked or trellised

Beets do best in cool weather with adequate water, loose, sandy soil. Greens are edible, best picked when young

Carrots do best in cool weather with adequate water, loose, sandy soil. May be interplanted with lettuce

See cress in Chapter IV

Bush varieties are compact, and produce less; others will climb a stake or trellis. Hand pollinate all except the seedless varieties

Can be seeded in large pots containing other plants

Not very space-efficient in terms of productivity, but an attractive plant

Plant cloves in very early spring and set outdoors. Harvest when plant top dies. May be interplanted with other vegetables

Will survive until the soil freezes in fall

Will bolt to seed in hot weather. Does best in cool weather in rich soil with plenty of water

Prefer well-drained soil kept fairly dry. Bring indoors in fall

deep as the transplant root ball or, in the case of tomatoes, as deep as the first true leaves. Water both the transplant and the new soil thoroughly. Then, carefully tap out single plants by holding them upside down, two fingers straddling the plant stem and held against the soil surface to support the

Given full sunlight, bush-type cherry tomatoes are ideal container plants and are also very attractive in hanging baskets

plant when it comes out of its pot. If there are several plants in one flat, cut between them with a knife to the bottom of the flat and pry out each one. In every case, keep as much of the root ball intact as possible. Set each transplant into the depression in the soil of the container, fill around it with soil, press down firmly on the surface around the plant stem and water again. Because transplanting is a shock to the plant, it should be kept watered and protected from severe winds and full, day-long sun for the first few days.

Seeds that are sown directly in pots must be kept moist until they sprout. Covering containers with glass or plastic will help retain soil moisture, although in very sunny conditions covers could raise soil temperatures too much. In all but the coldest areas, remove the covering as soon as the sprouts begin to appear through the soil.

Planting dates for container vegetables are similar to those of their less-restricted relatives, but the microclimate of a balcony or rooftop is likely to be so singular that some experimentation will have to be done. Richmond W. Longley noted in the *Canadian Journal of Plant Science*, for instance, that the

The Best Vegetables and Herbs for Container Growing (Continued)

Plant	Balcony requirements	Seeds or transplants	Survives light frost	Minimum container size	Days from planting to maturity	Recommended varieties
New Zealand spinach	some sun	S	No	10" dia., 8" deep for 1 to 3 plants	30-60	N/A
Onions, Chives & Scallions	some shade	S or T	Yes	6" deep, any dia.	20-75	Any
Parsley	some shade	S or T	Yes	12" dia., 12" deep for 2 plants	30-75	Any
Peas	some shade	S	Yes	12" dia., 12" deep for 6 plants	55-70	Edible-podded or snap peas make most efficient use of space
Peppers	full sun	T	No	12" dia., 12" deep for 1 plant	60-80	Choose early-maturing varieties
Radishes	some shade	S	Yes	Thin to 2" apart in soil 6"-12" deep depending on variety	20-50	Choose variety to suit container
Rosemary	some sun	T	Yes	4" dia., 4" deep for 1 plant	30-60	N/A
Sage	some sun	T	Yes	6" dia., 6" deep for 1 plant	30-75	N/A
Spinach	some shade	S or T	Yes	Plants 6" apart in 6" deep soil	40-50	Choose slow-bolting varieties such as Melody
Squash, summer	some sun	S	No	24" dia., 24" deep for 1 plant	50-60	Any
Summer savory	some sun	S or T	No	6" dia., 6" deep for 1 plant	30-60	N/A
Swiss chard	some shade	S or T	Yes	8" dia., 8" deep for 1 plant	30-60	Any
Tomatoes	some sun	T	No	6" dia., 6" deep for cherries; 12" dia., 12" deep for others	55-90	Bush or determinate plants are compact, early maturing. Indeterminate plants must be staked and pruned. In either case, cherry tomatoes are among the best for containers

Comments

Its trailing habit makes it best in hanging pots

Can be interplanted with other vegetables. In fall, bring pots indoors

A biennial, parsley will survive one winter indoors or outdoors before going to seed

Peas do best in cool weather with plenty of water. Insert stakes in pots when seeding or place pots by a railing or trellis

Stake plants in windy areas. Bring pots indoors in fall to overwinter or start new plants every spring

Can be interplanted with other vegetables. Resow as long as weather is cool. Keep watered

Will tolerate hot sun. Before heavy frost, move to a sunny window indoors for the winter. Perennial. Fertilize every spring

In some areas, sage may be left outdoors all year. Otherwise, bring indoors after the first heavy frost. The plant is perennial. Fertilize every spring

Will bolt in hot weather. Does best in cool, fertile soil with plenty of water

Bush varieties are compact, others will climb a trellis if trained, and are more productive. Constant picking of fruit prolongs harvest. Hand pollinate

Can be seeded sparingly in pots with other plants

Does best in cool, fertile soil with plenty of water

Insert stake in pot at planting time, or place pot by a railing to which stems can be tied as they grow

Edmonton growing season is longer than that of the surrounding countryside: "Heat from large cities tends to keep temperatures in the vicinity a few degrees higher than over the surrounding area, particularly on cool nights. This effect has caused late spring and early fall frosts to be less common at

Each leaf lettuce seedling should be allowed 4 inches of surface area when it is transplanted into its permanent container

the airport than in the country." The Montreal researchers found that their rooftop tended to be about 9 degrees F (5 degrees C) hotter than surrounding land, a boon in spring and fall, but perhaps too much of a good thing in summer.

Direct sun, too, is likely to be either very restricted or excessive. While a north-facing balcony will not mature fruiting plants, one that faces south may require a screen on one side to provide the plants with a little shade. Roofs and patios offer gardeners more options.

As we have noted, the container gardener works with some of the most challenging of limitations. But, as the Montreal team found, there are more rewards involved than those provided by growing most house plants. The researchers, whose work has since been published in Agriculture Canada's booklet "Container Gardening" (publication 1653 — see Sources for ordering information), noted that rooftop plantings could enhance the quality of urban living, improving the urbanite's surroundings aesthetically while giving him control over something directly affecting his life, "namely food production, albeit on a very limited scale."

Harvest Days, Frosty Nights

"That harvest was the happiest we have ever spent in the bush. We had enough of the common necessaries of life"

– Susanna Moodie
Roughing It In The Bush, 1852

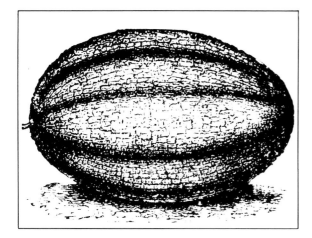

Fall is the time of reckoning. It is the time of recognition, too, of your successes and short-comings, of the quirks of climate in your own unique little patch of land. But it is also an extreme-ly busy time, all the more so if the garden has been a success. Almost everything must be harvested and much of that must be preserved. Tender plants have to be protected from frost and, at the end of it, the garden must be cleaned up, ready to await a new season under snow.

For Northerners, what most defines fall and, in fact, literally defines the growing season is the ex-pectation of that first frost. Frosty nights may, of course, have happened earlier in the summer, an untimely cold spell that the gardener may or may not have anticipated. But by late summer the ap-proach of killing frost is as inevitable as the fall of leaves from the trees.

Frost Hardiness

As we have already seen, different plants vary in their capacity to withstand cold weather. Some seeds were put into the garden as soon as the soil had thawed, while some transplants had to be kept indoors until all danger of frost had passed. Even then, they grew better under cover for the first few

weeks after they moved outdoors. Similarly, differ-ent plants stop growing and die at different times as the temperature drops in autumn.

There is nothing like that first fall frost to quickly and graphically demonstrate which crops are hardy and which are not. Most damage will be done to exposed tender plants. Although the first frost may not kill them, all the foliage that was frozen will appear limp and lifeless as soon as the temperature rises above freezing. Tender fruit that has been touched by frost will be discoloured and will soon rot, outdoors or in storage. The second light frost usually completes the job, killing the plants. Tender plants include tomatoes, peppers, eggplant, squash, melons, cucumbers, okra, and snap, lima and soybeans.

Indeed, even prolonged temperatures just above freezing will kill most tender plants. As fall ap-proaches and the temperature drops, their growth slows, then stops. Corn and beans cease growing as soon as the soil temperature drops below 50 degrees F (10 degrees C); tomatoes and squash stop grow-ing at 55 degrees F (13 degrees C).

But even as the foliage of the tender plants hangs like black rags after a few light frosts, many other

Although pumpkins are frost tender, their large leaves will usually protect the fruit from the first light frost in the fall

garden plants continue to be green, upright and very much alive. Of these, the next to die (or, at least, to lose their foliage) as the frosts become increasingly severe include lettuce, beets, sweet corn, cauliflower, celery, radishes, potatoes and asparagus. Peas and broad beans withstand lower temperatures than their pods, which freeze when the temperature dips to 30 degrees F (-1 degree C). Potato tuber growth will cease at about 41 degrees F (5 degrees C) and the foliage will die at 30 degrees F (-1 degree C), but underground tubers will remain unharmed, unharvested ones sometimes overwintering to sprout next spring. While asparagus shoots will be harmed by frost, the plant itself is a hardy perennial that will survive most northern winters.

The last plants to remain conspicuously alive in the garden are cabbage, Brussels sprouts, collards, carrots, corn salad, spinach, turnips, Swiss chard, salsify, parsley, rutabagas, parsnips, kale, leeks and onions — whose greens are very hardy though the bulbs will not keep well if touched by frost.

This does not mean that these hardy plants continue to grow at their summer pace during frosty weather. Some are noticeably weakened with each frost. Spinach ceases growing at 36 degrees F (2.2 degrees C), lettuce at 40 degrees F (4.4 degrees C). The planting dates of even the hardiest crops such as kale or Brussels sprouts are calculated so that the plants will mature by the first frost date, even though they may survive weeks longer. Little growth will take place after the first severe frost, 25 degrees F (-4 degrees C). With the hardy plants, the plus for gardeners is a prolonged harvest of fresh vegetables.

Why some plants withstand frost and others do not is not yet fully understood, but the process of natural selection ensures that those plants native to cooler climates will be hardier than those that come from the tropics. However, knowing that his tomato plants are fully hardy in a South American winter is little comfort to a Yukon gardener who has just lost the entire crop in mid-August. What could have been done?

Frost Damage Prevention

The proverbial ounce of prevention is a good starting point. As outlined in Chapters I and III, the northern gardener must plan his garden to take

Tender plants such as tomatoes are most easily protected from frost in the spring, when they are at their smallest

best advantage of what sun is available, avoiding lingering shade, frost hollows, severe winds and northern exposures. The tenderest or slowest-maturing plants go into the most favoured spots. Because warm air rises, any hills or raised beds are likely to afford a little frost protection to plants.

Careful attention to the best planting dates also makes sense where every warm day is valuable. Some plants, as we have seen, need a considerable head start indoors in order to mature before fall frost. And not only are some plants, such as the cabbage relatives, more frost hardy when they are young than when they are old, but also small plants are far easier to protect than the big ones. Where a hot cap or cloche might suffice for frost protection in spring, bulky tarps, bed sheets and yards of plastic may be required in fall.

And, of course, the selection of fast-maturing cultivars helps avoid frost kills. Some tomatoes are ready to harvest by the middle of July, while others may not have a single ripe fruit until September. Almost all vegetables are likewise available in both fast- and slow-maturing selections. Seed catalogues that list days to maturity are a great help to anyone

seeking the fastest-maturing selections. Do not fertilize plants after mid-summer, as this encourages tender growth that is less frost hardy.

But if the day has been cool, the sky is clear and the weatherman warns of frost "in low-lying areas," the gardener has a number of options. Many tender vegetables can be picked right away: tiny summer squash for delectable dining, small cucumbers for pickling. Tomatoes that have begun to turn colour, appearing white or pinkish, will probably ripen if they are brought indoors, spread out, not touching, on paper, and left in a dry room at a temperature of 55 to 70 degrees F (12 to 21 degrees C). Wrapping each fruit in paper enhances ripening by reducing air circulation around the tomatoes. Light is neither essential nor harmful in the ripening process. Muskmelons that are full-sized but not yet ripe will ripen in the same way. Immature peppers can be eaten, as can young peas and beans.

Sometimes part or all of the plant can be brought indoors. Cuttings of tomato plants – snap off the suckers growing in stem joints – will easily root indoors in water or soil. These are unlikely to produce fruit indoors, but they can be hardened off in late spring and planted outdoors in the manner of other tomato transplants. If they become too large, continue to start new suckers, discarding the larger plant. As soon as the suckers have rooted, they should be planted in soil mix and kept watered and fertilized throughout the winter.

Dig up a few pepper plants and, keeping the root ball as intact as possible, put each one in a 12-inch pot and bring it indoors, drench the plant and soil with diluted insecticidal soap to control aphids and whiteflies, and place the plants in a sunny window. Kept watered throughout the winter, the plants will probably not set fruit, but should provide very early peppers when they are planted outdoors the next spring after all danger of frost has passed. Several herbs, too, can be potted in fall for indoor use in winter, as described in Chapters VII and VIII.

The next strategy, particularly recommended if the weather is expected to improve soon, providing a few warm weeks of Indian summer, involves covering the plants. This prevents damage caused by dew settling on either the leaves or the fruit and freezing. While it will not protect tender plants from really low temperatures, any sort of covering – blankets, bed sheets, garbage bags, sheets of plastic or newspaper laid over plants in the early evening and secured so they won't blow off – will keep the plants alive through frosts that are just a

Potato foliage that has not already died will be killed by frost, but the underground tubers may survive through the winter

degree or two below freezing. Some gardeners choose to make special large, plastic-covered wooden frames just for this purpose. Low-growing plants can be lightly covered with mulch. If the plants are already growing under cover they are out of danger from light frost, but adding another layer of covering will help protect them from lower temperatures. Opaque coverings should be removed as soon as the temperature rises above freezing in the morning.

The fruit of summer squash, winter squash and pumpkins, hidden under huge leaves, is virtually self-protected from the first frost. But thereafter the

Preferred Vegetable Storage Methods

Artichokes, globe	Use fresh only
Artichokes, Jerusalem	Mulch and dig from garden as needed. Store a short time in polyethylene bags in refrigerator or cold room
Asparagus	Freeze or pressure can
Beans, shelled	Dry on the plant or indoors
Beans, snap or fresh shelled	Freeze or pressure can
Beets	Store in root cellar or refrigerator or dice and freeze. Greens may be frozen or dried
Broccoli	Freeze
Brussels sprouts	Freeze
Cabbage	Slice and freeze or make sauerkraut. Undamaged heads store several weeks in a root cellar
Carrots	Mulch and dig from garden as needed, or store in root cellar or refrigerator, or slice and freeze or dry

foliage will be dead, leaving the fruit exposed, and so it must be picked before the next frost if it is to be stored successfully.

Sprinkling crops helps protect them from even lower temperatures but, because of the labour, the difficulties and the quantity of water involved, the method is usually practised only by commercial growers with large fields and investments to protect. A garden sprinkler can, however, be useful in small areas. In this case, plants are sprinkled with water from the time the temperature drops to freezing until it rises above freezing again, usually from night until late morning. The method works because water releases heat as it freezes, although increasing amounts of water are needed as the temperature falls. In experiments in the Yukon Territory in the 1960s, Agriculture Canada scientist Gerard H. Gubbels found that "potato foliage and

Cauliflower	Freeze
Celery	Chop and freeze or dry, or replant in pots in root cellar
Corn	Freeze, pressure can or dry
Cucumbers	Pickle, relish
Eggplant	Use fresh only
Kale, Kohlrabi	Freeze
Lettuce & other sweet leafy greens	Use fresh only
Mushrooms	Slice and freeze or dry
Muskmelon	Chop and freeze in sugar syrup
Onions, Garlic, Shallots	Store in a dry, cool room or slice thinly and then dry
Okra	Freeze
Parsnips	Mulch and dig from garden as needed, or store in root cellar or refrigerator, or slice and freeze or dry

Peas, with or without pods	Freeze or pressure can
Peppers	Freeze or slice thinly and dry. Small peppers may be dried whole
Potatoes	Store in a cool, dark room
Radishes	Use fresh only
Rutabagas	Store in root cellar or slice and dry
Spinach & other dark leafy greens	Freeze, pressure can or dry
Squash, summer	Best fresh
Squash, winter	Store in a cool, dry room, or cook pulp and freeze
Tomatoes	Prepare by blanching (boiling for about a minute before plunging into ice water); then peel and core. In a hot water bath, can them whole, as sauce or ketchup. Or freeze whole tomatoes or sauce
Turnips	Freeze greens; store roots in root cellar
Watermelon	Chop and freeze in sugar syrup

peas were not injured seriously when maintained above 30 degrees F (-1.1 degree C). To maintain plant temperatures above 30 degrees F required .9 mm per hour of water when the air was down to 27 degrees F (-2.8 degrees C), 1.2 mm per hour down to 26 degrees F (-3.3 degrees C), 1.6 mm per hour down to 24 degrees F (-4.4 degrees C), 2.2 mm per hour down to 22 degrees F (-5.5 degrees C) and 2.9 mm per hour down to 19 degrees F (-7.2 degrees C)."

Space heaters or smoky bonfires spaced throughout the garden also help keep temperatures above freezing on frosty nights, but are so labour-intensive and fuel-consumptive that they are not recommended for most home gardens. A heated greenhouse is an obvious exception. In the 1960s, experiments were done in Canada to test a protein-based foam for plant protection. Although the foam protected tomatoes to 20 degrees F (-6.6 degrees C), it had to be washed off in the morning and was not considered practical enough to be adopted by commercial growers.

The Garden Cleanup

While harvesting will have been going on in a small way all season, as fall approaches the most tender plants, quite naturally, must be harvested first. Attention is then paid to those that are a little hardier, and lastly to those that are the most frost hardy. Roots or tubers can generally be left until just before the soil freezes, even though plant foliage may be quite dead. By the time the gardener gets around to digging the potatoes, only a dead stem is likely to mark the position of each hill of tubers. Onions are the opposite, with frost-hardy tops growing above bulbs that should be harvested before the first frost. Harvesting, curing and storage instructions for each vegetable are described in Chapter IV.

Approximate Dates of the First Fall Frost – Canada

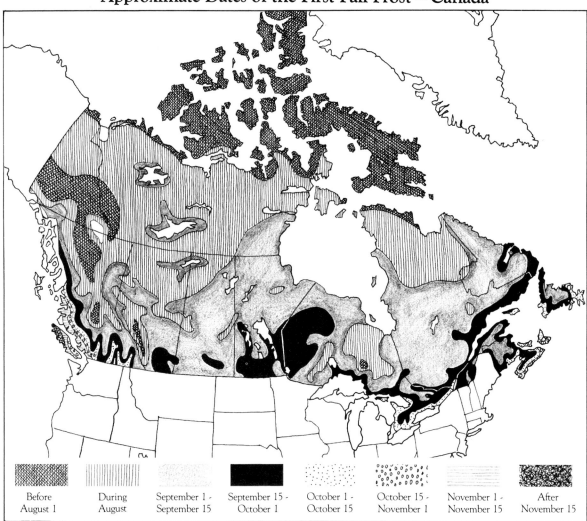

Before August 1	During August	September 1 - September 15	September 15 - October 1	October 1 - October 15	October 15 - November 1	November 1 - November 15	After November 15

As each crop is harvested, any remaining plant refuse should be carted out of the garden and added to the compost heap. This is not only a matter of neatness, but also one of future crop health. Many pests and diseases overwinter in the garden on crop refuse. For example, bean rust and bacterial wilt remain on infested debris; corn ear worms and European corn borers spend the winter inside corn stalks; Colorado potato beetles and striped cucumber beetles overwinter in the debris of their respective hosts. Burn any diseased plants or send them off with the garbage collector, and, particularly, avoid growing a related plant in that spot next spring. Thick stems such as those of broccoli and corn will not degrade readily on the compost pile.

Put them through a compost shredder or power lawnmower, or pile them separately where their gradual decomposition will not slow the working of the compost pile.

After each row or bed has been completely cleared, the soil can be tilled or spaded, or a cover crop such as rye grass can be sown for green manuring in spring (see pages 36 and 37). If the ground is spaded or tilled, leave it rough and let winter's freezing and thawing break up the clumps. In spring, the seed bed can be levelled with a rake.

Some root vegetables can be left in the ground to overwinter under a heavy layer of mulch. Carrots, beets, salsify, parsnips and Jerusalem artichokes may be kept this way. Parsnips and Jerusalem arti-

Approximate Dates of the First Fall Frost – United States

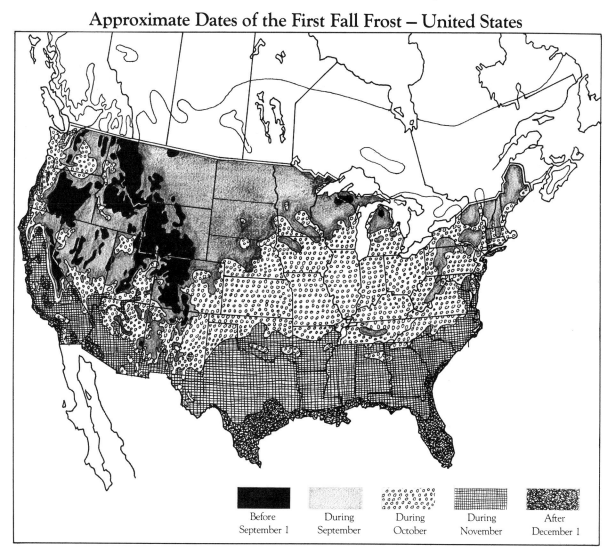

| Before September 1 | During September | During October | During November | After December 1 |

chokes will, in fact, survive most winters without mulching, although if this is done, they cannot be harvested until the soil thaws in spring.

The gardener faces a number of other end-of-season tasks:

• Fall is a good time to have a soil test done. See the list of addresses on page 45. Organic materials and lime or sulphur in amounts recommended by the report may be tilled or spaded in after the crops are harvested

• Write down all the harvest dates and comments on the success of each crop in your garden notebook, along with frost dates and a description of the weather. Make a note of anything you might want to try next year

• Rake up fallen leaves and pile them to compost for use in later years as mulch or organic matter

• Plant corn salad, garlic, and perhaps seeds of spinach, carrots, parsley and other cold-hardy vegetables which may sprout early next spring. Fall seeding is a gamble, but may mean extra-early crops for adventurous gardeners. Writing in the 1982 edition of *The Prairie Garden*, Joe Tsukamoto noted that in Brandon, Manitoba, he had been successful with carrots, lettuce, onions, parsley, radishes, beets and spinach sown "as close to the time of freeze-up as possible." These fall-sown seeds emerged earlier and matured faster than their spring-sown counterparts. Fall is also an alternative planting time for asparagus, Jerusalem artichokes,

Vegetables whose own acid content is too low for safe water bath canning can be preserved that way if sufficient salt and vinegar are added to them. It is important to follow the recipe exactly to ensure that the proportion of preservative is adequate

horseradish and rhubarb roots. While early spring is usually preferable, eager gardeners can plant them now, not long before the soil freezes

• The foliage of perennials such as asparagus may be cut back after the soil freezes but, if you prefer to leave it to catch snow in the garden, which will increase moisture reserves, cut it back in early spring

• If you wish to enlarge the garden or start a new one, begin preparing the site as soon as possible, as described in Chapter II

• Clean tools, sharpen them if necessary, wipe metal blades with an oily rag and store them under cover for the winter. Collect plant stakes, trellises and any other garden hardware, and store it all under cover. Power mowers, shredders and tillers should be prepared for winter according to the manufacturer's directions

Vegetable Storage

Most crops are stored indoors over the winter. Methods of storage include pickling, canning,

freezing, drying, cool storage and the preparation of jellies and jams. In every case vegetable maturation and spoilage is slowed or stopped, sometimes with the help of the plant's own ability to remain dormant, sometimes by artificial means that exclude decay organisms from food. Each method has its own advantages and disadvantages, and suits a few crops best.

Home Canning

Home canning rarely involves metal cans nowadays. Although it's still called canning, the foods are now usually put in sturdy glass jars capable of holding an airtight seal thanks to specially designed close-fitting lids. When food is processed in such jars at high temperatures for a specified time, harmful microorganisms are destroyed. If the canning has been done properly, the airtight seal prevents further microorganisms from entering the jar, and the food will store safely at room temperature.

The most dangerous contaminant of canned

food is the spore-forming bacterium *Clostridium botulinum*, which is present in soil and on most produce. In the oxygen-free environment of a sealed container, it can multiply, producing a deadly toxin. Only high-acid foods discourage the multiplication of *Clostridium botulinum*, and thus are the only ones

two inches. If only pint jars are to be used, a shallower bath will suffice. Do not use a steam canner. Although these devices are on the market, they have not yet been proven capable of sustaining the temperatures required for safe canning.

Suitable jars are also needed. Strong commercial

The tomato harvest is often large enough to allow plenty for fresh use as well as for homemade sauce, soup and ketchup

Available in several sizes, the canning jar which is most used today has a sealing metal lid and a metal screw band

that can safely be canned at a temperature as low as the boiling point of water; low-acid foods, including all vegetables except tomatoes, should be processed at 240 degrees F (116 degrees C), a temperature that can only be reached in a pressure canner.

Tomatoes are the only vegetable with a high enough acid content to allow processing in hot water, but even tomatoes are considered by Agriculture Canada to be borderline in acidity, so the addition of ¼ teaspoon (1 millilitre) of citric acid or 1 tablespoon (15 millilitres) of reconstituted lemon juice to each pint (500 millilitres) of stewed tomatoes is recommended. Add twice that amount to quart (litre) jars. Citric acid is a natural constituent of tomatoes, so its addition will have little effect on the flavour of the canned produce. Because its acid content is variable, fresh lemon juice must not be substituted for reconstituted bottled juice.

The principal piece of equipment used for the canning of high-acid foods is called a canning kettle or a hot water bath, which can be purchased in many hardware stores and country general stores. This large pot must be deep enough so that, when it is filled, water will cover quart (litre) jars by one or

jars now have securely fitting metal lids and screw bands that may be purchased separately whenever they need replacing. Older canning jars featured a rubber ring that rested on the jar rim and was held in place by a glass lid and retaining metal screw band. These, too, are reliable if used properly, and replacement rubber rings are still available. Rather than buying jars, many cooks use recycled jam jars, pickle jars and the like. They do, of course, save money, and they often come with sealer lids or will fit standard commercial lids, but they are made of lightweight glass that can shatter when exposed to high canning temperatures. Also, canning times have been calculated to suit commercial jars. Food experts such as those at Agriculture Canada recommend that recycled jars never be used for processing. Use them, instead, for the storage of dried foods.

With a hot water bath and a supply of strong, washed jars and lids, anyone wishing to preserve fruits, tomatoes, pickles, relishes and jams needs little else except perhaps a ladle, a pair of pot holders and standard kitchen equipment. The food to be canned is washed and, if necessary, hulled, trimmed or peeled. Whole tomatoes peel easily after they have been boiled for about a minute and then dipped into ice water. In some cases, the tomatoes or fruits are cooked before they are processed (in making strawberry jam or tomato ketchup, for instance), but this is a matter of personal preference only, and not a matter of safety.

Fill only as many jars as can be processed in one batch – usually seven. Pack the whole or sliced fruits into the jars to within an inch of the rim (that empty top inch is called "head space"), and then fill the jar with boiling water, juice or (if appropriate) sugar syrup, leaving ½ inch of head space in quart jars, ¼ inch in pint jars. Sugar syrup may contain from ¾ to 3 cups of water to every cup of sugar, honey or corn syrup, depending upon one's preference. Your choice of the amount and type of sweetener will have a distinctive effect on the flavour of the food. Sweeteners help maintain or enhance the flavour of the food, but they are not necessary for safe preservation.

Once the jars are filled, insert a rubber spatula down the inside edge of each jar to release air bubbles, adding more liquid if needed. When juices, sauces and syrups are being canned, water is not added. Just pour in the juice, sauce or syrup until only the appropriate head space remains.

Wipe the rim of each jar with a wet cloth, wet the lids or rubber rings (depending upon which system you are using), place one lid or ring on each jar, and then screw the retaining band on tightly. With the rubber ring system *only*, the band is then slightly loosened – turn it not more than one inch – before the jar is ready for processing.

Fill the water bath about halfway with hot water and place the jars on the rack that fits inside it. Lower the rack to rest on the bottom of the bath, and add enough water so that it covers the jars by an extra inch or two. Put the lid on the kettle, set it on high heat and, as soon as the water reaches a rolling boil, begin timing. The processing times given on this page are for altitudes less than 2,000 feet above sea level. At altitudes from 2,000 to 3,000 feet, add one-fifth to the time listed; from 3,000 to 4,000 feet, add two-fifths; and so on, adding one additional fifth for each successive rise of 1,000 feet above sea level.

• Whole berries, except strawberries, are processed for 15 minutes in pints, or 20 minutes in quarts
• Berry and rhubarb juices and syrups are processed for 10 minutes* in pints and quarts
• Whole or sliced strawberries are processed for 15 minutes in pints, or 20 minutes in quarts

Fruits, berries and tomatoes have a sufficiently high acid content that they can be safely canned in a hot water bath

• Tomatoes are processed for 55 minutes in pints, or 60 minutes in quarts
• Tomato juice, sauce and ketchup are processed for 40 minutes in pints and quarts
* When the processing time is less than 15 minutes, the jars should first be sterilized. Immerse them in boiling water for 15 minutes just before they are filled with hot produce.

A full boil must be maintained throughout the timing. When the time is up, turn off the heat, remove the kettle lid, lift the basket – it should have handles that will hook over the edges of the canning kettle – and carefully remove each jar, using pot holders or a jar lifter. Place the jars, not touching, on a dish towel on a counter where they can sit undisturbed until cool.

Any hissing during cooling indicates an unsealed jar. A loud "ping" during cooling, on the other hand, indicates a good seal on a "snap lid," a type of metal lid designed to emit that reassuring signal. When the jars are cool, check each seal. The metal lids should be indented and, as with glass lids, will not leak when the jar is turned upside down. The screw bands may be *gently* removed for further seal

Often difficult to seal, and hence unsafe, antique jars are best relegated to decoration or the storage of dried foods

checking and for jar storage – but be careful, as tightening or loosening the band vigorously may break the seal. You should not be able to remove either glass or metal lids with your thumb. Any jars that are not sealed can be given a new lid or rubber ring and reprocessed, or they can be refrigerated and the food used as soon as possible.

Store full jars upright in a cool, dark cupboard. Properly canned food will store for several years, but most cooks try to estimate their yearly needs so that fresh produce is canned as soon as the previous year's supply runs out. If food looks at all suspect when you open the jars, discard it where it will not be tasted by people or animals. The jars must then be washed and sterilized in boiling water for 15 minutes. *Never* taste canned food that looks spoiled in any way.

Pressure Canning

Except for fruit and tomatoes, all produce must be canned under pressure, using a specially designed pressure canner. To pressure can vegetables:

• Choose fresh, young, top-quality produce, trim and wash it thoroughly and, if appropriate, cut it into pieces

• Vegetables must be packed hot. Cook them according to the instructions in the table "Pressure Canning Instructions" on page 170

• Fill containers (only as many as the canner will accommodate at one time) with hot vegetables and then boiling water or vegetable cooking liquid to within ½ inch of the jar rim. For shelled peas and kernel corn, leave 1 inch of head space

• Add ½ teaspoon (2 millilitres) of salt to each pint (500-millilitre) jar, 1 teaspoon of salt (5 millilitres) to each quart (litre) jar

• Run a spatula down the inside edge of each jar to release air bubbles, adding more liquid if necessary

• Close jars as you do for hot water bath canning, described on the opposite page

• Pack jars in the canner and adjust its lid, fastening it securely. Place the canner over high heat and leave the vent open until the steam escapes with a hissing sound. Let it escape for 10 minutes or according to the manufacturer's instructions and then put on the pressure regulator or turn off the petcock to close the vent

• Continue heating until the gauge indicates the correct pressure. Start to measure the processing time, regulating the heat to keep the pressure constant for the length of time required. Processing

Harvested honeydew melon does not keep long. Its flesh can be cubed and frozen or canned, or used in chutneys and pickles

pressures and times are indicated in the chart "Pressure Canning Instructions" on page 170

• When the time is up, remove the canner from the heat and place it on a heat-proof surface. Allow the pressure to drop of its own accord. In 30 minutes to an hour, after the gauge has indicated zero for several minutes, very slowly open the vent

• Let the canner cool for several minutes, and then open the lid, being careful that the steam is directed away from your face

• Remove jars from the canner, cool them and check for seals as for hot water bath canning (see pages 164 and 165)

• Before eating home-canned vegetables, boil them in a covered pot for 10 minutes

Jams, Jellies, & Pickles

Jams and jellies make use of the naturally acidic properties of fruit for preservation. Pectin, gelatin and other thickeners are usually added, along with honey or sugar for flavour, thickening and preservation. Pickles and relishes use the acidity of vinegar and the preserving power of salt or sugar so that low-acid foods such as cucumbers and corn can be stored safely without pressure canning. Sauerkraut is a fermented cabbage product that includes salt. Such processing causes the greatest alteration in vegetable flavour – which is, in fact, its attraction.

When making pickles or relishes, it is important that the cook follow a recipe exactly – measurements have been proved to render the food safe for water bath canning. When making jams and jellies, some cooks choose to top the jars with a double layer of paraffin (let one layer cool before adding the second) rather than using a sealer lid. Make sure that the fruit goes above the shoulder of the jar, or the paraffin will be very difficult to remove.

Before being filled with jams, jellies or pickles, the jars should be sterilized. Do this by immersing washed jars in boiling water for 15 minutes, and then filling the hot jars with boiling produce. Unless it is recommended in the recipe, processing is not necessary for pickles and relishes. Tests by Agriculture Canada have indicated that processing these foods makes the product less crisp and does not improve its keeping quality.

Vegetables on Ice

The preparation of food for freezing requires less energy and less equipment, but freezing itself is expensive, requiring the maintenance of a closed environment of about 0 degrees F (-18 degrees C).

Blanching Times

Asparagus	medium spears	3 minutes
	large spears	4 minutes
Beans (green or wax)	cut	3 minutes
	whole	4 minutes
Beets	cook until tender and peel, then slice or dice and freeze	
Broccoli	1-inch florets	3 minutes
Brussels sprouts	small sprouts	3 minutes
	medium sprouts	4 minutes
	large sprouts	5 minutes
Cabbage	shredded	1 minute
Carrots	¼-inch slices	3 minutes
Cauliflower	1-inch florets	3 minutes
Corn, kernel	Boil husked cobs, cool in ice water, slice off kernels and freeze	4 minutes
Corn on cob	Boil husked cobs 7 to 11 minutes, depending upon cob size. Cool in ice water. Freeze	
Leafy greens		2 minutes
Parsnips	¼-inch slices	1 minute
Peas	shelled	2 minutes
	edible-podded	3 minutes
Potatoes*	⅜-inch slices or fingers	2 minutes
Pumpkins & Winter squash	Cook pieces until tender, cool, mash, pack and freeze	
Squash, summer*	¼-inch slices	2 minutes
Turnips, rutabagas	Diced	2 minutes

*Because of their high water content, these vegetables do not freeze very successfully under home conditions

Frozen food is, however, safe to eat and, in most cases, of high quality. Certain vegetables, properly prepared and frozen, are almost identical in flavour and texture to fresh ones that have been cooked.

Most vegetables should be blanched before freezing. The only items not blanched are those that would become mushy if they were: herbs, toma-

Vegetables intended for drying should be sliced thin for best air circulation. Cabbage for sauerkraut is also cut in this way

toes, peppers, mushrooms, and onions.

Spread most of these food items in a single layer on cookie sheets and place in the freezer. When frozen, pour the food into plastic bags or recycled containers. Tomatoes and tomato products may be frozen in bags or jars. Fruits can be packed with or without sugar, the latter method leaving the fruit in the most useful form to be used later in cooking, while sweetened fruit is best for eating raw when thawed. If sugar is to be added, it may be dry or in syrup. You may wish to add the amount of sugar recommended for a favourite pie recipe, for instance. Syrup for freezing, which may contain from ¾ to 2 cups of water to every cup of sugar or honey, should be cold. Pour it into containers packed with berries, chopped rhubarb or melon. Leave 1 inch of head space between the surface of the fruit and the rim of the container, as the liquid will expand when it freezes.

All other foods should be blanched to destroy enzymes that otherwise cause the texture, flavour and nutrients of vegetables to deteriorate in storage. Studies have indicated a greater loss of vitamin C in blanched green beans, broccoli, spinach and squash than in the unblanched food after three months' storage. Other research has shown that carotene (vitamin A) levels remain higher in blanched vegetables. (Unblanched food is, however, safe to eat.) To blanch vegetables, bring a large kettle about half-filled with water to a boil, add the vegetables — and begin to time the blanching according to the chart on page 167. The kettle is lidded and left on high heat during blanching.

As soon as the time is up, pour off the water. (If you are doing several batches of the same vegetable, retain the hot water and reuse it.) Pour the hot vegetables into a sink of ice water. As soon as they are cool, lift them into a colander to drain for a few minutes, and then pack in containers and place in the freezer as soon as possible. Any delay from garden to freezer will result in loss of food quality.

The container should be as full as possible, because any air enclosed with the vegetables will lower the food quality. With a drinking straw, suck the air out of filled freezer bags, then pinch the top shut and secure it with a twist tie. The freezer itself should be set at 0 degrees F (-18 degrees C) for best food preservation. If possible, place the new bags of vegetables in the freezer so that they will not touch, and so can freeze as quickly as possible. Once frozen, the bags can be stored together in one area of the freezer. Also, freeze no more than 3 pounds of food for every cubic foot of freezer capacity at one time.

Home-frozen vegetables usually retain enough blanching water that none need be added when they are heated to serve. Without adding water, heat the frozen vegetables gently in a lidded pot, turning them occasionally, and serve them as soon as they are hot. Frozen cobs of corn, however, are buttered, wrapped in foil and baked for 20 minutes at 400 degrees F (205 degrees C).

Dried Produce

Home-dried food is often markedly altered in flavour and texture from fresh, even after reconstitution, but its preparation is easy and inexpensive and storage takes very little space (usually just a kitchen cupboard). Some foods adapt particularly well to freezing. Herbs, mushrooms, onions, carrots, parsnips, spinach and other leafy greens are a

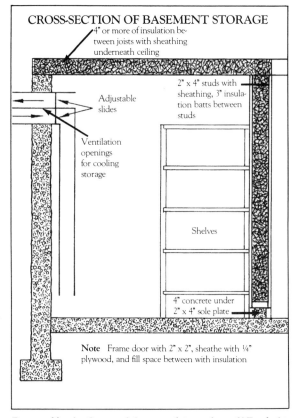

CROSS-SECTION OF BASEMENT STORAGE

4" or more of insulation between joists with sheathing underneath ceiling

2" x 4" studs with sheathing, 3" insulation batts between studs

Adjustable slides

Ventilation openings for cooling storage

Shelves

4" concrete under 2" x 4" sole plate

Note Frame door with 2" x 2", sheathe with ¼" plywood, and fill space between with insulation

Designed by the Ontario Ministry of Agriculture & Food, this 5-by-8-foot root cellar will hold about 30 bushels of food

few of these. As is the case with frozen food, items that will otherwise become mushy, such as herbs, peppers, tomatoes, onions and mushrooms, need not be blanched before drying. Other foods should be blanched according to the times on page 167, or the flavour and nutrient content of the food will gradually deteriorate in storage.

Vegetables to be dried should be sliced ¼ to ⅛ inch thick, if appropriate, before blanching. Leafy vegetables and herbs can be left whole (see the information on drying herbs in Chapter VII). Blanched vegetables that are to be dried need not be cooled. Just drain the vegetables, blot them dry and then place them, still hot, in a single layer on cookie sheets or on cheesecloth or screening (not galvanized) stretched on a frame. Set the trays in a warm, dry spot with good air circulation. The ideal temperature range for drying is 100 to 140 degrees F (37 to 60 degrees C), hot enough to discourage quick drying but not hot enough to cook the food.

The ideal root cellar temperature range of a couple of degrees above or below freezing is easily maintained in an outdoor root cellar that is entirely underground. More exposed structures such as this one in British Columbia are best where the winters are not severe

Good drying locations include the sill of a sunny, open, screened window, the open oven of a warm cook stove, a sunny spot outdoors, an electric oven at its lowest setting with the door left open, a greenhouse, a cold frame with the glazing slightly open and, of course, a dehydrator, many models of which are commercially available.

Food must never be allowed to become damp once drying has begun. Food that is drying outdoors must be brought in overnight or when the weather is damp. Under good conditions, leafy vegetables and herbs should be dried in half a day; other vegetables in two days. Drying may take much longer if conditions are not optimal.

Berries, snap beans, mushrooms, root vegetables, squash and pumpkins will feel tough and leathery when ready to store. Herbs, leafy vegetables, onions, cabbage, broccoli, potatoes, cucumbers and celery should be paper dry and crumbly or brittle. Corn, shelled peas and beans should be too hard to dent with a fingernail. If in doubt, let the food dry longer. Insufficiently dried foods will spoil.

As soon as the food is dry and cool, pour it into clean, labelled glass jars with lids (recycled jars are fine). Store them in a cool, dry cupboard. The food will gradually deteriorate while in kitchen storage, and so should be used within a year and replaced with a fresh stock. While dried fruits are ideal snack foods, dried vegetables are especially suited to use in dishes that have enough liquid to reconstitute the vegetables: soups, stews, puddings or pies. Remember that dried foods may be less than half as bulky as their fresh counterparts, so add correspondingly less to the recipe, and be prepared to use extra liquid.

Root Storage

Some foods designed by nature to be dormant through the winter can be stored without any special equipment at all — they just need the right environment. While whole plant storage is bulky and

Pressure Canning Instructions

The processing times given are correct for altitudes under 2,000 feet above sea level, where the recommended pressure in the canner is 10 pounds per square inch. From 2,000 feet to 4,000 feet, set the canner at 11 pounds; from 4,000 feet to 6,000 feet, at 12 pounds and so on, adding 1 pound for each 2,000 additional feet above sea level.

Add ½ tsp (2 mL) of salt to each pint (500 mL) jar and 1 tsp (5 mL) of salt to each quart or litre jar.

Using sound commercial jars, new lids and a reliable pressure canner, follow these processing times exactly. When serving canned foods, boil them for 10 minutes in a covered pot, before tasting, as an added precaution to destroy harmful microorganisms. Because the high temperatures necessary for safe pressure canning cannot be ensured in canning quarts of cream-style corn, this product should be processed in small jars only.

Vegetable	Preparation	Pints	Quarts
Asparagus	Wash, trim and steam. Pack hot, tips up. Cover with hot cooking liquid, leaving ½ inch of head space. Add salt	30	35
Beans	Wash, trim and boil for 3 minutes. Pack hot into jars, cover with hot cooking liquid, leaving ½ inch of head space. Add salt	30	35
Beets	Boil beets until skins slip off easily. Small beets may be canned whole, others sliced or cubed. Pack hot, adding salt and boiling water, leaving ½ inch of head space	30	35
Carrots	Wash, peel and boil for 5 minutes. Small carrots may be left whole, others sliced lengthwise or crosswise. Pack hot, add salt, cover with boiling water, leaving ½ inch of head space	30	35
Corn, whole kernel	Boil cobs for 4 minutes. Cool in ice water and slice kernels from cobs into a saucepan. Add half as much boiling water as corn. Bring to boil and pack hot, very loosely, leaving 1 inch of head space. Add salt	60	85
Corn, cream-style	Slice the kernels off cobs into a saucepan, then scrape cob for juice. Add half as much boiling water as corn. Bring to boil, stirring to prevent scorching. Pack hot, very loosely, leaving ½ inch of head space. Add salt. Do not can cream-style corn in quart jars	105	no
Greens	Steam or boil until wilted. Pack hot, loosely. Add salt and boiling water, leaving ½ inch of head space. To remove air bubbles, cut greens crosswise with a sharp knife to bottom of jar	70	90
Peas	Cover shelled peas with boiling water and boil 1 minute. Pack hot, loosely. Add salt. Cover with hot cooking liquid, leaving 1 inch of head space over peas	40	45
Pumpkins, Winter squash	Remove stringy fibres and seeds. Cut in pieces and cook until tender. Scrape meat from skin and mash in saucepan. Boil, adding water if necessary to prevent scorching. Pack hot, leaving ½ inch of head space. Add salt	75	90

the correct conditions may be difficult to maintain, such a system is economically attractive and actually affords the gardener fresh produce in winter, although the flavour will deteriorate over time.

The best place for root storage is a root cellar, which may be constructed either out of doors or indoors. The advantage of the outdoor cellar, which is built underground or bermed with earth, is the natural temperature regulation by the surrounding soil, which maintains an ideal temperature of close to freezing throughout the winter. The optimum relative humidity in a root cellar is 80 to 95 per cent. Most hardware stores stock a combination thermometer/hygrometer (for humidity measurement) that can be installed in the root cellar, where a too-low humidity reading can be altered by placing pans of water on the shelves. Package vegetables in polyethylene bags where storage conditions are dry.

Indoor root cellars have the decided advantage of easy accessibility. While an unheated basement is the perfect environment for such a storage room, a heated basement will also be serviceable if the cellar is well insulated and provided with a window that will allow cold outside air to enter. During winter, the window will need to be opened only infrequently to keep the temperature within the correct storage range. A storage room 5 feet by 8 feet will hold about 30 bushel hampers (see the illustration on page 168). Alternatively, a refrigerator set at its highest temperature will keep a small quantity of poly-bagged produce crisp and moist.

Root cellars should be outfitted with shelves to hold baskets and boxes of packed produce. As well, they are usually suitable for the storage of canned goods, although the screw bands on the jars may rust and be unsuitable for reuse.

Not all foods should be stored together. Apples, pears, peaches, plums, apricots, muskmelons and tomatoes produce ethylene gas, which speeds up the aging process of vegetables, shortening their storage life. Onions, celery and cabbage produce strong odours that may be picked up by other vegetables. Most of these foods would not be stored together in any case, but where they are together, consider packing one item in polyethylene, or keeping them as far removed from each other as possible. Avoid the following combinations:
- celery with onions or carrots
- apples, pears or tomatoes with celery, cabbage, lettuce, carrots, rutabagas, potatoes or onions
- root crops with fruit or leafy vegetables

Store only sound, whole produce; bruises, cuts and insect damage provide excellent places for the growth of moulds. Beets, carrots, parsnips, horseradish, winter radishes, salsify and scorzonera can be packed in perforated polyethylene bags and stored at 32 degrees F (0 degrees C), or they may be layered in peat, sand or straw and left in boxes in a dark, cool root cellar at a temperature just at or above freezing. Potatoes should also be in darkness, although their environment should be drier and warmer, preferably about 45 to 50 degrees F (7 to 10 degrees C). The top of the basement stairs might be a good spot for a bag of potatoes. Cabbages will keep a few weeks in most root cellars. Either wrap them in newspaper and store them on a shelf in the root cellar, or pack them in polyethylene bags in the refrigerator. Winter squash and pumpkins will store best in a dry place at about 50 to 60 degrees F (10 to 16 degrees C), in or out of light. Watermelons can be stored in the same place, where they will keep for about a month. Onions need the driest surroundings of all and, although they keep best at temperatures just above freezing, the hard winter-keeper varieties will often keep well even at room temperature. They may be stored loose in bags, boxes, baskets or nylon stockings; or the dried onion tops can be braided with a string and the completed braids hung in a cool, dry room.

To store well, these vegetables should first be cured for a day. This dries the skin of the produce so that it helps contain the moisture within. Squash, pumpkins, roots and tubers should be harvested on a dry morning and spread out in a single layer on newspaper or a sunny porch. After a few hours turn each vegetable over, exposing the damp underside and rubbing off any clinging lumps of soil. Onions should be cured for several days, until the skins are papery and the tops are dry. Cover them or bring them indoors during damp weather or overnight. Alternatively, they can be cured in a warm, dry room with good air circulation.

The Regional Gardener

"Any garden is better than no garden and any piece of ground will make a garden of some kind"

– Adolph Kruhm
Home Vegetable Gardening from A - Z, 1918

Whatever we can do with our soil or plants, there is very little we can do about the weather except talk about it – or read about it. Looking like the latest in avant-garde experimentation from the Museum of Modern Art, the map of Canada's plant hardiness zones is, nevertheless, far more useful than decorative. The map is the result of a considerable amount of work done in the '60s, when data was collected from 108 stations across Canada. As well as recording the hardiness of 174 species and cultivars of "indicator shrubs," the Agriculture Canada scientists coordinating the project also noted seven meteorological variables at each station: low winter temperatures, the frost-free period, summer and winter rainfall, summer high temperatures, snow depth and wind speed. A complex formula was used to assess the information from each station, and then to divide the country into 10 zones, numbered 0 to 9, each higher number denoting a slightly more benign climate than its predecessor. As well, each zone was divided into two parts: A and B.

Several years before the Canadian map was printed, the U.S. Department of Agriculture published its own map of climatic zones. This one also included 10 zones, but covered the area from central Canada to southern Florida. In this case only one variable was taken into account, minimum winter temperature. Each zone has an average winter minimum which is 10 degrees F (5.6 degrees C) warmer than that of the previously numbered zone; subzones represent 5-degree-F intervals. The U.S. map and the Canadian map are similar in zoning patterns, but because they are based upon different criteria the two do not, unfortunately, mesh. Alberta has also published its own quite different zone map, as have Manitoba, Prince Edward Island and Nova Scotia. Always be sure that you know what map an author has in mind when he refers to a certain climatic zone. A gardener in southern Alberta could be simultaneously in zone 2 (Alberta Agriculture), zone 3 (Agriculture Canada) and zone 4 (USDA).

Climatic zones are most useful when you are trying to determine which trees and shrubs are hardy in a particular area. Sheridan Nurseries, for instance, includes a zone map in its catalogue, and notes the lowest-numbered (coldest) zone for which each tree is hardy. Most nurseries make some reference to climatic zones in their recommendations for each species. But, even for tree buyers, climatic zone maps have their limitations. Not only does

Climatic Zone Map — Canada

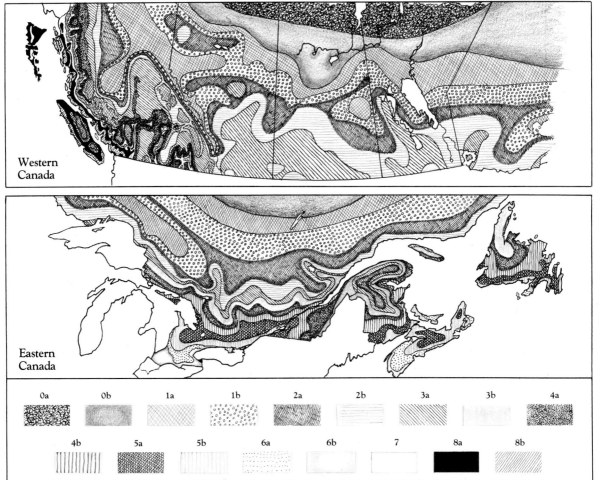

the map not include the far North, but it may not make note of small microclimates which exist throughout all zones. One example of a distinct microclimate was cited in a report, "The Frost-Free Period in Alberta," by Richmond W. Longley: "The Three Hills station is evidently in a frost-hollow, for its mean frost-free period of 86 days is a month shorter than those for Trochu Equity to the north and Hanna to the east." Yet this climatic blister is evident on no zone map.

Also, conditions at the border of each zone can be expected to differ from those nearer the centre of the zone. Climate does not really follow precisely demarcated outlines but changes gradually from area to area. As the scientists involved in the Agriculture Canada map project noted in the *Canadian Journal of Plant Science* in 1967, "Some plants rec-

ommended for a given zone may not survive every winter near the northern limit of that zone. Conversely, the southern limits may be more comparable to areas in the adjacent zone. . . . "

For vegetable gardeners, the climatic zone map has a more obvious lack: It is applicable mainly to woody perennials such as fruit or ornamental trees, not to herbaceous perennials such as sage, asparagus and Jerusalem artichokes, for which zone tolerances have not yet been established. The fate of plants that overwinter in vegetable gardens is largely unknown, and depends on snowfall, mulch, and the severity of any particular season. Because vegetable gardeners are, in any case, mostly concerned with growing annuals, the approximate spring and fall frost dates are of greater overall usefulness than are the climatic zones. Maps of spring frost dates

Climatic Zone Map – United States

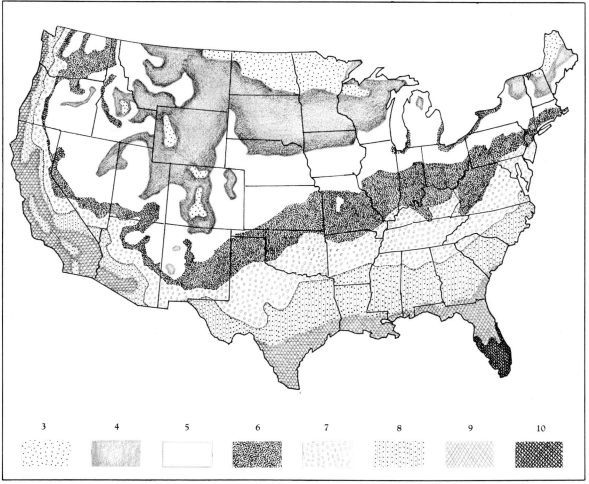

3   4   5   6   7   8   9   10

are on pages 48 and 49, and those for fall frost dates are on pages 160 and 161.

A further measure of climate, the number of heat units or growing degree-days that can be expected in each area, is mainly used by commercial growers who need to be sure that their crops will mature. Agriculture Canada's pamphlet, "Farming Potential of the Canadian Northwest," offers the following definition: "Heat for plant growth is measured in terms of heat units or growing degree-days. The basic temperature for cool-season crops is 42 degrees F (5.6 degrees C). This temperature is subtracted from the mean temperature for the day to give the heat units. Thus, a day with a mean temperature of 43 degrees F would have one degree-day and a day with a mean of 64 degrees F would have 22 degree days." (An accumulation of 1,000 growing

degree-days is considered the basic necessity for dependable production of frost-hardy vegetables.)

Home gardeners can afford to be far more daring and experimental. Whether they find themselves with a plot of zone 9 or zone 0 soil, or with a balcony overlooking zone 4, they might as well do all they can with what they have. "Any garden is better than no garden and any piece of ground will make a garden of some kind."

The Pacific Northwest

Canada's westernmost province and the most northwesterly states include a greater climatic diversity than any other region. The fact that climatic zones 1 through 9 are represented here is merely numerical evidence of the contrasts that are much more remarkable when seen or felt. There is the semi-desert sagebrush country around Cache

Creek, the almost impenetrable, foggy rain forests of coastal Washington, Oregon and British Columbia, the prairie of Dawson Creek, the alpine meadows near Golden, and the endless, wild forests of British Columbia's northland. Gardeners in one part of the northwest have little in common

Supporting cucumbers on a fence encourages air circulation while discouraging fungus diseases in wet gardens

with those in other parts save for their use of some of the same seed companies. Interior and Okanagan gardeners should read the gardening information for the Prairies, while Northerners should read that for the North.

Gardeners on the Pacific coast, Canada's "banana belt," have little in common with those anywhere else in the country. Along with their U.S. neighbours directly to the south, they live in a unique corner of the northland, with more rain, more flowers and more trees than almost anybody, except perhaps Macmillan Bloedel, knows what to do with. Gardeners there seem to work overtime. Eric Nicol wrote in his book *Vancouver* that the city observes the sabbath "in the pew of a row of carrots to be thinned" and does so almost all year. Sidney, British Columbia charts a frost-free season of 230 days. When frost does come, the temperature seldom dips much below 32 degrees F (0 degrees C). Meanwhile, most of the province's sparsely inhabited mountainous areas experience less than 60 frost-free days. Acknowledging this climatic diversity, the British Columbia Ministry of Agriculture and Food's publication 81-8, "The Home Vegetable

Garden," includes two garden plans, one for coastal areas and one for the interior, the former designed for a longer growing season than the latter.

Unfortunately for those who live in the southern and coastal regions, that long frost-free season does have its price. About 130 inches of rain fall each

In one of the drier areas of the Pacific Northwest, an Okanagan garden produces a plentiful and varied harvest

year on some westerly facing slopes. Heavy rains produce very acidic soil as well as pests, weeds and generally soggy conditions. Gardeners in really rainy areas can experiment with organic mulches, but are likely to find that the mulches encourage slugs and fungus diseases while conserving moisture in soil that is already too wet. Instead, try to ensure good air circulation, as much sun exposure as possible, adequate soil drainage by using raised beds and, whenever possible, keep fruit off the ground. Tomatoes can be supported in cages or on stakes, vining varieties of cucumber, squash and melon trained to climb a trellis or fence, and peas and pole beans allowed to climb.

Rain means not only wet acidic soil but also overcast skies and reduced light. Some areas of British Columbia receive less sunshine than anywhere else in the country, despite the long growing season. Although Prince Rupert has a frost-free season of 180 to 220 days, it records less than 1,200 hours of sunshine a year, about half that of Calgary or Regina, which have a frost-free season of only 110 days. The result is that sun-loving crops such as sweet corn actually have a much better chance of success in Winnipeg or Calgary than in Prince Rupert.

It is not that coastal gardeners cannot grow corn, but they are unlikely to do so on a commercial scale. In fact, like gardeners throughout the North, Pacific Northwest gardeners will obtain the best results with early varieties of tender, heat-loving vegetables such as tomatoes, peppers, melons and cucumbers.

Cold-tolerant vegetables, however, are likely to do very well in the Pacific Northwest, provided they can be protected from slugs and other pests. Cabbage relatives and leafy greens will often over-winter with, or even without, mulch. Hardy plants can be sown as early as February in some gardens, allowing for bumper crops in fall. Seeds planted in mid or late summer and sheltered by a cold frame will provide winter greens.

Publications Steve Solomon's *Growing Organic Vegetables West of the Cascades* (Pacific Search Press, 1985) and Ann Lovejoy's *The Year in Bloom* (Sasquatch Books, 1987) are excellent guides for gardeners in the area. Further information can be obtained from the British Columbia Ministry of Agriculture & Food, Parliament Buildings, Victoria, British Columbia V8W 2Z7. Or contact the cooperative extension service at the appropriate university: Washington State University, Pullman, Washington 99163; Oregon State University, Corvallis, Oregon 97331; University of Idaho, Moscow, Idaho 83843.

The Prairies

The plains of British Columbia, Alberta, Saskatchewan, Manitoba and the northern United States certainly have their climatological differences, but they have some notable similarities as well. Winters are harsh, summers dry and hot. Regina, for instance, has an average January low of -9.4 degrees F (-23 degrees C) and an average July high of 78.9 degrees F (26 degrees C). Drought is a common occurrence. Three climatic zones predominate: 1, 2 and 3, with the 0 zone banding the northern third of each province. The growing season is short, varying from less than 60 days to about 125, but because the prairie skies tend to be clear the area supports many tender garden plants that flourish in the abundant sunshine, and greenhouses can be very successful. The south-central part of the Canadian Prairies, including Calgary and Regina, records more sunshine than anywhere else in Canada.

If there is one overriding horticultural limitation here, aside from the brevity of the growing season, it is a shortage of rain. To counteract dryness, organic mulch is a real boon to prairie gardeners. As in other northern areas, mulch should not be applied until about mid-June, when the soil has warmed, but then a 4- to 12-inch bed of straw, hay or grass clippings placed around plants will retain moisture while adding organic matter to the soil. Heavy mulches applied in late summer will help protect roots and hardy plants over the winter, when light snow cover coupled with low temperatures will often cause winterkill. Remove them in early spring to allow the soil to warm.

Much of Alberta is subject to chinooks, warm winter winds that can melt away all snow cover, leaving plants vulnerable to the icy temperatures that almost inevitably follow. In drawing up the Agriculture Canada zone map, the researchers had to make special adjustments to chinook-prone areas because, although the chinooks raised the average winter temperatures, making the areas appear relatively benign, they actually had a destructive effect on plants. They melted the protective snow cover, thereby encouraging some non-native plants to resume growth even though winter temperatures would soon recur. In these areas, heavy winter mulches are particularly important.

Watering is critical on the Prairies, and must be geared to conservation. Water the drills (furrows) before sowing seeds. Later, when you do water, be sure that the watering is deep and thorough. Trickle irrigation systems, with perforated hoses, help conserve water by applying it directly to the soil around plants, not to paths or foliage where it is not needed. Covering the trickle pipes with mulch will conserve even more moisture. Vining crops such as cucumbers, squash and melons should be allowed to sprawl, so that their leaves can act as additional, elevated mulch.

Because rainfall is scarce, some prairie soil tends to be alkaline, requiring applications of sulphur for neutralization. This is not always the case, however. The soil may be acidic, requiring lime or wood ashes. It may also be salty, a more difficult problem to treat. Have a soil test done before applying any amendments or fertilizers. Organic matter is often lacking in prairie soils and its addition in the form of manure, green manure, compost and mulch adds to the moisture-holding and tempera-

The Sub-Arctic series of tomato plants was developed in Alberta and Ontario for cultivation in short-season gardens

ture-buffering capabilities of the soil. For information on soil-building techniques see Chapter II.

Early vegetable varieties are especially important here, and not just early tomatoes and corn, but early broccoli, cauliflower, and cabbage as well. They should be given an indoor start in most areas, then transplanted outdoors under cloches or hot caps anchored against the wind. In general, hardy seeds go into the prairie garden between late April and mid-May, while tender seeds and transplants go outdoors from late May until mid-June.

Fortunately, a great deal of vegetable-breeding work has been aimed at prairie and northern gardeners. From Alberta come some of the Sub-Arctic series of tomatoes – Brookpact, Earlinorth, Earlicrop and Rocket – Limelight beans and Earligold melons. From Saskatchewan comes the Swift tomato. Manitoba cultivars include Prairie Pride and Ping Pong cherry tomatoes, Harper Hybrid melon, Early Arctic corn, Morden Early cucumber, Supersweet pea, and Pee Wee, Little Leaguer, Junior and Morden Midget cabbages. Cooperative work among the Prairie provinces has produced the Starfire tomato and Far North melon, while coopera-

tive work between Canada and the northern states is devoted to developing potatoes especially suitable for the Prairies.

Publications Friends of the Devonian Botanic Garden, University of Alberta, Edmonton, Alberta T6G 2E9 offers memberships, which include the tri-

A rural garden in southern Ontario illustrates the broad variety of vegetables that can be grown in the mid-continent

monthly newsletter *Kinnikinnick*, a seed list, tours, as well as an exchange of gardening information.

The Prairie Garden, an annual publication, is available for a small fee from the Winnipeg Horticultural Society, P.O. Box 517, Winnipeg, Manitoba R3C 2J3.

Gardening in the Upper Midwest by Leon C. Snyder deals with growing vegetables, flowers, lawns and trees on the Prairies. Available from the University of Minnesota Press, Minneapolis, Minnesota 55414.

Agriculture Canada offers publication 1033, "Growing Vegetables in the Prairie Garden." Copies are available from the provincial departments of agriculture as well as from Information Services, Agriculture Canada, Ottawa K1A 0C7.

Further information is available from Alberta Agriculture, 9718-107 Street, Edmonton, Alberta T5K 2C8; from the Saskatchewan Department of Agriculture, Administration Bldg., 3085 Albert Street, Regina S4S 0B1; and from Manitoba Agriculture, 411 York Avenue, Winnipeg, Manitoba R3C 0V8. Or contact the cooperative extension service at the appropriate university: Montana

In all areas of the North, from coast to coast, potatoes are among the most reliable of crops as they require a long season of fairly cool, wet weather. Ideal conditions exist in the Maritimes, although suitable cultivars have been bred for drier and warmer gardens

State University, Bozeman, Montana 59715; North Dakota State University, Fargo, North Dakota 58102; South Dakota State University, Brookings, South Dakota 57006.

The Mid-Continent

Typified by deciduous forests and a continental climate, most of Ontario, Quebec and the American Midwest are known for cold winters, fairly hot summers, and moderate amounts of rainfall and snow. There is also a surprisingly balmy area here, a region that benefits from the moderating effects of Lakes Erie and Ontario. The Niagara region of southern Ontario and the United States, whose latitude is close to that of northern California, has a climate so benign that peaches, tomatoes and corn can be grown commercially there. Next to those of coastal and southern British Columbia, the gardeners of the Niagara peninsula enjoy one of the longest growing seasons in the country, lasting about 164 days, and having so much sun that the area's accumulation of growing degree-days is also the highest in the country. Blessed with just enough rain – 31 to 35 inches (80 to 90 centimetres) a year – gardeners living in the Niagara region

can grow just about anything they wish to.

But for most gardeners of the mid-continent, conditions are much more strenuous, with cold winters and fairly cool summers – the average summer temperature on Quebec's north shore does not exceed 60 degrees F (15 degrees C). As in the Niagara peninsula, however, precipitation is close to ideal – neither so high that raised beds are soggy, nor so low that watering is a routine procedure. And while the season is relatively short, skies in most areas are sufficiently clear and sunny to encourage fairly constant crop growth.

For these gardeners, then, almost any crop and any technique is worth a try, its success dependent upon the conditions of each garden's own peculiar microclimate. Plastic or organic mulches will often be beneficial. Plastic mulches will be of most use further north and organic mulches are preferable nearer the Great Lakes and the St. Lawrence River. Heavy organic mulches applied in the fall to overwintering crops will help ensure their survival. Snowfall is variable, and may or may not provide adequate coverage.

In general, southern mid-continent gardeners

sow hardy seeds outdoors from late April until mid-May and plant tender seeds or set tender plants outdoors from late May until mid-June. Gardeners who live further north will follow the schedule for Northerners.

Soils in this region tend to be acidic, a situation worsened by industrially caused acid precipitation. The opposite conditions may prevail, however, where the bedrock is alkaline. Have a soil test done before applying any pH-adjusting amendment.

Agriculture research stations in Ontario and Quebec have done considerable breeding work to produce vegetables suitable for Northerners in general and the mid-continent in particular. Several seed companies in the region cater to the continental climate. The "vee" series of tomatoes and sweet corn – Basketvee tomatoes, Polarvee corn, and others – are among the best-known Ontario cultivars, while others include Moira, Rideau, Earlirouge and Earlibright tomatoes and a series of potatoes including Nipigon, Trent, Rideau and Longlac. Butter King lettuce from Ottawa was an All-America winner in 1964. Coming from Quebec are Mac Pink, Perron 50, Square and the Quebec series of tomatoes.

Publications The New Alchemy Institute of Massachusetts has anthologized several of their informative brochures under the title *Gardening for All Seasons* (Brick House Publishing Co., 1983). The book, which includes information on aquaculture, fruit growing and food preservation, is suitable for organic growers in the Northeastern states and eastern Canada.

Introduction au Jardinage Ecologique by Yves Gagnon (self-published, 1984, available from 800 rang du Portage, St. Didace, Quebec J0K 2G0) is a good French-language guide to organic vegetable growing.

In addition, many books that are published by Rodale of Pennsylvania are appropriate for mid-country gardens. Most comprehensive is their *Encyclopedia of Organic Gardening*; almost as useful is the *Encyclopedia of Natural Insect and Disease Control*.

For further information, contact the Ontario Ministry of Agriculture and Food, Information Branch, 801 Bay Street, Toronto, Ontario M7A

1A5; Ministry of Agriculture of Quebec, 200A Chemin Ste-Foy, Quebec City, Quebec G1R 4X6. A number of publications are also available from Cornell University. Write: Distribution Center C, 7 Research Park, Cornell University, Ithaca, New York 14850. Or contact the cooperative extension

Brassicas such as cauliflower are often the most successful crops in the cooler gardens of the wet Atlantic region

service at the appropriate university: University of Minnesota, Minneapolis, Minnesota 55455; University of Wisconsin, 432 North Lake Street, Madison, Wisconsin 53706; Michigan State University, 113 Agricultural Hall, East Lansing, Michigan 48824; Ohio State University, 2120 Fyffe Road, Columbus, Ohio 43210; Pennyslvania State University, University Park, Pennsylvania 16802; University of Vermont, Burlington, Vermont 05401.

The Atlantic Coast

Canada's four Atlantic Provinces and the northeastern corner of the United States exhibit a remarkable diversity of climate, as is illustrated by the reports of two early visitors. In his journals of 1794, able seaman Aaron Thomas declared that, in Newfoundland, "the only vegetable which at present can be procur'd here is the Dandelion which grows wild. I have a salad of it most days." In 1856, Isabella Lucy Bird recorded a quite different impression of Prince Edward Island, which, she wrote, "bears the name throughout the British provinces of the 'Garden of British America.' That this title has been justly bestowed, none who have ever visited it in summer will deny."

Newfoundland gardens, cooled by the Labrador current that keeps coastal summer temperatures around 55 degrees F (12 degrees C), are also hampered by a lack of good topsoil, notably in the seaports. Gardeners there must often find garden space inland where conditions are more favourable. New Brunswick, Nova Scotia, and Prince Edward Island, however, possess very good conditions for the growth of many crops, and are well known for their possession of one of the world's most ideal climates for potatoes. Moist and fairly cool, New Brunswick and Prince Edward Island together account for 40 per cent of the country's total potato production.

Parts of Nova Scotia, warmed by the Gulf Stream, have winter temperatures that seldom dip below 32 degrees F (0 degrees C). As on the continent's northwest coast, all that rain, 77 inches in Saint John, 68 inches in Halifax, encourages the growth of potatoes, cabbages, carrots and lettuce, but the frequently overcast skies have a slowing effect on the growth of sun-loving plants. Here, too, the choice of suitable varieties is important. Fortunately, several seed companies such as Johnny's, Vesey's, Rawlinson, Gaze and Halifax specialize in seeds that have a fighting chance in the northeast.

Soils here are usually very acidic, demanding liming for neutralization. Have a soil test done and apply lime or wood ashes as directed. For most Maritimers, seaweed is easy to come by for use as a soil conditioner. While it makes a good mulch, many gardens will be too wet to need it in that capacity. Instead, compost the seaweed for use throughout the season. Researchers at the Ark project where various gardening methods were tried at Spry Point, Prince Edward Island, reported in 1980 that eel grass proved to be a decidedly good mulch for the area. Many cold-tolerant crops will overwinter under a heavy blanket of snow — 120 to 160 inches in northwestern New Brunswick, 80 inches in Prince Edward Island.

Publications *Adventures in Gardening* by Maritime gardener Gordon Warren (Lancelot Press, P.O. Box 425, Hantsport, Nova Scotia B0P 1P0) is a compendium of advice for Atlantic gardeners. Warren favours nonorganic methods of pest and disease control, but most of his growing techniques are suitable for all gardeners in this type of climate.

Agriculture Canada offers publication 1274, "Potherbs or Greens for the Maritimes." Write to Information Services, Agriculture Canada, Ottawa K1A 0C7. For further information, contact the

Two Klondike pioneers displayed their lush northern cabbages and potatoes to a turn-of-the-century photographer

New Brunswick Department of Agriculture, P.O. Box 6000, Fredericton, New Brunswick B2N 5E3; Nova Scotia Department of Agriculture and Marketing, Box 550, Truro, Nova Scotia B2N 5E3; the Department of Rural Agriculture and Northern Development, Prudential Building, 49-55 Elizabeth Avenue, St. John's, Newfoundland A1C 5T7; Prince Edward Island Department of Agriculture and Forestry, Provincial Administration Building, Box 2000, Charlottetown, Prince Edward Island C1A 7N8. All four provinces have cooperated to produce a series of factsheets on vegetable production in the Atlantic region. Or contact the cooperative extension service at the appropriate university: University of Maine, Orono, Maine 04473; University of New Hampshire, Taylor Hall, Durham, New Hampshire 03824; University of Massachusetts, Amherst, Massachusetts 01002; University of Connecticut, Storrs, Connecticut 06268.

The Far North

Many surprisingly productive gardens appear north of 55 degrees north latitude, some thanks to the skill of the gardener, some because the climate can be munificent. Tomatoes planted outdoors from seed have ripened in some of the protected western valleys. Minimum January temperatures in Whitehorse are similar to those in Regina and Winnipeg, while Fort Norman, Northwest Territories has a July mean temperature as warm as Fort Nelson, British Columbia. Still, for most Northerners gardening is an unpredictable adventure. An Inuvik gardener lamented that she put her seedlings outdoors in early July, and they were promptly snowed upon, hailed upon and then rolled upon by dogs ecstatic to find a patch of cool soft soil. On Mackenzie River permafrost some bounteous crops have been produced, but further east or north only one crop is really reliable — bean sprouts, grown indoors.

As a rule, northern gardeners have very little rainfall, cool soil and plenty of summer sun. Although the sun never rises very high in the sky, summer days are long in compensation. Fairly fast-maturing hardy crops are reliable stand-bys: early cabbage, cauliflower and broccoli, leaf lettuce, carrots, kale, bunching onions, bolt-resistant beets, Swiss chard, potatoes, radishes, peas and broad beans. Tender vegetables must be grown under cover for part or even all of the season. Supplementary heating for a greenhouse is a must unless only cold-tolerant plants are grown in it. Experiments by the University of Quebec at Chicoutimi demonstrated that double-tunnel greenhouses are particularly economical and effective for northern tomatoes. Tunnels 1 metre high and 1 metre wide were placed over the growing beds, which were covered with an aluminized transparent polyethylene thermal curtain. Only the area under the tunnels, not the entire greenhouse, had to be heated.

Soil is often scarce in the North, and must occasionally be trucked in. Under such circumstances, container gardens or small permanent raised beds are sensible. They not only limit the amount of soil needed but also help the soil warm in spring. Because they increase drainage, however, raised beds should be mulched with clear polyethylene to retain soil moisture while helping to warm the soil. The soil itself may range from acidic to alkaline. Have a soil test done before adding any fertilizer, even wood ashes. Because the soil's level of organic matter is often very low, compost should be used as a fertilizer and soil conditioner before planting, even though composting tends to be a very slow procedure here.

Hot caps, crop covers and cloches will help almost every crop mature. In fact, because frost can come at almost any time, it is best to have a supply of portable crop covers on hand for the protection, at a few hours' notice, of uncovered tender or half-hardy plants.

The long, harsh winters do have one advantage for gardeners: They kill most insect pests. But even in the far North plants in greenhouses are susceptible to the usual aphids and whiteflies. Ladybugs, insecticidal soap and sterile soil will help prevent or control infestations.

Throughout most of the arable North, hardy vegetables are not planted outdoors until mid or late May, while tender vegetables go outdoors under cover in early June.

After its 1980 trials, the Agricultural Experiment Station in Fairbanks, Alaska, produced the following vegetable variety recommendations:

Artichokes Grand Beurre (Thompson and Morgan) — yielded 24 pounds per 100 feet at 24-inch spacing

Beans, snap Roma (Twilley) — flat bean, high quality

Beets Little Egypt, Spring Red (Stokes) — good

Broccoli Green Duke (Park) — nice, large heads

Cabbage Erin (Alberta Nurseries and Seeds) — excellent flavour

Carrots Supreme Long Chantenay (Stokes) — excellent flavour

Cauliflower Dominant (Stokes) — large head, nice curd, consistent high yield

Celery Transgreen (Ferry-Morse) — average size 2.8 pounds at 12- by 18-inch spacing

Corn Polarvee (Stokes) — first harvest August 17 yielded 215 ears per 100 feet. Sweet corn was seeded May 7 and covered with 1.5 mil clear polyethylene. When plants were approximately 4 inches tall, slits were made to allow plants to emerge from beneath the plastic

Cucumbers Suyo Long (Johnny's) — slicer, long shape with ridges, good flavour

Kohlrabi Grand Duke (many) – earliest, good quality

Leeks Giant Elefant (William Dam) – largest size

Lettuce Salad Bowl (Northrup-King) – very dependable

Peas Snowbird (Burpee) – edible pod, very early harvest but overmatured rapidly

Peppers Early Prolific (William Dam) – turns red early. Greenhouse-grown plants 65 days old were transplanted June 6. Plants were grown through 1.5 mil clear polyethylene in tents constructed from clear polyethylene

Radishes Tokinashi (Johnny's) – large, Daikon-type, satisfactory

Squash Greenzini (Ferry Morse) – consistent high yield and quality

Swiss chard White King (Stokes) – did not bolt

Tomatoes Earlirouge (Johnny's) – yield was 2.14 pounds per plant, average fruit size 4.9 ounces. Greenhouse-grown plants 52 days old were transplanted June 6 and were grown through 1.5 mil clear polyethylene

For the addresses of the seed companies noted above, see Sources, beginning on the next page.

Publications Summaries of vegetable variety trials are available from the Agricultural Experiment Station, University of Alaska, 309 O'Neill Resources Building, 905 Koyukuk Avenue North, Fairbanks, Alaska 99701.

Agriculture Canada offers publication 1575, "Northern Gardening." Write to Information Services, Agriculture Canada, Ottawa K1A 0C7.

Gardens for Alaskans by Lenore Hedla (Lenore Hedla, 6440 West Diamond Blvd., Anchorage, Alaska 99502) is a personal account of the gardening experiences of the author and her friends in Alaska.

Cities have unique microclimates that are more benign than their surroundings. In a sunny Montreal back yard, the gardener has devoted every inch of space to the cultivation of crops that will come to maturity in a growing season that lasts about four months

Mail-Order Sources

Plants Across the Border

Most serious gardeners prefer to order their seeds by mail rather than buying them at the corner store. Mail-order catalogues offer the gardener a comprehensive seed selection that can be reviewed at one's leisure. Catalogues can be marked, and prices can be compared from company to company and from year to year. For gardeners wishing to order from companies outside their own country, there is both good news and bad news. The good news is that the movement of garden *seeds* between Canada, the U.S. and Great Britain is not restricted. The bad news is that the importation of plant materials such as tubers, bulbs, trees and seedlings is strictly regulated. Canadians wishing to purchase such plant materials from the U.S. must first write to the following address to receive an information packet and an identification number that must accompany the order to the U.S. nursery:

The Food Production and Inspection Branch
Plant Protection Division
Agriculture Canada
K.W. Neatby Building
Ottawa, Ontario K0A 0C6

Gardeners living in the United States must obtain importation permission from:

Permit Unit
Plant Protection and Quarantine
APHIS, USDA
Federal Building, Room 638
Hyattsville, Maryland 20782

Tools, accessories and such are, of course, subject to duty when imported. Get details from the Customs office for your own country.

Mail-Order Catalogues

The following alphabetical listing of seed, plant and garden-supply sources gives an indication of the area of specialization of each company and includes the 1992 catalogue price. Items sold by any company will vary from year to year, as will the catalogue price. There are several ways in which the gardener can keep up to date on current listings and prices. One is to send the company a self-addressed, stamped envelope requesting ordering information. Another is to purchase the early-spring issue of *Har-*

rowsmith magazine, which includes an updated list of seed catalogues. In addition, many companies advertise in consumer magazines in early spring.

When forwarding payment for the catalogue (and, later, for seeds), remember to pay in the currency of that country. U.S. companies request that Canadian buyers pay with a postal money order in U.S. funds. In most cases, if you order seeds from a company one year, you will automatically receive its catalogue again the following spring.

Abundant Life Seed Foundation
Box 772
Port Townsend, Washington 98368
A nonprofit foundation dedicated to acquiring, propagating and preserving plants of the North Pacific Rim. Also heirloom vegetables and flowers, all nonhybrid and untreated. Catalogue $1 (U.S.).

Alberta Nurseries and Seeds, Ltd.
Box 20
Bowden, Alberta T0M 0K0
Vegetables, flowers and herbs for the western prairies. Catalogue free to Canada, $2 to the U.S.

Becker's Seed Potatoes
RR 1
Trout Creek, Ontario P0H 2L0
The largest selection of seed-potato varieties in Canada. Catalogue free, to Canada only.

Bishop Seeds Ltd.
Box 338
Belleville, Ontario K8N 5A5
Large and small quantities of grains, lawn seeds, green manures ("plowdowns"), forage seeds and a few vegetables. Catalogue free, to Canada only.

Bountiful Gardens
18001 Shafer Ranch Road
Willits, California 95490
Organically grown seeds from several places, including Chase Organics of England. Catalogue $2 (U.S.) to Canada, free to the U.S.

W. Atlee Burpee & Co.
300 Park Avenue
Warminster, Pennsylvania 18974
Hundreds of vegetables and flowers, including many of their own. Catalogue free, to U.S. only.

Butterbrooke Farm
78 Barry Road
Oxford, Connecticut 06478-1529
Old-fashioned "tried and true" varieties of vegetables. Customers also receive a quarterly co-op newsletter. Price list 50 cents (U.S.).

Chiltern Seeds
Bortree Stile, Ulverston
Cumbria LA12 7PB, England
This thick catalogue that lists just about everything is a delight for experienced gardeners and beginning adventurers alike. Catalogue $3 to Canada, $4 to the U.S.

Companion Plants
7247 North Coolville Ridge
Athens, Ohio 45701
Herb plants will be shipped to U.S. addresses only, but seeds, gathered mostly from their own plants, can be sent to Canada. Catalogue $2 (U.S.).

Comstock, Ferre & Co.
263 Main Street
Old Wethersfield, Connecticut 06109
Vegetable, herb and flower seeds, including some heirlooms. Catalogue $2 (refundable), to U.S. only.

DeGiorgi Seed Co.
6011 N Street
Omaha, Nebraska 68117
Hybrid and nonhybrid vegetables, herbs, flowers. Catalogue $2, to U.S. only.

Evergreen Y.H. Enterprises
Box 17538
Anaheim, California 92817
Seeds of about 140 varieties of Oriental vegetables. Catalogue $2.

Fungi Perfecti
Box 7634
Port Angeles, Washington 98362
All you need to grow mushrooms at home, indoors or out. Catalogue $3 (refundable).

Garden City Seeds
1324 Red Crow Road
Victor, Montana 59875
Nonhybrid seeds "adapted to our special growing conditions in the valleys of the northern Rocky Mountains and the northern Great Plains." Catalogue $1 (U.S.).

Gleckler Seedmen
Metamora, Ohio 43540
Unusual vegetables for garden fun. Catalogue free.

The Gourmet Gardener
4000 West 126th Street
Leawood, Kansas 66209
Domestic and imported seeds for gourmet gardeners. Catalogue $2 (U.S.).

Gurney Seed & Nursery Co.
110 Capital Street
Yankton, South Dakota 57079
A mainstream inventory of flowers and vegetables from a company more than a century old. Catalogue free, to U.S. only.

Harris Seeds
Box 22960
Rochester, New York 14692-2960
A good selection of vegetables and flowers for the Northeast and Midwest, intelligently described. Catalogue free, to U.S. only.

Heirloom Seed Project
Landis Valley Museum
2451 Kissel Hill Road
Lancaster, Pennsylvania 17601
A project managed by a museum dedicated to re-creating and interpreting Pennsylvania "Dutch" life of the 18th to 20th centuries. Catalogue $2.75 to Canada, $2 to the U.S.

Heirloom Seeds
Box 245
West Elizabeth, Pennsylvania 15088-0245
Older varieties of vegetables. Catalogue $1 (U.S.) (refundable).

The Herb Farm
Norton, New Brunswick E0G 2N0
Herb plants and seeds from a pesticide-free farm. Price list $2 and a SASE; catalogue $5, including complementary seeds.

Heritage Seed Program
RR 3
Uxbridge, Ontario L9P 1R3
Heather Apple's boundless dedication – and perhaps her prophetic name – has helped make this seed-preservation program a great success. Annual membership – $15 regular, $9 fixed, $20 supporting, $18 U.S. – brings a thrice-yearly magazine and access to a list of heirloom, rare and endangered vegetables, fruits, grains, herbs and flowers grown by members.

J.L. Hudson, Seedsman
Box 1058
Redwood City, California 94064
Open-pollinated, adventurous seeds from around the world. Catalogue $1 (U.S.).

Johnny's Selected Seeds
Box 299
Albion, Maine 14910
One of the best lists of seeds for cool and short-season gardens. Catalogue free.

J.W. Jung Seed Co.
Randolph, Wisconsin 53957
A broad inventory of seeds and plants, both ornamental and edible. Catalogue free, to U.S. only.

Liberty Seed Co.
Box 806
New Philadelphia, Ohio 44663
A comprehensive list of vegetables and flowers. Catalogue free, to U.S. only.

Lindenberg Seeds Ltd.
803 Princess Avenue
Brandon, Manitoba R7A 0P5
Flower and vegetable seeds for prairie and northern gardens. Catalogue free to Canada, $1 to the U.S.

Mapple Farms
Hillsborough, New Brunswick E0A 1X0
Sweet-potato roots, Jerusalem artichokes, French shallots. Send a SASE for price list, to Canada only.

McFayden Seed Co. Ltd.
Box 1800
Brandon, Manitoba R7A 6N4
Two free catalogues a year: a spring one for seeds, a fall one for bulbs and equipment.

Meadowbrook Herb Garden
Route 138
Wyoming, Rhode Island 02898
Biodynamically grown herb plants and seeds. Send a SASE for order form.

Mellinger's Nursery
2310 West South Range Road
North Lima, Ohio 44452-9731
A big catalogue of the usual and unusual, from kohlrabi to kiwi. Catalogue $2.50 (U.S.) to Canada, free to the U.S.

Native Seeds/Search
2509 N. Campbell #325
Tucson, Arizona 85719
A nonprofit group selling heirloom seeds of the Southwest. Catalogue $1 (U.S.).

Ontario Seed Company, Ltd.
Box 144
Waterloo, Ontario N2J 3Z9
A colour catalogue with a bit of everything. Catalogue free, to Canada only.

Pacific Northwest Seed Co, Inc.
Site 14A, Comp. 2, RR 5
Vernon, British Columbia V1T 6L8

Vegetables, flowers and herbs for western gardens. Catalogue $1 to Canada, $2 to the U.S.

Park Seed Co.
Cokesbury Road
Greenwood, South Carolina 29647-0001
A big colour catalogue of flowers, herbs and vegetables, including some exclusives. Catalogue free.

Peace Seeds
2385 SE Thompson Street
Corvallis, Oregon 97333
Vegetable and herb seeds from their own organic fields. Catalogue $4.

Pinetree Garden Seeds
Route 100
New Gloucester, Maine 04260
A good selection of seeds at low prices. Catalogue free, to U.S. only.

Prairie Grown Garden Seeds
Box 118
Cochin, Saskatchewan S0M 0L0
For Jim Ternier's chatty list of home-gathered vegetables, send two first-class stamps from Canada, $1 from the U.S.

Rawlinson Garden Seeds
269 College Road
Truro, Nova Scotia B2N 2P6
More than 300 Maritime-tested, untreated vegetable cultivars at low prices. Catalogue free to Canada, $1 (refundable) to the U.S.

Redwood City Seed Co.
Box 361
Redwood City, California 94064
A selection of items gathered from around the world. Catalogue $2 (Cdn.) or $1 (U.S.).

Richters
357 Highway 47
Goodwood, Ontario L0C 1A0

Hundreds of herb-seed varieties and plants to Canada. Catalogue $2.

W. Robinson & Son, Ltd.
Sunny Bank, Forton, nr. Preston
Lancashire PR3 0BN, England
Famous for mammoth vegetables. Catalogue free.

Ronniger's Seed Potatoes
Star Route 31
Moyie Springs, Idaho 83845
Close to 200 types of potatoes. Catalogue $2, to U.S. only.

Salt Spring Seeds
Box 33
Ganges, British Columbia V0S 1E0
More than 100 different beans and some unusual grains. Catalogue $2.

Seed Savers Exchange
RR 3, Box 239
Decorah, Iowa 52101
Much like Canada's newer Heritage Seed Program, this nonprofit organization protects heirloom vegetables from extinction by recruiting gardeners to grow them and distribute their seeds. Annual membership $30 (U.S.) in Canada, $25 in the U.S.

Seeds Blüm
Idaho City Stage
Boise, Idaho 83706
"Heirloom Seeds and other Garden Gems," all nonhybrid. Catalogue $3, to U.S. only.

Seeds of Change
621 Old Santa Fe Trail #10
Santa Fe, New Mexico 87501
Organically grown seeds, mostly heirlooms. Catalogue $5 (U.S.) to Canada, $3 to the U.S. (refundable).

Seeds Trust, Inc.
High Altitude Gardens
Box 1048
Hailey, Iowa 83333

A good place to look for short-season vegetables, especially tomatoes. Catalogue $4 to Canada, $3 to the U.S.

Shepherd's Garden Seeds
6116 Highway 9
Felton, California 95018
Varieties for gardeners who love to cook – and the recipes for them. Catalogue $1 (U.S.).

Stokes Seeds Ltd.
39 James Street, Box 10
St. Catharines, Ontario L2R 6R6
or
Box 548
Buffalo, New York 14240
Respected for fresh seeds and detailed cultural directions for hundreds of vegetables, flowers and herbs. Catalogue free.

T & T Seeds
Box 1710
Winnipeg, Manitoba R3C 3P6
Short-season varieties, both seeds and plants. Catalogue $2.

Talavaya Seeds
Box 707
Santa Cruz Station
Santa Cruz, New Mexico 87507
Native, nonhybrid, organically grown seeds. Catalogue $1.50 (U.S.) to Canada, $1 to the U.S.

Territorial Seeds Ltd.
Box 825
206-8475 Ontario Street
Vancouver, British Columbia V5X 3E8
or
Box 157
Cottage Grove, Oregon 97424
An emphasis here on year-round varieties for Pacific gardeners. Catalogue free.

Thompson & Morgan Inc.
Box 1308
Jackson, New Jersey 08527

A colourful digest-type catalogue that is almost all flowers, including many otherwise hard-to-find species and cultivars. Catalogue free.

Totally Tomatoes
Box 16216
Augusta, Georgia 30903
Some 250 tomatoes from cherry to beefsteak. Catalogue $2 (U.S.) to Canada, $1 to the U.S.

Vermont Bean Seed Co.
Garden Lane
Fair Haven, Vermont 05743
Untreated vegetable seeds, both hybrids and heirlooms. Catalogue $2 to Canada, $1 to the U.S.

Vesey's Seeds Ltd.
York, Prince Edward Island C0A 1P0
Only varieties that have passed trials in their own gardens. Catalogue free.

Western Biologicals
Box 283
Aldergrove, British Columbia V0X 1A0
Mushroom spawn and the equipment and information for growing them. Catalogue $3.

William Dam Seeds Ltd.
Box 8400
Dundas, Ontario L9H 6M1
Untreated seeds, including many European vegetables. Also organic supplies. Catalogue $2 (refundable).

Organic Gardening Magazine
Emmaus, Pennsylvania 18099-0003
A monthly magazine on growing and using vegetables and herbs without chemicals.

The Prairie Garden
Winnipeg Horticultural Society
Box 517
Winnipeg, Manitoba R3C 2J3
An annual magazine on growing flowers, trees and vegetables on the prairies.

Rural Delivery
Box 1509
Liverpool, Nova Scotia B0T 1K0
A monthly newspaper on gardening, husbandry and rural lifestyles in the Atlantic Provinces.

U.S. Department of Agriculture
Office of Public Affairs
Publishing Division, Room 507-A
Washington, D.C. 20250-1300
Ask for the "List of Available Publications of the U.S. Department of Agriculture."

Publications
See Chapter X for publications suitable for particular regions.

Harrowsmith
7 Queen Victoria Road
Camden East, Ontario K0K 1J0
A bimonthly magazine featuring self-reliance, environmental preservation and alternatives for life in the country and, increasingly, the city.

Glossary

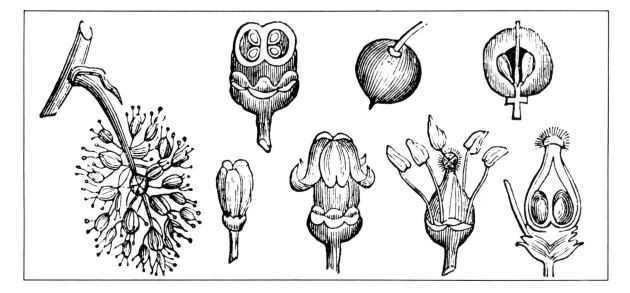

Acidic refers to a soil with a **pH** below 7, which is neutral. For the best growth of most plants, an ideal garden soil is slightly acidic, with a pH of about 6.5. Sulphur compounds tend to make soil more acidic or "sour." Acidic soils are usually found in areas of high rainfall. Peanuts, potatoes, radishes and sweet potatoes all do best in acidic soil.

Alkaline the opposite of **acidic**, and refers to soil with a **pH** above 7. Liming compounds such as calcium carbonate or magnesium carbonate make soil more alkaline. Alkaline soils are usually found in areas of low rainfall or where the bedrock consists of alkaline materials. Onions, asparagus, beets, rhubarb, peas, and **brassicas** do best in alkaline soil.

Annual a plant that completes its entire life cycle within one year. Dill, sunflowers, tomatoes, nasturtiums and lettuce are all annuals. Many garden plants that would survive the winter in their native environment die during the northern fall and are, for practical purposes, considered annuals.

Axil the crotch between a large stem and a smaller stem or a leaf. The flowers of some types of mint develop in leaf axils as do tomato **suckers**, which should be snapped off staked plants.

Biennial a plant that must survive one winter or a certain period of low temperatures before it will produce seed. Beets, carrots, cauliflower and parsley are all garden biennials.

Blanch in the garden, the process of shading a vegetable so that its colour is lightened and its flavour becomes milder. Strong-tasting vegetables such as dandelions, chicory and endive are best after being blanched for a week or two. Cauliflower is blanched by tying leaves over the developing head, which then stays white; unblanched heads turn green or purple and have a stronger flavour. Blanched vegetables are somewhat lower in nutrients than their unblanched counterparts.

In the kitchen, blanching denotes the processing of some vegetables prior to freezing or drying. They are steamed or boiled just long enough to kill destructive enzymes, but not long enough to cook the food. They are then rapidly cooled so that they remain crisp.

Bolt the process in which plants produce seed stalks quickly. Lettuce and spinach are said to bolt to seed in hot weather. When crops bolt, the edible parts deteriorate in flavour and texture.

Brassica a member of the *Brassica* **genus** of plants, including broccoli, Brussels sprouts, cabbage, collards, cauliflower, kale and kohlrabi. All brassicas suffer from similar diseases and pests.

Clone an exact genetic replica of the parent, propagated from part of the parent rather than from seed. **Cuttings**, potato eyes, **rhizomes** and runners all produce plants that are clones of the parent. The word may also be used as a verb that denotes such propagation.

Compost organic matter in a state of partial and continuing decay. Compost is usually a mixture of leaves, animal manure, hay and other biodegradable ingredients that is kept wet and aerated until it decays, releasing heat and killing harmful microorganisms. As soon as it is crumbly, which may take from two weeks to several years, depending upon the amount and type of materials in the pile, the size of pile and the ambient temperatures, compost can be used as a fertilizer, as **mulch**, or as a potting mixture. The word is also used as a verb that denotes the process of composting.

Cotyledon the first leaf produced by a plant; also called a seedling leaf. The cotyledon looks different from later-developing **true leaves**. Cotyledons are usually very simple in structure and appearance, lacking indentations and other characteristics of all later developing leaves. Monocotyledons (or monocots) such as corn produce only one cotyledon, while dicotyledons (or dicots) such as tomatoes produce two.

Cross-pollination occurs when pollen is passed from the male part of one flower to the female part of another. Also called crossing or crossbreeding.

Cultivar a man-made plant **variety**, short for **cul**tivated **vari**ety. For example, while *Brassica oleracea capitata* designates cabbage (*capitata* being the variety name), Stonehead is a cabbage cultivar.

Cutting a shoot or twig of a plant that can be used for propagation. Placed in water or a wet growing medium to root, it produces a **clone** of the parent.

Damping off a **fungus** disease that spreads in unsterilized soil, especially when it is cool and wet and when plants are overcrowded. The disease kills seedlings either before they emerge through the soil or soon after, when the base of the stem becomes pinched and the seedling finally topples and dies.

Determinate a type of tomato that is bush-like in habit, usually produces an early crop of fruit, and should not be pruned. The opposite type is **indeterminate**. Seed catalogues or packets often refer to determinate **cultivars** as bush tomatoes.

Drip line the ground under the outermost extent of the foliage of a plant. Its name comes from the fact that rain that is shed off the plant will first fall most heavily along this line.

Flat a container about 3 inches deep and up to 18 inches long and wide which is filled with growing medium and used for germinating seeds and for holding seedlings before they are transplanted into deeper soil.

Fungicide a substance that kills fungi (plural of **fungus**). The word usually applies to any of a number of synthetic substances used mostly by commercial growers.

Fungus a plant that does not manufacture its own chlorophyll, and so must live off other plants or organic materials. Mushrooms are fungi as are many diseases that infect garden plants. Most fungi thrive in wet conditions.

Genus a grouping of closely related plants within a larger family. Members of the Solanaceae family, both the potato and the garden huckleberry belong to the genus *Solanum*; the first is known as *Solanum tuberosum*, the latter as *Solanum nigrum*. The plural is genera.

Germination the sprouting of a seed.

Green manure a crop that is grown for the purpose of being plowed under while still immature, thus adding nutrients and organic matter to the soil. Common green manure crops include buckwheat, rye grass and field peas.

Grey water household waste water from washing or bathing. As long as it does not contain detergents, borax, bleaches or other chemicals (although some soap is all right), it may be used sparingly in the garden.

Harden off acclimatize a plant to a change in its environment, usually a change from indoors to outdoors. Plants that are not slowly acclimatized, or hardened off, before making such a move may die. In hardening plants off, then, the gardener gradually exposes them to increasingly long periods of time in the conditions of their new environment, a process that usually takes several days.

Herbicide a substance that kills certain plants. The word usually applies to a number of synthetic substances used mostly by commercial growers.

Hybrid a plant that does not have the same genetic makeup as either of its parents, which are members of different **species, varieties** or **cultivars**. These plants possess "hybrid vigour," some of the best characteristics of both parents, and so may be superior in some ways to nonhybrid, open-pollinated or "standard" plants.

Indeterminate a type of tomato that continues to grow and blossom throughout the season. It is usually staked and pruned by the removal of the **suckers** growing in leaf **axils**. The opposite type is **determinate**. Seed catalogues often refer to indeterminate **cultivars** as staking tomatoes. Semi-determinate tomatoes possess characteristics of both determinates and indeterminates.

Inflorescence a flower. The term usually denotes a tight cluster of flowers whether opened or closed, such as the head of broccoli or cauliflower.

Inoculation the process of inoculating **legume** seeds with the proper type of *Rhizobium* bacteria to ensure **nitrogen fixation** in the soil, enhancing soil fertility. Inoculant can be purchased from many seed houses. Seeds are coated in the inoculant powder before they are planted.

Insecticide a substance that kills insects, bugs, larvae and such. The word usually applies to any of a number of synthetic substances used mostly by commercial growers.

Larva the stage between egg and adult of a moth, butterfly, beetle or fly. Larvae are often called caterpillars, loopers, grubs or maggots.

Leggy describes a plant, especially a **seedling**, that has become tall and weak, usually as a result of too little light, often in combination with too much fertilizer, water and warmth.

Legume a member of the pea family, Leguminosae. These plants, which include beans, lentils, peanuts and vetch, have the ability to obtain or fix nitrogen from the air with the help of certain bacteria.

Manure tea the liquid produced after a quantity of livestock manure has been allowed to steep for about a day in five to 10 times as much water. The tea is then used as a mild fertilizer.

Mulch a covering on the soil that is meant to slow or stop the growth of some plants (usually weeds) and encourage the growth of others (vegetables, herbs, trees or flowers). Mulches may be of inorganic materials such as plastic or carpeting, or they may be organic, consisting of leaves, seaweed, straw or sawdust. Plastic mulches help warm the soil; organic mulches may cool the soil, but also provide it with additional organic matter and nutrients as they decay.

Nitrogen fixation the process of changing the nitrogen in the atmosphere into a form that can be used by plants, thus enhancing soil fertility. Certain bacteria of the *Rhizobium* genus, which inhabit small nodes or nodules on the **legume** roots, actually "fix" the nitrogen.

Perennial a plant that, under normal circumstances, will live more than two years. It may set seed every year or less frequently.

Pesticide an **insecticide, herbicide** or **fungicide**; a substance, usually synthetic, that kills a selected type of living thing.

pH a scale that denotes acidity or alkalinity, and that ranges from 0 to 14. The higher the number, the more **alkaline**; the lower the number, the more **acidic**. The number 7 represents neutral. Thus numbers lower than 7 indicate acidic conditions and numbers higher than 7 indicate alkaline conditions. The scale is logarithmic, so each number denotes a value 10 times greater than its predecessor. The symbol pH stands for potential hydrogen.

Pollination the process by which pollen is transferred to the female part of a flower from the male part. Pollination is usually accomplished by wind, insects, water or animals.

Potpourri French for "rotten pot," a mixture of dried or preserved herbs and/or flowers that is kept for its appearance and fragrance. Preservatives such as pickling salt or orris root are often added to make the scent last longer.

Rhizome the fleshy, underground stem used by some plants for food storage and for spreading over a larger area. Perennial grasses such as quack grass have rhizomes.

Seedling a young plant, usually with only its **cotyledons** or its first **true leaves**.

Self-sterile a flower in which fertilization will not occur if its own pollen is used on its own **stigma**. Such plants must **cross-pollinate** if fertilization and eventual seed production are to occur.

Set a small bulb, especially of an onion or shallot. It is planted in spring to develop into a full-sized bulb by fall.

The term "set fruit" means that **pollination** and fertilization have occurred in a flower, and that the fruit has begun to swell.

Side-dressing a method of mid-season fertilization by which nutrients are spread on the soil beside plants, usually under the **drip line** of their foliage. In this way, fertilizer is gradually utilized.

Solanaceous describes a plant of the family Solanaceae, which includes tomatoes, potatoes, peppers, ground cherries, garden huckleberries and nicotiana.

Species a subdivision of a **genus**; members of the same species appear similar and are capable of interbreeding. Swiss chard and beets belong to the same species, as do celery and celeriac.

Stamen the male part of a flower, consisting of a thread-like stem, the filament, which supports an anther upon which pollen is produced. There are usually several stamens surrounding a central **stigma**, although some flowers produce only stamens.

Stigma the part of a flower which receives pollen. The stigma is the top of the female part of a flower, the pistil, at the base of which is an immature ovary, an undeveloped fruit.

Sucker a fast-growing shoot that may develop at the expense of the rest of the plant. It often grows where shoots are not desirable for reasons of plant health, longevity, neatness or the size of the harvest.

Taproot a swollen root where the plant stores food that is usually used when the plant resumes growth in spring. Carrots, parsnips and dandelions all have taproots.

Tendril a slender shoot that twines itself around anything it touches, thereby supporting the plant from which it grows. Peas and vining cucumbers have tendrils.

Transplant as a verb, denotes the transfer of a live plant from one growing medium to another. As a noun, transplant refers to the plant that will be moved, is being moved, or has recently been moved.

True leaf any leaf produced by a plant subsequent to its development of the **cotyledons** or seedling leaves.

Tuber a swelling on an underground stem which the plant uses for the storage of food that, in most cases, it uses when it resumes growth in spring. The edible part of the potato plant is the tuber.

Umbel a seed head in which the flowers have stalks that originate at a common point on the stem. The head may be globe or umbrella shaped. Plants of the Umbelliferae family such as dill, carrots and parsley derive their family name from their umbels. Onions and dandelions also produce umbels.

Variety the narrowest botanical classification by which a plant is identified; subdivision of a **species**. A variety refers only to one distinct type of plant, such as a tomato, whether red, yellow or cherry.

Index

Credits

Drawings and maps on pages 17, 20-21, 22, 23, 32-33, 43, 48-49, 60, 61, 62, 132, 133, 148, 149, 160-161, 168, 174-175 by John Mardon.

Illustrations in Chapters IV and VII from *The Vegetable Garden* by M.M. Vilmorin-Andrieux, originally published in 1976 by the Jeavons-Leler Press, reprinted by permission; and from *Indian Herbalogy of North America* by Alma R. Hutchins, originally published in 1969 by Merco.

Reprint Permission: page 47: J.M. Dent & Sons (Canada) Ltd. Page 62: information on row covers from "Slitted Row Covers for Intensive Vegetable Production" by Otho S. Wells and J. Brent Loy, published by the Cooperative Extension Service, University of New Hampshire.

Credits for charts, photographs and other illustrations are listed below, by 2-page spread, clockwise from top left, where applicable:
6-7: Camera Art. 12-13: William Lammers; *Cyclopedia of American Agriculture*, by L.H. Bailey, published by Macmillan Company, 1909. 14-15: John Hatch; Michael Burzynski. 16-17: Helene Leonard-Contant; Gabrielle Klein. 18-19: *Harrowsmith* files. 22-23: *Harrowsmith* files; National Garden Bureau. 24-25: *Harrowsmith* files; chart adapted from Johnny's Selected Seeds. 28-29: Hans Wendler/Image Bank of Canada. 30-31: Barbara K. Deans/Masterfile;

Harrowsmith files. 34-35: Harold Burton; *Harrowsmith* files; *Harrowsmith* files. 36-37: United States Department of Agriculture. 38-39: *Harrowsmith* files. 42-43: Illustration from *Drought Gardening*, courtesy of Garden Way Publishing, Charlotte, Vermont 05445. 44-45: United States Department of Agriculture. 46-47: Frank Foster. 50-51: *Harrowsmith* files; *Harrowsmith* files; Wayne Barrett. 52-53: Based on an illustration from the Ontario Ministry of Agriculture & Food. 54-55: *Harrowsmith* files; *Harrowsmith* files. 56-57: Public Archives Canada. 58-59: United States Department of Agriculture. 60-61: Based on a diagram from the Ark Institute of Man & Resources, P.E.I. 62-63: Based on an illustration from "Slitted Row Covers for Intensive Vegetable Production," University of New Hampshire. 64-65: Gabrielle Klein; L. Black. 70-71: *Harrowsmith* files. 76-77: Kerry Banks. 82-83: *Harrowsmith* files; *Harrowsmith* files. 86-87: Kerry Banks. 88-89: Kerry Banks. 98-99: *Harrowsmith* files. 104-105: Jett Korber; Joe Soucy. 106-107: *Harrowsmith* files; Stephen Brooke. 108-109: *Harrowsmith* files; *Harrowsmith* files. 110-111: Gabrielle Klein; *Harrowsmith* files. 112-113: Gwen Pepper; Bruce Kennedy; J.B. Childs. 114-115: Mojtaba Ghadery; *Harrowsmith* files; *Harrowsmith* files; Larry Gritzmaker. 118-119: *Harrowsmith* files; National Garden Bureau. 120-121: United States Department of Agriculture; United States Department of Agriculture; *Harrowsmith* files. 122-123: Based on "Pollination of

Vegetable Crops," Ontario Ministry of Agriculture & Food. 124-125: *Harrowsmith* files; *Harrowsmith* files. 126-127: Bill Milliken; Stokes Seeds Ltd. 128-129: *Harrowsmith* files; Edmund Haag. 130-131: Frank Foster; from *The Herbalist*, Clarence Meyer; *Harrowsmith* files. 134-135: *Harrowsmith* files; *Harrowsmith* files. 138-139: Richard Allison. 140-141: Stephen Errington. 146-147: *Harrowsmith* files; *Harrowsmith* files. 150-151: W. Atlee Burpee Co. 152-153: Stephen Errington. 154-155: *Harrowsmith* files; Anton Gross. 156-157: J.B. Childs; Ecological Agricultural Project, Macdonald College. 158-159: Scott Haynes. 162-163: R. Nüttgens/Image Bank of Canada; *Harrowsmith* files; Agriculture Canada. 164-165: *Harrowsmith* files; *Harrowsmith* files. 166-167: *Harrowsmith* files: Agriculture Canada; Robert Mariner. 168-169: Based on design by the Ontario Ministry of Agriculture & Food; Scott Haynes. 170-171: Based on Agriculture Canada's publication number 1560, "Canning Canadian Fruits and Vegetables." 172-173: Gabrielle Klein; William Lammers. 176-177: F. Moshenko; Al Harvey/Masterfile. 178-179: *Harrowsmith* files; *Harrowsmith* files; *Harrowsmith* files. 180-181: Bob Romerein; Public Archives Canada. 182-183: Maggie Crothers. 184-185: Bill Milliken; *The Compleat Farmer*, Mayflower Books, 1975. 194-195: *Chambers Information for the People*, 1874, W & R Chambers. Photograph of Jennifer Bennett on dust jacket by Peter Emmerson.